Gender, politics and the state

Over the last two decades our understanding of the relationship between gender, politics and the state has been transformed almost beyond recognition. *Gender, politics and the state* provides an overview of this dynamic and growing field. It reflects both the expanding empirical scope and the accompanying theoretical development and debate.

Following an introductory chapter, the next three essays in this collection focus on conceptual and theoretical issues: the meaning of 'gender', the state's role in the construction of gender within the public and private sphere, and the political representation of gender differences within liberal democracy. Six essays then provide analysis of more concrete issues of state policy and participation in differing national political contexts – abortion politics in Ireland, the local politics of prostitution in Britain, the impact on women's political participation of economic change in China and Latin America and political change in Russia, and the gender impact of state programmes of land reform, while the final chapter draws together the issues raised throughout the collection.

The book is a unique exploration of its subject's central themes – the difficulties inherent in the task of identifying and organising politically around gender differences and interests, the necessity of engaging with the state while simultaneously recognising both its complexity and variation, and the need for a more inclusive conception of politics that does justice to women's political agency.

Vicky Randall is a Reader in Government at the University of Essex. **Georgina Waylen** is a Lecturer in Politics at the University of Sheffield.

Gender, politics and the state

Edited by Vicky Randall
and Georgina Waylen

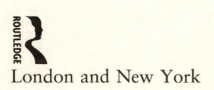

London and New York

First published 1998 by Routledge
11 New Fetter Lane, London EC4P 4EE

Simultaneously published in the USA and Canada
by Routledge
29 West 35th Street, New York, NY 10001

© 1998 Selection and editorial matter Vicky Randall and Georgina
Waylen; individual chapters, the contributors

Typeset in Sabon by
BC Typesetting, Bristol
Printed and bound in Great Britain by
Redwood Books, Trowbridge, Wiltshire

British Library Cataloguing in Publication Data
A catalogue record for this book is available from the British Library

Library of Congress Cataloging in Publication Data
Randall, Vicky.
    Gender, politics and the state/Vicky Randall and Georgina
Waylen.
        p.   cm.
    Includes bibliographical references and index.
    1. Women in politics. 2. Feminism. 3. Women–Government
    policy.
    I. Waylen, Georgina. II. Title.
    HQ1236.R259 1998
    320'.082–dc21   98-9382
                                                       CIP

ISBN 0–415–16401–X (hbk)
ISBN 0–415–16402–8 (pbk)

Contents

Contributors

Terrell Carver is professor of political theory at the University of Bristol. He is the author of *Gender is Not a Synonym for Women* (Lynne Rienner 1996) and co-editor of *The Politics of Sexuality* (Routledge forthcoming).

Nikki Craske is lecturer in politics at Queen's University, Belfast. She has also held posts at the Institute of Latin American Studies and the University of Manchester. She is the author of *Corporatism Revisited* (ILAS Research Paper 1994) and co-editor of *Dismantling the Mexican State?* (Macmillan 1994) and *Mexico and the North American Free Trade Agreement* (Macmillan 1996). Her forthcoming book is *Women and Politics in Latin America* (Polity Press).

Barry Gilheany is currently writing up his PhD research at Essex University on 'Irish Abortion Politics 1992–95: Historical and Comparative Dynamics'. He is also a part-time tutor in politics in the Department of Government. He has previously written about women's participation in the Republic of Ireland for his master's thesis from Queen's University, Belfast. He is also a qualified librarian and has general interests in reproductive rights issues and mental health, currently serving as a Formal Advocate for the Colchester branch of MIND.

Barbara Gwinnett is senior lecturer in sociology at the University of Wolverhampton. Her research interest in prostitution and gender inequalities is part of ongoing research in Birmingham (UK). She is currently working on a co-authored book *Social Inequalities: Sociological Perspectives*.

Jude Howell is a senior lecturer in politics and development at the School of Development Studies, University of East Anglia. She is the author of *China Opens its Doors: The Politics of Economic Transition*, Lynne Rienner/ Harvester Wheatsheaf, 1993, and co-author with G. White and Shang Xiaoyuan of *In search of Civil Society: Market Reform and Social Change in Contemporary China* (Oxford University Press 1996). She is the author of several articles and book chapters on gender, market reform and labour in China.

Susie Jacobs teaches sociology at Manchester Metropolitan University. She is the author of numerous articles on gender, land resettlement and the law in Zimbabwe, and on land reform comparatively. She is also co-editor of *States of Conflict: International Perspectives on Gender, Violence and Resistance* (Zed Press, forthcoming).

Kate Nash is lecturer in sociology at the University of East Anglia. She has recently published *Universal Difference: Feminism and the Liberal Undecidability of 'Women'* (Macmillan 1988).

Vicky Randall is reader in government at Essex University. Her books include *Women and Politics* (Macmillan 1982, 2nd edn 1987) and, with Joni Lovenduski, *Contemporary Feminist Politics* (Oxford University Press 1993); articles and chapters cover a range of related issues, including abortion politics, feminist politics and women's political participation. Recently her primary research interest has been the politics of childcare provision: she has published several articles on this subject and is currently completing a book on the politics of childcare in Britain.

Valerie Sperling holds a PhD from the University of California, Berkeley, in political science. Her dissertation is entitled *Engendering Transition: The Women's Movement in Contemporary Russia*. She is currently a post-doctoral fellow at Harvard University's Davis Center for Russian Studies (1997–8).

Ursula Vogel is senior lecturer at the Department of Government, University of Manchester. Her research and teaching interests cover the political and legal thought of the Enlightenment, theories of citizenship, feminist conceptions of rights. Publications include *The Frontiers of Citizenship* (Routledge 1991) (together with M. Moran) and a variety of articles on women's property rights, the institution of marriage, and German Romanticism. She is currently completing a book on marriage and the political order.

Georgina Waylen is lecturer in politics at the University of Sheffield. She is the author of *Gender in Third World Politics* (Lynne Rienner/Open University Press 1996). She has written a number of articles and chapters on women's political participation, democratisation and political economy; and is currently completing a book on *Gender, Democratic Consolidation and Economic Reform*.

Preface

This book explores the relationship between gender relations, the state and politics, examining both policy and political activity. To some extent the volume is interdisciplinary, incorporating perspectives from political science, sociology and political theory. It also combines theoretically and empirically based pieces. The geographical areas covered by the contributors range over the developed, developing and communist and ex-communist world including examples from Latin America, Europe (Russia, Britain, Ireland, France and Germany), Africa (Zimbabwe) and Asia (Vietnam, India and China).

With the exception of one person, all the contributors participated in a British Sociological Association/Political Studies Association women's group one-day annual conference organised by the editors on the theme 'Gender, Politics and the State' which was held at the London School of Economics. One further piece, on transition politics in Russia, was expressly commissioned. We decided on the overall structure of the volume after much thought. As the editors, we wrote the introductory and concluding chapters to give the volume a context and overall coherence and to bring out its recurrent themes. The introductory chapter focuses on the state while the concluding chapter looks primarily at women's political activity before concluding the volume as a whole. The other contributions have been organised in a particular order. The first three essays (Carver, Vogel and Nash) deal with some of the theoretical issues surrounding the meaning and construction of gender, the relationship between the state and the construction of gender historically and the implications of this for liberal democracies. The subsequent contributions take up many of the themes raised in the early chapters through more empirically based work. Gilheany and Gwinnett examine particular aspects of the construction and regulation of gender relations through women's bodies, by examining abortion and prostitution. The remaining case study chapters (Craske, Jacobs, Sperling and Howell) deal with gendered aspects of varying state actions and different types of women's political activity in differing political formations ranging from the democratising to the communist/ex-communist and the formally liberal democratic.

The volume as a whole addresses many of the issues which we believe should inform future development of the study of gender, politics and the state. It seeks, first, through the elaboration of gendered analyses, to help to 'bring the state back in' to feminist accounts and, second, to combine this with an examination of women's political activity and women's engagement with the state in different political contexts. In so doing, it aims to bridge the gap which so often characterises studies in this field between structure and agency.

Both editors have debts to acknowledge in the making of this book. Georgina would especially like to thank Liz Harvey, Vicky would like to thank Aletta Norval and both are grateful to the contributors to this book for their valuable comments on the first drafts of Chapters 1 and 11.

Vicky Randall
Georgina Waylen

1 Gender, feminism and the state

An overview

Georgina Waylen

This collection begins from the premise that while there is more and more literature on gender and politics, as yet there is little which usefully links the analysis of gender, politics and the state. As editors we believe that this is a lack which should be addressed. There is a pressing need to do a number of things. First, to use the term politics as defined more widely to include activities often undertaken by women which fall outside the boundaries of conventional politics and therefore not usually deemed to be 'political'. Second, to examine the interrelationship between 'politics' and the construction of gender relations and gendered identities. And third, to analyse satisfactorily in gendered terms both political activity and processes together with the institutions/structures which constrain them – the main structure in this case being the state. As Terrell Carver makes clear in his contribution to this volume, gender is often seen very unhelpfully as 'loosely synonymous with "sex" and lazily synonymous with "women"'. However, following the arguments of Joan Scott (1986) we see gender not only as a 'constitutive element of social relationships based on perceived difference between the sexes', but also as 'a primary way of signifying relationships of power'. Within Scott's formulation, while it has often been overlooked, the contextually specific ways in which politics constructs gender and gender constructs politics become an important subject of inquiry.

Assuming that men's activities are on the whole already more widely analysed (albeit using gender-blind presumptions which assume that men are the 'normal' or generic humans), this task entails considering not only the impact of different women and women's movements on institutions and structures but how these institutions and structures can shape and alter gender relations and women's activities in particular contexts. The articles in this collection therefore look not just at the impact of the state on women and how the state helps to construct gender relations, but how the activities of different women and women's movements impact on the state and are in turn impacted on by the state. It is clear that this problematic raises the question of the relationship between structure and agency. However, any analysis has to occur in ways which avoid both excessive voluntarism and the opposite tendency to simply examine the determining impact of structures. There is increasing recognition in many parts of the social sciences that there is a need to do away with the rigid dichotomy between structure and agency; we, the editors, share this view and intend that this collection will go some way towards achieving this aim within feminist theorising. Indeed, the relationship between women's actions and institutions is a theme of many of the contributions. Vicky Randall takes up this question in terms of circularity in the concluding chapter.

This introductory chapter focuses on how the state acts to construct gender relations and impacts on different groups of women The concluding chapter by Vicky Randall will look at women engaging with the state, construction of gendered identities and questions of representation, which all bring up notions of power. Therefore the present chapter deals directly with the institution of the state while the concluding chapter focuses much more on 'politics' defined in the widest sense and intervening chapters deal with various aspects of these themes. However, as editors we believe that it must be borne in mind that this division between the subject matter of the first and last chapters is a somewhat false separation instituted for practical as well as intellectual reasons. The actions of different groups of women cannot be understood outside of the structures which constrain them, just as those structures cannot be understood without some consideration of the impact of the choices made by actors both inside and outside of them in creating and changing those structures. The inescapable links between these two aspects are demonstrated by the recurrence of many of the same themes, such as the centrality of the public–private divide and concepts of citizenship in both chapters, but they are taken up in different ways.

So far greater emphasis has been placed in much of the feminist literature on women's political activities which take place outside the formal arena, particularly their participation in various kinds of social movements in both the developed and the developing worlds. At the same time there has been a lack of useful feminist theorising on the state. This collection intends to go some way to remedy this lack but without prioritising one over the other. One objective of this book is therefore to help to 'bring the state back in' rather belatedly to feminist analyses. The introductory and concluding chapters will outline the current state of the debate as we see it and what we believe is needed to push it forward. We wish to avoid the over-universalising which has ignored the experience of the post-colonial state that much western feminist theorising on the state has been criticised for up until now (Rai 1996). And we simply aim, while remaining aware of the specificity of the state in different contexts, to give an indication of some of the most important processes involved in particular cases which may help to illuminate questions and frameworks for the examination of other contexts in both the developed and the developing world. Therefore we want to further both the gendered analysis of politics and the state and the development of feminist theories of the state.

The contributors to this volume share a commitment to feminism defined in terms of a shared belief that women are subordinated, but with differing analyses of the nature of that subordination and of the strategies needed to change that situation. The starting point of this collection is therefore that there are differing feminist analyses of the state and as a consequence different strategies for dealing with the state which range from autonomy to integration (termed by some as the dilemma of 'in and against the state' (Rai 1996)). This diversity of views is reflected in this collection, but all the contributors share a commitment to the need for more sophisticated analysis of state institutions/structures in gender terms. In order to provide a context for the subsequent articles, this chapter addresses a number of themes. First, it outlines the nature of the feminist writings on the state to date. Having examined some of the different approaches, including their major strengths and the deficiencies which most obviously need to be remedied, the piece goes on to discuss: first, a number of improved ways to understand the nature of the state; second, the nature of different state policies in gendered terms; third, the relationship of the state to citizenship; and fourth, the relationship of the state to the debates around the public–private divide.

Feminist theorising of the state so far

Despite the centrality of the analysis of the state to many different disciplines such as politics, sociology and history and the increasing agreement among many feminist academics that adequate analyses of the state are still essential, there have not been many gendered analyses of the state produced after the initial flurry of activity in the late 1970s and early 1980s, in comparison to some other areas. Amongst the huge traditional western literature on the state emerging from liberalism and Marxism, gender relations do not feature explicitly as part of the analyses despite the implicit assumptions about gender which lie at their foundation (Connell 1990). On the other hand, it is impossible to argue that a coherent feminist theory of the state exists but instead a variety of positions can be discerned. At one end of the continuum, some feminists have even questioned whether a feminist theory of the state is necessary. Judith Allen (1990: 22) for instance has argued that:

> Feminism has not been guilty of oversight or failure in *not* developing a distinct theory of 'the state'. Instead, feminist theorists' choices of theoretical agendas with priorities other than 'the state' have a sound rationale that deserves to be taken seriously. 'The state' as a category of abstraction that is too aggregative, too unitary, and too unspecific to be of much use in addressing the disaggregated, diverse and specific (or local) sites that must be of most pressing concern to feminists. 'The state' is too blunt an instrument to be of much assistance (beyond generalizations) in explanations, analyses or the design of workable strategies.

Allen (1990: 34) argues that it is more profitable to develop instead theories of a large number of other more significant categories and processes, among which she cites policing, bureaucratic culture and masculinity as important. However, as we will see below, the conclusion that the analysis of the state up until now has been too aggregative does not necessarily imply that trying to theorise the state is a worthless enterprise, but can imply instead that more sophisticated analyses are necessary.

Despite the scepticism of feminists like Allen, others have 'taken the state seriously' and engaged in trying to understand it from a gendered perspective. As we will see, while a variety of analytically distinct positions can be discerned, much of this work produced up until the 1990s shares certain characteristics. The majority of feminist analyses focus on the liberal-democratic state in the first world while comparatively little attention has been paid to the gendered analysis of the post-colonial and Third World state (Afshar 1987; Charlton *et al.* 1989; Rai and Lievesley 1996). Much of the work either tends to be rather over-general, consisting of overarching macro-theoretical analyses, for example analysing society in terms of patriarchy and capitalism and seeing the state as a mechanism to reconcile the two systems (Eisenstein 1979); or it consists of detailed empirical micro-analyses with very little in between. A great deal of the literature sees women as the objects of state policy: within this framework the state is something 'out there' and external to women's lives and women are 'done to' by a state over which they have little control. Those who have looked at women's struggles with the state have often used a 'them and us' framework in which women make demands upon the state. This kind of approach assumes a number of things: that the state is a homogeneous entity and a given which lies almost outside of society rather than being something which is created in part as a result of interaction with different groups (Watson 1990).

Until recently, few feminist analyses went beyond seeing the state as either essentially potentially good or bad for women as a group. A number of positions identify the state as good in that it can be empowering for women when it can offer them the opportunity to make some gains in economic and political terms. It is in the social democratic Scandinavian context that some of these arguments have been developed most fully. In a benign analysis of the Scandinavian welfare state, analysts such as Drude Dahlerup (1987: 121) have claimed that it has become a mechanism to avoid dependence on individual men. She writes:

> Some studies conclude that in fact women have just moved from dependence on husbands to dependence on the state, while their subordination remains. I will argue that this shift has in general improved women's general position and has given women new resources for mobilization, protest and political influence.

This view has been shared by some American feminists such as Barbara Ehrenreich and Frances Fox Piven (1983) in their writing on the welfare state. In the context of the developing world, Deniz Kandiyoti (1991) has highlighted a similar tendency around the time of political independence, often for nationalists to see the state as a benign and potentially modernising force which would bring benefits to women. Frequently, liberal feminists have also tended to share a relatively benign view of the state because they ultimately rely on the pluralist view that the state can be a neutral arbiter between different groups within society. While it cannot provide a very sophisticated understanding of why the state does not always play this role with regard to women, this analysis does provide a justification for 'state feminism' and other forms of engagement with the state. Therefore both these social democratic and liberal feminist analyses have implications for feminist strategy towards the state, which we will consider below.

Other feminists have been more sceptical about the potential of the state to be a progressive force for women, but from differing perspectives. Socialist feminists of the 1970s have been criticised for simply adding the oppression of women to a Marxist framework which saw the state as primarily an instrument of the ruling class, and as a result gender oppression becomes functional for capital. In their view, women's subordination plays a role in sustaining capitalism through the reproduction of the labour force within the family and the state helps to reproduce and maintain this primarily through the welfare state (Wilson 1977; McIntosh 1978). Radical feminists have seen the state as inherently patriarchal, simply reflecting the male dominated nature of society, and therefore the state acts to uphold and defend male interests at the expense of women. Analysts such as Catherine Mackinnon (1983) have outlined how the state institutionalises male interests, for example through the law. Some feminists such as Zillah Eisenstein (1979), often emerging from a socialist feminist tradition, have put forward a dual systems analysis which attempts to reconcile these two separate systems of capitalism and patriarchy by arguing that the state plays the role of mediator between the two and acts in the interests of both. The implications for strategy of the radical feminist, socialist feminist and dual systems analyses of the state as an agent acting to control women for either patriarchy or capitalism or both are that on the whole it should be avoided. The partial exception to this was the way in which the potential of the local state, for example the Greater London Council (GLC), was viewed by some socialist feminists during the early 1980s. However, the conclusion of the majority of feminists was that women should steer clear of the state. Within all three frameworks the power of structures is seen as being overwhelming, leaving little room for agency.

By the late 1980s other feminists were beginning to criticise the various approaches outlined above. They took issue with the incipient functionalist analysis reflected in the notion that the state can act on behalf of particular groups in any simple way, as suggested by some Marxists and feminists

(Franzway *et al.* 1989). Rosemary Pringle and Sophie Watson (1992: 54) argue that 'the state itself remains an important focus. But the state, the interests articulated around it, and feminist political strategies need to be reconsidered in the light of post-structuralist theory.' Furthermore, it is claimed that it is impossible to assume unitary interests between men, women and sections of capital or that these interests are fully formed outside the state. The state is therefore seen as an arena where interests are actively constructed rather than given (Watson 1990: 8). This approach is linked to a Foucauldian analysis of power in which power is relational and something to be exercised rather than possessed. The emphasis shifts to practice and discourse rather than to institutions with much greater focus on the state as a process. What emerges from this type of analysis is the view that '"the state" as a category should not be abandoned, but for a recognition that, far from being a unified structure, it is a by-product of political struggles' (Pringle and Watson 1992: 67). Clearly this forms one way around the dichotomy between structure and agency discussed at the beginning of this chapter by not making the separation between the two and leaves open the potential not just for approaching and working through the state but also for being 'in' the state. It is in the Australian context that both the post-structuralist analysis of the state and the role of the 'femocrat', that is feminists working as bureaucrats within the state arena, have been considered the most. Indeed, within this framework the two are inter-connected.

The advocacy of this kind of analysis parallels developments among some other feminists who do not directly employ a post-structuralist analysis but who also have taken issue with the notion of a unitary state on the one hand and a unitary set of women's interests on the other. Sonia Alvarez (1990: 271), for example, in the conclusion to her ground-breaking study of transition politics in Brazil argues that the state is not monolithic and suggests 'a need for a more complex, less manichean perspective on gender and the State' which emphasises the importance of looking at different conjunctures and periods. These conclusions resonate with those arguments about the capacity of the local state often to be more 'women friendly' than the national state. At the same time, many orthodox analysts were also returning in more sophisticated ways to the analysis of the state and institutions. Institutions have been defined by North (1990: 3) very broadly as 'the rules of the game in society or, more formally, the humanly devised constraints that shape human interaction'. Historical institutionalism has emerged as one way of engaging in middle-level theorising which can help to illuminate cross-national differences, processes of change and the ways in which political struggles are mediated by the institutional setting in which they take place (Steinmo *et al.* 1992; Migdal 1996). As such, its discussion of the interaction of structures and agents can also be of some use in the gendered analysis of the state. By the early 1990s, therefore, a number of different and more sophisticated ways of conceptualising the state were beginning to emerge from both feminist and orthodox analysts. As is clear from the preceding analysis, while it may not be possible to have a feminist theory of the state, there are certain questions and themes which it is valuable to pursue in the gendered analysis of the state.

The nature of the state

As we have seen, while many discourses and disciplines agree on the centrality of the state, there are many formulations and little consensus. The starting point of any analysis has to be the complexity of the state historically, now and in different political formations such as liberal democracy, colonialism and state socialism. The nature of the state is not fixed and it has no necessary relationship to gender relations, but this relationship is evolving, dialectic and dynamic. However, although not inevitably patriarchal and while showing significant differences over time and space, most historical studies have demonstrated that the state has in general acted to enforce women's subordination up until now. But this cannot be assumed or taken for granted.

In addition to the specificity of different state formations, 'the state' itself can rarely, if ever, be seen as a homogeneous category. It is not a unitary structure but a differentiated set of institutions, agencies and discourses, and the product of a particular historical and political conjuncture. A number of the contributions to this volume draw attention to the heterogeneous nature of the state by examining the different levels and arenas of state activity, ranging from the local to national. As Barbara Gwinnett shows in Chapter 6 on prostitution in one district of Birmingham, the various agencies and branches of the state, both local and national, do not always act in concert. Barry Gilheany (Chapter 5) highlights the different role played by a number of Irish institutions such as the Supreme Court and the Catholic Church which can be identified as part of the state nexus in the development of Irish policies towards abortion.

If the state is not a homogeneous entity but a collection of institutions and contested power relations, it is far better to see it as a site of struggle, not lying outside of society and social processes, but having, on the one hand, a degree of autonomy from these which varies under particular circumstances, and on the other, being permeated by them. Gender (and racial and class) inequalities are therefore buried within the state, but through part of the same dynamic process, gender relations are partly constituted through the state. The state therefore partly reflects and partly helps to create particular forms of gender relations and gender inequality. State practices construct and legitimate gender divisions, and gendered identities are in part constructed by the law and private discourses which emanate from the state. Carol Smart (1989), for example, has investigated how the power of the law as a discourse, while it is not unified, can act to disempower women and alternative feminist paradigms. The state therefore plays a key role in constructing gender and regulating relationships between men and women, that is, gender relations. As a result of these new understandings recent feminist analyses have moved from looking at ways in which state treats women differently to men, for example in terms of state policies, to ways in which particular states act to construct gendered subjects. As Vicky Randall discusses in the concluding chapter, identities can be constructed as part of a process of engagement with the state which relates to the analysis of women's political activity and questions of representation.

If the nature of the state or the relationship between the state and gender relations is not fixed and immutable, battles can be fought in the arena of the state. The state is therefore 'an uneven and fractured terrain with dangers as well as resources for women's movements' (Rai and Lievesley 1996: 1). Consequently, while the state has for the most part acted to reinforce female subordination, the space can exist within the state to act to change gender relations (Alvarez 1990). At different times and within different regimes, opportunity spaces can be used to alter the existing pattern of gender relations. This theme is taken up by Valerie Sperling (Chapter 9) in her discussion of Russian women's movements and their dealings with various parts of the state and it will recur in the concluding chapter. This kind of analysis again leads to questions of feminist strategy and provides a very different justification for engagement with the state to either that of liberal feminists or those who have a benign social democratic view of the welfare state. 'State feminism' becomes a potentially effective tool within this framework. The state therefore is not to be avoided. As many of the contributions to this volume demonstrate, in certain contexts, for example in some political formations or during moments of regime change, that is transition or fluidity, there may be greater potential for actions and strategies which will act to alter gender relations.

The state as a gendered hierarchy

If institutions, very widely defined by North (1990: 4) as frameworks for socially constructed rules and norms and organisations which have developed as a result of those frameworks, are important in any gendered analysis of the state, it then becomes crucial to analyse the state in gendered terms as a complex bureaucratic organisation. While Savage and Witz (1993) make the distinction between the state as nominally patriarchal (that is, staffed at the top levels by men) and substantively patriarchal (it can act in the interests of men), Franzway *et al.* (1989) point out that the state is almost invariably a gendered hierarchy. Large numbers of women are employed at the bottom of the hierarchy but the numbers decrease as the top of the pyramid is approached. Some parts of the state such as the military and the police are also disproportionately staffed by men at all levels, while women are found only rarely in central banks, economic ministries or foreign trade departments. There have been a number of attempts to examine the character of the bureaucracy in gendered terms. These range from a rather optimistic early liberal feminist revisioning of Weber's views which argues that, while women are often less powerful than men within bureaucracies, the truly rational objective structure envisioned by Weber can be achieved with men and women playing a truly equal part within it. In contrast, Katherine Ferguson (1984) puts forward a radical feminist analysis which blends Weberian and Foucauldian insights to argue that bureaucracies embody male power with their embedded masculine style and have little to offer women. Ferguson advocates that women should develop alternative ways of organising instead of trying to change the ways in which bureaucratic structures operate.

Those more influenced by post-structuralist analyses and the experience of 'femocrats' have been interested to analyse the ways in which the state constitutes arenas in which different men use a variety of strategies to construct their interests and women can use various strategies and counter-strategies to constitute their interests (Watson 1990). Within this framework, the state bureaucracy becomes an area in which feminists attempt to play an active role from within, trying to change its structure and the ways in which it operates as well as influencing its policies at a number of levels and areas. From a slightly different perspective, feminist academics and practitioners working in development have been attempting to improve their understanding of gendered institutional structures and practices in order to promote gender equity more effectively. Anne Marie Goetz (1995) has argued, for example, that gendered public-sector institutional failures cannot be seen simply as the result of 'discriminatory attitudes or irrational choices on the part of individuals, or unintended oversights in policy. Nor are they deliberate policy outcomes. They are embedded in the norms, structures and practices of institutions.' Despite the frequent appearance of gender neutrality, it is therefore necessary to understand not simply the nature of the structures but also the history of social choices made by particular groups embedded in those institutions.

State policies

Even if, throughout the world, there are few women to be found at the top of state hierarchies and in decision-making positions within conventional politics, the preceding analysis makes clear that the state is a gendered structure and that the policies which emerge from states are also gendered. The ideas outlined above will help to give us a different way of examining state policies. This will entail looking at different kinds of policies from a perspective of constructing and regulating gender relations and seeing policies as emerging from battles which take place in the arena of the state. In the introduction to their collection on women, the state and development, Charlton *et al.* (1989) have divided state policies into three major categories.

Within their framework, the first category consists of policies which are aimed particularly at women. 'State feminism' could also fall within this category and it has been the subject of increasing attention both in the developed and more recently the developing world (Franzway *et al.* 1989; Watson 1990; Stetson and Mazur 1995; Waylen 1996). However, I will not discuss it any further here because some of the issues surrounding state feminism which emerge from the chapters by Jude Howell (Chapter 10) and Nikki Craske (Chapter 7) are taken up in some detail by Vicky Randall in the concluding chapter.

Many of the policies directed solely at women often focus around so-called protective legislation and reproduction, for example abortion and laws surrounding childbirth, such as maternity leave. One way to understand these policies is in terms of the role played by the state in constructing and regulating women's (and men's) bodies. Feminist academics have used the concept of the body as one method to comprehend the complex ways in which women and men are positioned by legislation and discourse in different cultural and political contexts. As Terrell Carver (Chapter 2) and Vicky Randall (Chapter 11) discuss, the relationship between gender identity and the biological body cannot be taken for granted. The body has not been a historical constant, the ways in which it has been perceived and experienced have changed. Often influenced by Foucault, many feminist academics have recently begun to emphasise the power of discourse to define and control the body (Abrams and Harvey 1996). As demonstrated by Barry Gilheany (Chapter 5), practice and policies relating to abortion in the Irish context show how women's bodies are subject to scrutiny and control in the situation of unwanted pregnancy. While policies regulating abortion show crude and direct forms of intervention, women's bodies are also controlled and disciplined in more subtle ways. Measures to control 'sexual indiscipline' and 'unruly sex' were often expressed through the disciplining of sexual women. In Chapter 6, Barbara Gwinnett considers this type of regulation in her study of prostitution in Birmingham, showing how it is women prostitutes and not their male clients who are subject to regulation by various agencies of the state.

A second category outlined by Charlton *et al.* (1989) is those policies which deal with relations between men and women, particularly property rights, sexuality, family relations, the area where power relations between men and women and therefore gender relations are often institutionalised. The laws and regulations surrounding these issues frequently become an area of contestation when attempts are made to alter existing patterns of power relations. A number of historians have explored how, during the enforcement of colonial rule in Africa, the regulation of marriage, divorce and women's mobility became highly contested as the colonisers attempted to control the societies they taken over (Channock 1982; Barnes 1992; Manicom 1992). In Chapter 3, Ursula Vogel focuses on the changing ways in which marriage has been the dominant site which has produced 'men' and 'women' through the meanings which the law prescribed and enforced in the status of husband and wife in parts of nineteenth-century Europe. She shows some of the ways in which the construction of gender took place in the marriage law of the Napoleonic civil code and was subject to some alteration in the later nineteenth century.

The third category, general policies, is ostensibly gender-neutral but frequently has a different impact on men and women. These policies can be further subdivided between those policy areas linked to the public sphere and somehow seen as 'masculine', such as state-defined politics, war, foreign policy, international trade, resources extraction and long-distance communication, and those concerned with welfare and social reproduction. Women have traditionally been excluded from the so-called masculine areas of policy. The most extreme example of this has been war, where women have until very recently participated on a very different basis to men. In Chapter 8, Susie Jacobs takes the supposedly gender-neutral area of land reform policies in varying political formations to demonstrate that these policies have very different implications for men and for women in rural areas, and that women have generally been disadvantaged relative to men by the reforms which have been implemented.

Those policy areas more intimately connected with the private sphere and social reproduction, for example housing, health and education, fall under the general rubric of welfare and the welfare state. In contrast to the 'masculine' policies of the public sphere, welfare states have for sometime been the subject of feminist analyses, particularly in the first world, looking at how they were established assuming particular patterns of gender relations or with the effect of creating or maintaining particular gender roles and emphasising issues of control and empowerment for women. As we have already seen, some analysts of the Scandinavian welfare state have stressed the positive impact the welfare state can have on women while others have stressed the policing and disciplining role played by the welfare state and its agents. Recently there has been increasing recognition by feminist academics that feminist analyses of welfare states and mainstream welfare research have taken place quite separately. Mainstream work has often concentrated on understanding differences between welfare states but its explanations for different welfare regimes have rarely considered gender relations within their frameworks (Lewis 1992). As a result, Diane Sainsbury (1994: 2) argues:

> mainstream comparative analysis tells us little about how women have fared in different welfare states or about dissimilar policy outcomes for men and women. Nor has the mainstream research paradigm considered one of the most interesting aspects of the development of welfare states: how women have been incorporated in the core policies of welfare states and the politics of entitlement.

However, while feminist studies have provided critiques of this mainstream work and attempted to bring gender into the analysis of the welfare state, they have rarely attempted comparative analyses or an understanding of the variations in the gender content of systems of welfare provision (Orloff

1993). Some of the recent historical analyses, often looking at Europe, provide a partial exception to this tendency (Bock and Thane 1991; Koven and Michel 1993). However, this general omission results in part from the functionalist tendency, discussed above, which sees the welfare state as an expression of patriarchy, capitalism or some combination of the two and therefore tends to ignore differences between welfare regimes. Ann Orloff (1993; 1996) goes on to argue that it is necessary to engage and engender the conceptual frameworks of the mainstream literature, thereby transforming them, rather than develop an alternative schema. One of the key tasks is therefore to gender some of the basic concepts used in the analysis of (not just) the welfare state such as 'citizen' and 'social rights'. Others, however, believe that alternative theories are necessary.

While none of the contributions in this volume addresses the welfare state as the sole focus of its analysis and none are based on the kinds of assumptions about the relatively 'woman friendly' nature of the welfare state which has informed some of the analyses of the Scandinavian welfare states, Nikki Craske (Chapter 7) discusses a welfare regime associated with the neoliberal state in the Latin American context. Social sector adjustment which encompasses poverty alleviation programmes and social investment funds as part of its emergency measures is being promoted as part of the neoliberal economic restructuring taking place in many parts of the world. As yet there have been few analyses of the type that Craske undertakes, which attempt to assess the gendered implications of such policies that aim to alter the balance of welfare provision between the state, the market, the community and household and which, according to Veronica Schild (1998), reposition women in a different form of citizenship as the 'subjects of rights'.

Citizenship

As one of the most important ways in which the relationship of individuals to the state and polity has been theorised, the concept of citizenship and an exploration of the ways in which it has been used is essential in any discussion of the relationship between gender, politics and the state. Citizenship provides a major link between states, individuals and collectivities (Lister 1996). It is 'a status bestowed on those who are full members of a community generally the nation state. All who possess the status are equal with respect to the rights and duties with which the status is endowed' (T.H. Marshall 1950, quoted in Yuval Davis 1996: 2). In the twentieth century, citizenship, couched as it is in terms of the individual, has been seen as gender neutral. However, as many writers have argued, including Vicky Randall in Chapter 11, feminists have advocated very trenchantly that citizenship is and always has been gendered and that at worst women are excluded from full citizenship and at best incorporated into citizenship in different ways to men. In western states the notion of the '*citoyen*' was initially masculine, and citizenship was restricted to men (for long periods excluding working-class men and men of different races such as black slaves in the United States); men were incorporated as soldiers and then as wage earners, that is through their activities in the public sphere. Only later were women incorporated as citizens, often on the basis of their activities in the private sphere as mothers rather than as workers or soldiers.

Many feminists, building on the gender-blind analyses of Marshall and Turner, define citizenship in terms of civil, political and social citizenship and the associated rights which go with this, analysing the ways in which women are unable to access those rights (Walby 1994). Indeed, Orloff (1993: 308) argues that 'just as the independent male householder serves as the ideal-typical citizen in classical liberal democratic theory, the *male* worker serves as the ideal-typical citizen in the literature on social rights'. As we have seen above in the discussion of the welfare state, women have experienced social rights very differently to men. The British welfare state was set up with a very particular vision of the role of men as breadwinners and women as homemakers, with welfare benefits constructed accordingly.

Feminist theorists have also tried to envision different models of citizenship which can incorporate both men and women. In this volume Kate Nash (Chapter 4) assesses three feminist attempts to 'think beyond the "false" universalism of liberal individualism in order to develop a universalism that would be genuinely universal, inclusive of all citizens of a democratic society, and in the case of Chantal Mouffe, self-conscious about the limits of that inclusiveness'. Taking this further, Nira Yuval Davis (1996: 1) has stressed the need to consider the 'issue of women's citizenship not only by contrast to that of men, but also in relation to women's affiliation to dominant or subordinate groups, their ethnicity, origin and urban or rural residence. It should also take into consideration global and transnational positionings of these citizenships.' Feminists should ensure that the use of the terms inclusion and exclusion refers to more than simply gender-based factors but also includes other factors such as race, ethnicity and sexuality.

The public–private divide

The discussion of themes such as citizenship and the welfare state highlights the importance of construction of the public–private divide. Indeed, the identification of women with the private sphere has served to underpin their exclusion from full citizenship, and according to Lister (1997) the rearticulation of the public–private divide provides the starting point for challenging women's exclusion from full citizenship. The public–private divide has therefore become an important theme throughout much feminist writing in politics and political theory and recurs in many of the contributions to this volume. The assumptions underlying the separation of the public and the private are of huge significance to the study of gender and politics. Liberal political theory, while appearing gender neutral, by maintaining a division between the public and the private as central to liberal democracy maintains a division between men and women, where only men can be abstract individuals (Pateman 1983; 1989). The political is therefore defined as masculine in a very profound sense which makes it hard to incorporate women on the same terms as men and excludes many activities in which women are involved as being not political.

The nature of the public–private divide is not fixed and ideas about the nature of the public and private have been recast in different historical periods. Indeed, the state has played a key role in defining and enforcing the different spheres of action which are seen as encompassing the public and the private. An exploration of the ways in which the state helps to construct the public–private divide in particular contexts therefore forms a crucial part of the gendered analysis of the state and politics. Ursula Vogel (Chapter 3) details one example of this in her analysis of the intervention of the state into the private sphere through the construction of marriage laws in nineteenth-century France and shows how as a result men and women were positioned very differently within these legal frameworks. In a contrasting context in the contemporary period Nikki Craske argues that state-imposed neoliberal policies are reasserting, often in complex and contradictory ways, the public–private dichotomy in much of Latin America.

However, there is also a lack of consensus as to just what is entailed in the private domain and these 'inconsistencies and confusions' have led Nira Yuval Davis (1996: 11) to argue that instead of the public–private distinction we should differentiate between three distinct spheres: the state, civil society and the domain of family and kinship relations. Along with citizenship, the discussion of civil society has been become increasingly important in recent years as another way of understanding the relationship between state and society. Civil society is seen as an arena where citizens can play a role in the associational life which helps to give democracy its vibrancy, and the lack of a dense civil society is seen as problematic. However, as with the public–private distinction, a number of analysts have warned of the dangers of over-dichotomising the division between the state and civil society. On the Left in particular there has also been a tendency to have an over-romanticised vision of the radical potential of civil society and of social movements, which are often seen as the embodiment of civil society whether in the established liberal democracies of the west or in the democratising states of Latin America and east and central Europe.

Within this formulation, women's movements of various kinds fall under the rubric of civil society. However, the majority of orthodox analysts, while recognising that many participants in a large number of social movements are women, do not attempt gendered analyses or attempt to assess the significance of this phenomenon. A number of the contributions to this volume, for example those of Sperling (Chapter 9), Craske (Chapter 7) and Howell (Chapter 10), address some of the themes raised in the civil society literature about the nature of the relationship between social movements and the state in the context of authoritarian and democratising systems and implement a gendered analysis in trying to understand their significance. The implications of the political activities of women's movements are taken up again by Vicky Randall in the concluding chapter.

Conclusions

This chapter has attempted to 'bring the state back in' to feminist analyses and to address some of the major themes involved in the study of gender and the state. It has attempted not only to summarise the extent of feminist debates up until now but also to provide some pointers for the analysis of the state in particular contexts and different political formations in the future. Many of these themes are taken up in various ways in subsequent chapters. In particular, we have seen that the state is not a monolithic category but a collection of different agencies, discourses and institutions at local and national (and international) levels. It is necessary to explore the gendered nature of these institutions not simply in terms of their personnel but also in terms of the norms and practices dominant within those institutions. The state plays a key role both in the construction of gender and gender relations and in the construction of the public–private divide. This role needs to be explored in different settings and in terms of different legal and policy outcomes. Furthermore, as the state cannot be seen as lying outside society but is itself a site of struggle, the relationship between different groups of women and the state needs to be explored. Indeed, at certain times it appears that 'opportunity spaces' can exist within the state. One way of exploring the complex relationship between the state and groups of women is in terms of the debates surrounding concepts of citizenship, civil society and social movements and their engagement with the state and polity. Another approach is to examine the activities of women inside the state, often in terms of 'state feminism' and their links to movements outside the state. All these dimensions bring up questions of structure and agency. I have argued that this is in many ways a false dichotomy and, as many of the contributions demonstrate, it is impossible to analyse actions without analysing the structures which constrain those actions.

References

Abrams, L. and Harvey, E. (1996) 'Introduction: gender relations in German history', in L. Abrams and E. Harvey (eds) *Gender Relations in German History: Power, Agency and Experience from the Sixteenth to the Twentieth Century*, London: UCL Press.

Afshar, H. (ed.) (1987) *Women, State and Ideology*, London: Macmillan.

Allen, J. (1990) 'Does feminism need a theory of "the state"?', in S. Watson (ed.) *Playing the State: Australian Feminist Interventions*, London: Verso.

Alvarez, S. (1990) *Engendering Democracy in Brazil: Women's Movements in Transition Politics*, Princeton, N.J.: Princeton University Press.

Barnes, T. (1992) 'The fight for control of African women's mobility in colonial Zimbabwe', *Signs: Journal of Women, Culture, and Society* 17(3): 586–608.

Bock, G. and Thane, P. (eds) (1991) *Maternity and Gender Policies: Women and the Rise of European Welfare States 1880s–1950s*, London: Routledge.

Channock, M. (1982) 'Making customary law: men women and courts in colonial Northern Rhodesia', in M. Hay and M. Wright (eds) *African Women and the Law: Historical Perspectives*, Boston University Papers on Africa no. 7, Boston, Mass.: Boston University.

Charlton, S.E., Everett, J. and Staudt, K. (eds) (1989) *Women, the State and Development*, Albany, N.Y.: SUNY Press.

Connell, R. (1990) 'The state, gender and sexual politics', *Theory and Society* 19(5): 507–44.

Dahlerup, D. (1987) 'Confusing concepts – confusing reality: a theoretical discussion of the patriarchal state', in A. Showstack Sassoon (ed.) *Women and the State*, London: Routledge.

Ehrenreich, B. and Fox Piven, F. (1983) 'Women and the welfare state', in I. Howe (ed.) *Alternatives: Proposals for America from the Democratic Left*, New York: Pantheon.

Eisenstein, Z. (ed.) (1979) *Capitalist Patriarchy and the Case for Socialist Feminism*, New York: Monthly Review Press.

Ferguson, K. (1984) *The Feminist Case Against Bureaucracy*, Philadelphia, Pa: Temple University Press.

Franzway, S., Court, D. and Connell, R. (1989) *Staking a Claim: Feminism, Bureaucracy and the State*, Cambridge: Polity Press.

Goetz, A.M. (1995) 'Macro–meso–micro linkages: understanding gendered institutional structures and practices', paper for SAGA Workshop on Gender and Economic Reform in Africa, Ottawa, October.

Kandiyoti, D. (1991) 'Identity and its discontents: women and the nation', *Millennium: Journal of International Studies* 20(3): 429–43.

Koven, S. and Michel, M. (eds) (1993) *Mothers of a New World: Maternalist Politics and the Origins of Welfare States*, London: Routledge.

Lewis, J. (1992) 'Gender and the development of welfare regimes', *Journal of European Social Policy* 2(3): 159–73.

Lister, R. (1996) 'Citizenship: towards a feminist synthesis', paper presented at the Women and Citizenship Conference, Greenwich, July.

Lister, R. (1997) 'Inclusion/exclusion: the Janus face of citizenship', paper presented at 'Towards a Gendered Political Economy Workshop', Sheffield, September.

McIntosh, M. (1978) 'The state and the oppression of women', in A. Kuhn and A.M. Wolpe (eds) *Feminism and Materialism*, London: Routledge.

Mackinnon, C. (1983) 'Feminism, Marxism, method and the state: towards a feminist jurisprudence', *Signs* 8(2): 635–58.

Manicom, L. (1992) 'Ruling relations: rethinking state and gender in South African history', *Journal of African History* 33: 441–65.

Migdal, J. (1996) 'Studying the state', paper presented to annual meeting of the American Political Science Association, San Francisco, August.

North, D. (1990) *Institutions, Institutional Change and Economic Performance*, Cambridge: Cambridge University Press.

Orloff, A.S. (1993) 'Gender and the social rights of citizenship: the comparative analysis of gender relations and welfare states', *American Sociological Review* 58: 303–28.

Orloff, A.S. (1996) 'Gender and the welfare state', Discussion Paper no. 1082–96, Madison, WI.: Institute for Research on Poverty, University of Wisconsin.

Pateman, C. (1983) 'Feminist critiques of the public–private dichotomy', in S. Benn and G. Gaus (eds) *The Public and the Private in Social Life*, London: Croom Helm.

Pateman, C. (1989) *The Disorder of Women: Democracy, Feminism and Political Theory*, Cambridge: Polity Press.

Pringle, R. and Watson, S. (1992) 'Women's interests and the post structuralist state' in M. Barrett and A. Philips (eds) *Destabilizing Theory: Contemporary Feminist Debates*, Cambridge: Polity Press.

Rai, S. (1996) 'Women and the state in the Third World: some issues for debate', in S. Rai and G. Lievesley (eds) *Women and the State: International Perspectives*, London: Taylor & Francis.

Rai, S. and Lievesley, G. (eds) (1996) *Women and the State: International Perspectives*, London: Taylor & Francis.

Sainsbury, D. (ed.) (1994) *Gendering Welfare States*, London: Sage Publications.

Savage, M. and Witz, A. (eds) (1993) *Gender and Bureaucracy*, Oxford: Blackwell.

Schild, V. (1998) 'New subjects of rights: women's movements and the construction of citizenship in the "New Democracies"' in S. Alvarez, A. Escobar and E. Dagnino (eds) *Politics of Culture/Culture of Politics*, Boulder, Col.: Westview.

Scott, J. (1986) 'Gender: a useful category of historical analysis', *American Historical Review* 91(5): 1053–75.

Smart, C. (1989) *Feminism and the Power of the Law*, London: Routledge.

Steinmo, S., Thelen, K. and Longstreth, F. (eds) (1992) *Structuring Politics: Historical Institutionalism in Comparative Analysis*, Cambridge: Cambridge University Press.

Stetson, D. and Mazur, A. (eds) (1995) *Comparative State Feminism*, London: Sage Publications.

Walby, S. (1994) 'Is citizenship gendered?', *Sociology* 28(2): 379–95.

Watson, S. (ed.) (1990) *Playing the State: Australian Feminist Interventions*, London: Verso.

Watson, S. (1993) 'Femocratic feminisms', in M. Savage and A. Witz (eds) *Gender and Bureaucracy*, Oxford: Blackwell.

Waylen, G. (1996) 'Democratization, feminism and the state: the establishment of SERNAM in Chile', in S. Rai and G. Lievesley (eds) *Women and the State: International Perspectives*, London: Taylor & Francis.

Wilson, E. (1977) *Women and the Welfare State*, London: Tavistock.

Yuval Davis, N. (1996) 'Women, citizenship and difference', background paper for the Conference on Women and Citizenship, Greenwich, July.

2 A political theory of gender
Perspectives on the 'universal subject'

Terrell Carver[1]

This chapter examines current usage of the concept 'gender' as loosely synonymous with 'sex' and lazily synonymous with 'women'. It considers the indeterminate and ambiguous construction of the term and proposes a conceptualisation that can be usefully related to political theory and political practice: 'the way that sex and sexuality become power-relations in society'. Using this perspective, it can be shown that the paradoxical construction of the 'universal subject' in politics and political theory as both masculine and de-gendered pushes important activities in society to the political margins and works to make change unthinkable for men.

Perspectives: feminist theories and gender studies

Amongst the perspectives employed, I would particularly draw the reader's attention to those of feminist theory, which I define as 'theorisations of women's oppression', and gender studies, which I define as 'investigations into the ways that sex and sexuality become power relations in society', where 'sex' is M/F and 'sexuality' is sexual behaviour. No doubt these are somewhat idiosyncratic and less than completely informative definitions, but I offer them just to hint at what to expect. Moreover, I have a particular project that has emerged from within both perspectives, namely a focus on men as problematic in two respects: their power over women and their use of gender in society.

One line of thought that has emerged very strongly in my mind is that recent work in the sociology of masculinities has something to say to political theorists about their trade. Recent sociology derived from Foucault has begun to expand our notions of power in society – where it is and how it works. And feminisms have begun to upset traditional distinctions between public–private and political/non-political – and the way that these terms are mapped onto each other. It seems to me that after these developments men are going to look different. While this has of course already happened in various ways within feminist theory, there is always room to move the discussion along, using material that is not yet commonly cited.

It also seems to me that it is important to move these kinds of discussions about men into the mainstream/malestream of academic and scholarly work. In my experience of this milieu I have detected not only ignorance of what feminist theorising has accomplished but also complacency with respect to feminist theorising as an activity. This complacency resides in a view that feminist theorising is always, necessarily and most usefully done by women, for women, about women. This could perhaps be summarised as a '(Separate) but Equal Opportunities' view of affairs that 'lets the girls get on with it'. In an oral and very public remark Wendy Brown once commented that feminist theorists would have to address mainstream/malestream political theory as such, changing its terms of reference and doing it differently, otherwise the work of feminist theorists would always be 'Mrs Political Theory', with all that that false honorific implies.

Perhaps I may be allowed one further illustrative anecdote, though I shall do my best to disguise the identity of my interlocutor. A male colleague in political science once explained that his work could not include *women* political leaders, because as a matter of fact there weren't any in his field of study. He apologised to all that his work regrettably 'had no *gender* dimension'. My immediate and no doubt overly forthright response was: 'Gender is not a synonym for women', and, urged on by a publisher, I made it the title of a book. One of the obvious reasons why there were no women political leaders to be found in that context is precisely the working of gender relations with respect to women. But it was also the case, as emerged in discussion, that gender relations of masculinities, as practised among men, played a large role in the formation of the political relations that ensured the subordination and loyalty of some men to other men and the concomitant exclusion of women.

Gender: the way that sex and sexuality become political

In many contexts one finds that a reference to gender is a reference to women, as if men, males and masculinities were all unproblematic in that regard, or indeed perhaps simply nothing to do with gender at all. This can very readily become a way of making women problematic, once again, in a way that marginalises them as 'a problem' and leaves men where they have always been, doing pretty much what they like or, more accurately, what some of them like. On the whole there have been only minimal concessions in power relations from men to women, and none at all in the basic construction of gendered, that is power-ridden, identities derived rather incoherently from presumptions about sex and sexuality. These identities, or perhaps rather identity-claims, are the real stuff of the asymmetrical social relationships that we have inherited. Few people, if any, really 'have' these identities with utter consistency and conviction. Rather, they claim them as they are performed, and in doing this they establish the symbolic codes from which disciplinary practices emerge (Butler 1990).

In the common parlance of recent times, gender has also become a euphemism for sex, i.e. male or female, M or F, man or woman, as biologically, socially and legally defined. These definitions, though, are hardly unambiguous. In doctrines of family, parenthood and personal dignity, considerations of individual preference and social functionality begin to cross-cut the commonplace stereotyping on which our elaborations of the two supposedly opposite yet co-requisite sexes are based. This synonymy of gender for sex seems a step backward, or at least it marks a kind of inertia. It constantly reinscribes the supposedly obvious and supposedly well-understood categories male and female, men and women, back into political ideas, just when these ideas are starting to be really problematic, politically interesting and interestingly complex. Why map gender onto sex as one-to-one, just when the term was helping to make visible the ambiguities of sexuality, orientation, choice and change that have been undercover for centuries? Indeed, modern technologies of the body and modern methods of political mobilisation have rendered these questions not just visible but very pressing within the media, the institutional apparatus of courts and legislatures, and all the professions in society.

A one-to-one mapping of gender onto a commonplace categorisation of sex as male/female is over-simple, even with respect to biology and medicine, as there are chromosomal variations and syndromes, not to mention morphological ones, that create genuinely ambiguous individuals. Even supposing that 'normality' with respect to the M/F distinction (as medically and socially enforced) is good enough for most analytical purposes, why then limit gender to a restatement of that? Indeed, the term was coined to do more than restate the (supposedly) obvious, by decoupling (simplified) biology from (stereotyped) behaviour. Gender was taken to be the way that sex was expressed in society in terms of behaviour, masculine or feminine. Feminine males and masculine females were then categorised and made problematic within psychoanalytic, psychological or sociological theories of normality and development.

Discourses and practices of toleration and liberation have to some extent replaced the more sinister approaches and institutions which historical and sociological work on the history of the human sciences have exposed. There is yet more room in life for discourses of variation or 'difference'. However, at the moment the vocabulary that is available is ambiguous and indeterminate, binary and hierarchical; or rather, I am arguing that this is so. Following through the conceptual history of sex and gender leads me to conclude that we simply do not know how many genders there are, because in practice the answer varies according to what is assumed about sex and sexuality before any particular concept of gender is then deployed. These various concepts of gender do not fit together in a coherent way, and so current usage allows and indeed encourages people to talk past each other.

When 'gender' came into use, as something distinct from 'sex', it was argued that there are normal or characteristic ways of *being of the male or female sex*, called masculine and feminine, and that these are socially learnt rather than biologically determined. Following through that logic, there are then four genders, rather than two, as masculine men, masculine women, feminine women and feminine men become logically possible and empirically observable. Indeed, observational checklists distinguishing masculinity from femininity were constructed.

The next development was to enquire into the relationship between gender as an expression of sex and orientation as an expression of sexuality, on the assumption that masculine men and feminine women are oriented to each other, whereas 'inverts' are not. Thus gender was also used to cover the way that *sexuality is expressed* between the sexes, on the assumption that 'normal' gendering (for example, of males as masculine and females as feminine) also encompasses 'normal' opposite-sex (and reproductive) sexuality, whereas same-sex sexuality was triply 'abnormal', in that it was non-reproductive, inversely gendered (feminine men and masculine women), and desirous of 'sameness' rather than an 'opposite'. Further research, especially in the 1950s as sexology developed, revealed complexities and varieties of sexual behaviour that gradually undermined this simplistic schema (Brod 1987).

None the less, the logic of these assumptions persists; and following it through, there are then two genders, heterosexuality and homosexuality (or three, if celibacy is an option), on the assumption that these categories include both Ms and Fs, depending on whether sexuality is M to F and F to M (heterosexuality) or M to M and F to F (homosexuality). Alternatively, perhaps there are four or six genders, as the lineup might then be heterosexual men, heterosexual women, homosexual women, homosexual men, celibate women and celibate men, once gender as orientation is mapped back onto gender as sex. Perhaps historically there were three genders (heterosexual men, heterosexual women, celibates) or four (heterosexual men, heterosexual women, celibate women, celibate men), before homosexuality as a sexual identity was developed, or at least as a sexual identity that we would recognise as homosexual or that the social actors themselves would identify as such (Weeks 1985). Adding bisexuality as either one further gender or two 'sexually' differentiated genders runs the total up further (Evans 1993).

If orientation is not mapped back onto sex, but is instead analysed in terms of object of desire (a male or a female), then the logic is that there are two genders, one encompassing heterosexual women and homosexual men (desiring men) and the other encompassing heterosexual men and homosexual women (desiring women). The former is actually a well-known combination as 'best friends', whereas the latter does not seem to have attained much social reality or visibility, as far as I know. If bisexuals are added, then in terms of object of desire they are definitely one gender unto themselves, as the differentiation into 'women who desire women and men' and 'men who desire women and men' becomes rather pointless, as genital identity seems transcended on both sides of the equation.

Once the mapping of gender has turned from bodily organs to objects of desire, whether human or otherwise, or to performance and 'dressing up', in which activities involving objects (whether human or otherwise) become the analytical focus, then the variations and possibilities move swiftly towards infinity. How one defines the bounds of sexuality itself as an activity is by no means unambiguous, so that in some conceptions reproduction is rigorously enforced as a criterion, whereas in other conceptions it is virtually erased. This divergence of strategy is relevant, for example, even to an activity that is often *presented* as somehow asexual and only guiltily of the body, namely parenting. This then raises issues of power and politics. If gender is part of a political identity, a group basis for political coalitions, a field of individual interest where people find common cause in *similarity*, then perhaps 'parent' is itself a gender, transcending the bodily differences that are usually identified as not just sexual but 'opposite'.

Considerations of *difference* can also be relevant here, as women in feminist politics were not the first to discover. But this immediately raises the question of *similarity* against which 'difference' is supposed to be pertinent. Class and 'race'/ethnicity amongst women were points of reference from which quite different notions of gender politics were constructed in terms of substantial demands and coalition strategies (Riley 1988; Bottomley *et al.* 1991). The notion of gender politics as necessarily a politics of sexual *polarisation* has been made highly problematic: could it be that the gender politics of working-class women should be oriented away from issues of male domination and towards *solidarity* with working-class men in an anti-imperialist struggle? Perhaps the masculine as a threat to feminist politics was correctly located in rich, white, capitalist societies, and not in 'men of colour' in any significant way?

If gender is tied to gender politics, rather than to individualised conceptions of sex and sexuality, then perhaps privileged white men and poor exploited men are in different genders as political subjects, as well as political objects? Gender politics amongst men is not a topic that often surfaces in political theory. It works to divide them as men, and, when divided, to draw them together in ways that may be hierarchical or egalitarian, 'homosocial' or homoerotic, within the divisions that are created around sex and sexuality (Hearn and Collinson 1994). Gender politics amongst men is thus by no means always in opposition to women or to conceptions of women's interests. On the one hand, naturalised or commonplace categories like sex, gender, class and 'race'/ethnicity are manipulated in politics to construct inclusions and exclusions with respect to groups, an inside and an outside with respect to a border or boundary-line, and various maps of identity and difference such that allies and enemies, partners and opponents, powerful and powerless are produced as societies apparently 'function'. But on the other hand, these constructions, despite all the disciplinary apparatuses employed, map poorly onto the varieties of experience that individuals can still manage to generate in living their lives as human agents, and which interpreters such as political theorists can construct as a 'recovery'. It is up to each of us to make our own interpretations and to generate our own purposive context, though we cannot do this just as we like.

Methodologically the way forward is to cease using gender as a synonym for sex or as a synonym for women. Both the concepts sex and women are problematic enough; merely redescribing them as gender, or as something to do with gender, is not in itself helpful, unless some further rigorous theorisation is undertaken. From the review above it is evident that sexual difference is not quite as sharp and binary as even thoughtful writers often imagine, and what exactly the differences are cannot themselves be located in some supposedly sacrosanct realm of truth such as biology, itself a realm of metaphor and anthropomorphic assumptions (Haraway 1991). This is not to say that there are no bodily differences, or that bodily differences do not matter, as obviously they do, but that conceptualisations of bodily difference are not power-neutral. Rather, they are undertaken for purposes involving power, claims to the contrary notwithstanding.

Thus a binary involving sex is socially created and enforced, but this enforcement swiftly raises other issues: reproduction, orientation, sexuality. Over the last 100 years the social sciences have unpacked a vast realm of differences involving class, 'race'/ethnicity, culture and sheer individuality. Having tipped all that out of the box, it seems of little use to deploy gender as a term that allegedly conceptualises all this complexity as if all the complexities could be resolved into something rather simple. My own solution is to use gender as a way of starting an investigation or discussion about sex, sexuality and power as social relations in the various ways that people construct them. It is, of course, important to remember that this construction occurs in two ways with respect to individuals: namely, individuals may have an identity or category ascribed to them, or they may themselves self-describe in terms of an identity or category. My point is that these identities or categories do not exist in a realm where they just are what they are; rather, they are constantly defined and re-defined in the discourses through which real power relations are conducted. Thus political studies, whether empirical or theoretical (and there is less difference between the two than is often pretended), must deploy concepts that are carefully tailored to the needs of the writer but are also sensitively constructed with respect to the discursive realm in which the subjects of any study actually live.

In particular, the intersection between categories of gender, broadly conceptualised in the way that I have indicated, are co-defined with concepts of class, 'race'/ethnicity and the myriad other concepts from which localised cultures are constructed. This is not to say that abstraction and generalisation are impossible, rather that they are of course essential to any study of politics, provided they are tailored to the complexities of the issues under discussion. Whether the gender politics of some working-class women is or should be oriented towards solidarity with working-class men is very much up to them, which means that theoretical conceptualisations of gender should be broad enough to valorise this and not so narrow as to claim that all gender politics must fracture along a sexual binary. Similarly, the sexual power that men exercise over men, whether of a directly abusive kind (such as male rape in wartime, as well as female rape) or of an indirect and excluding character (for example, controlling women generally, and in particular controlling men's access to them in class terms) can be usefully conceptualised as gender politics, not only incorporating the sexual binary, but also expanding the analysis of power beyond it. What emerges is a richer and more explanatory account, but only if the theoretical terms from which the explanation derives are flexible enough to embrace complexity and to consider self-descriptions as well as social ascriptions.

What follows is a largely theoretical discussion, but it does touch on familiar discourses and problems, and I hope it illustrates productive use of gender as ways in which sex and sexuality become power relations in society.

Private man: two critiques

The 'universal subject' is a familiar person in the discourse of politics and of political theory. This is 'man', 'mankind', 'the individual', 'human nature', the citizen of the polity or the subject of government. In recent years there has been considerable feminist analysis of this way of abstracting from and generalising about the humans that form any society. However, there have also been feminist-inspired studies of men in terms of the history and variety of masculine experience, and also in terms of the dynamics of dominant masculinities that create hierarchies and exclusions amongst men as well as the oppression of women.

The most striking ambiguity in 'private man', as he appears in liberal political theory and as he is explicated in the feminist critique, is that he is both male and de-gendered. This is also mentioned in Hearn's 'critique of men' when he comments that 'generic universal Man . . . [appears as] both neutral (neutered?) humanity . . . and as "male"' (Hearn 1992: 3).

In the first instance, as we have seen, this 'man' has a 'masculine body' and 'is inherently male'. Maleness here is theorised negatively as not displaying female bodily characteristics. But masculinity is theorised positively as a psychology of competitive self-interest in material things, rather than a focus on nurturing and emotion.

However, in the second instance, this 'subject' is paradoxically identified as de-gendered or neutered (Phillips 1992a: 27; Mendus 1992: 214–15). In political theory, as we know, the generic human is traditionally presented as unsexed, because sex is generally backgrounded as irrelevant. But when sex is made relevant, it is clearly a subordinate element in the way that human identity is conceived (Brown 1987).

The 'abstract individual' appears de-gendered because it is in the public realm. This realm is defined in opposition to the private precisely through a particular kind of abstraction, an abstraction away from sexual activity and reproductive attributes altogether. However, this is not to say that actual practice always respects this (Butler 1993). Thus the 'abstract individual' exemplifies an absence of pregnancy and other female bodily characteristics that arguably play a major role for females in self- and social-identity formation, and in the formation of political interests, whereas in political theory the 'individual' that emerges is monotonically singular, unreproductive and apparently sexless. Moreover this 'individual' is sometimes theorised as a rational consciousness in a way that suggests disembodiment altogether, as the body never really appears except as a presumed material substratum. The body is certainly not the site of the dramas of female corporeal existence nor indeed of sexual reproduction or sexual activity that need concern 'us' in the presumed audience.

The presentation of what is dominantly masculine as 'de-gendered' or 'neutered' can be understood as a misogynist political strategy pursued within the founding narratives of political theory. This is a perspective 'which hides behind a mask of gender neutrality in order to subordinate women' (Bock and James 1992: 6). It pushes sexuality, domestic labour, reproduction and childcare into a private sphere and makes them women's work – except when this sphere requires public regulation, in which case 'public man' does the job, and what was 'private' becomes the public realm (Walby 1990). Indeed, theorising this 'subject' as disembodied altogether seems to negate the need for any very serious theory of the body and any very challenging account of bodily violence, most especially of male violence towards women, at home and on the street or indeed anywhere else.

Thus in liberal theory various characteristics of dominant masculinities are smuggled into the supposedly de-gendered 'abstract individual' as normal or natural behaviour through an imputed psychology of rational individualism. Moreover, these theorisations have also been shown to slip into revealing or admitting that this supposedly de-gendered subject is in fact male in reproductive terms, rather than womanly, and masculine in dominant modes, rather than feminine. Gender-neutrality and dominant masculinity are both affirmed and denied for a reason.

Besides the relegation of sexuality, reproduction, childcare and domestic labour into the realm of 'private woman', there is this further result: *male* sexualities and reproductive capacities are also pushed into the background, as well as a *male* role in childcare and domestic labour (Bacchi 1991). These are issues that have not been on the theoretical and political agenda, as it has come down to us in traditional politics, for public (or indeed much private) discussion. Indeed, the point of these theorisations, on feminist analysis, was precisely to structure and direct the definition of politics, and the course of debate, in this way in the first place. A theorisation of 'the family' or of 'generation' (i.e. reproduction) occasionally appears in the classic narratives, albeit peripherally and contradictorily (Coole 1992; Gatens 1992; Pateman 1988). Arguably, theorists and politicians themselves are not anxious to give to men's differences from women even the limited attention that they give to women's differences from men. This is because sustained attention to these matters could well disturb the power relations that contemporary narratives of gender – including strategic silences – actually construct.

Thus what might be problematic about men in terms of sexual behaviour, reproductive responsibilities and domestic and childcare obligations is displaced into a realm where negotiated discussion need not take place. Indeed, these matters have been conveniently relegated to the feminist agenda, on the presumption that feminists may discuss it powerlessly amongst themselves. Over many years, feminist theory has identified precisely those areas of male activity as sites where men victimise women, and feminist research has given voice to women's experiences of men. Moreover, theorisations of gay sexualities are beginning to trace the political subordination that gay men experience in relation to dominant heterosexist masculinities. This is the point at which a critical re-theorisation of men should begin, and this means that the gender-neutral but archetypically masculinised 'subject' of political theory can no longer be unreflectively deployed. It is not a 'merely conceptual' construction but rather an artefact of power struggles that we are supposed to forget or never even to see.

Conclusions

Thus the de-gendered and disembodied male is a disguise. It covers an absence. This absence is the void, in traditional political theory and in traditional political discourse more broadly, of theorisation concerning male sexuality, reproductive capacities and domestic roles in childcare and other caring activities. Or rather, near-void. Paternity is sometimes deployed in political theory, and in politics, as a symbol, chiefly of men as founders of republics or 'nursing fathers', or as 'family men' acting as heads of households in a paternalist manner, ruling over dependants (see, for example, Locke 1988: 330–49). But there is very little interest in political theory, and in political discourse generally, in exploring those symbolisations in any detail in order to attempt to test their validity as abstractions from actual practice (Wolff 1978 is a very rare exception). This is because it might well be discovered that in general men are not engaged in these activities in the way that the symbolisation implies (Brown 1988: 205; Segal 1990; Seidler 1991a; Seidler 1991b). Fatherhood is mentioned strategically but 'forgotten' theoretically. This serves to protect a position of privilege by making critical discussion unthinkable.

'Woman' as a category of oppression needs to be reversed, and for feminist politics that aims to secure more positions of power for women, working from the category 'woman' has been and should continue to be successful (Phillips 1992b: 78; Jones 1993). Thus any defensible political theory ought to allow for group- and self-identification and equal opportunities to promote the visibility and power of excluded groups (Phillips 1991; Young 1990). However, it is also true that women themselves differ over why, how and where they ought to be visible, and what they might do with such power as they are able to gain individually. Thus what constitutes an 'opportunity' and what 'equal' ones might be are both up for grabs in theory and in practice (Bacchi 1991).

However, it does not follow that these issues are best conceptualised in terms of 'woman', as a trade-off develops between relative ease of organisation and unnecessary or counterproductive exclusions. Organising directly on the sex boundary risks reinforcing the function of gender as a catch-all source of categorisations and distinctions, and in particular the risk of reinforcing the particular way that these categorisations and distinctions are popularly understood today. Organising around 'woman' does not necessarily put childcare on the agenda, or necessarily put it on the agenda in a way that is child-centred or even 'woman'-centred. As has been noted, there is a risk that by making something a 'women's issue' it seems to become something that women naturally or necessarily do *and men don't*.

Note

1 The argument in this chapter is based on the Introduction and Chapter One of my *Gender Is Not a Synonym for Women*, © 1996 by Lynne Rienner Inc. Used with permission of the publishers.

References

Bacchi, Carole L. (1991) *Same Difference: Feminism and Sexual Difference*, Sydney: Allen & Unwin.

Barrett, Michèle and Phillips, Anne (eds) (1992) *Destabilizing Theory*, Cambridge: Polity Press.

Bock, Gisela and James, Susan (1992) *Beyond Equality and Difference: Citizenship, Feminist Politics and Female Subjectivity*, London: Routledge.

Bottomley, Gill, de Lepervanche, M. and Martin, Jeannie (eds) (1991) *Intersexions: Gender/Class/Culture/Ethnicity*, Sydney: Allen & Unwin.

Brod, Harry (ed.) (1987) *The Making of Masculinities: The New Men's Studies*, Winchester, Mass.: Allen & Unwin.

Brod, Harry and Kaufmann, Michael (1994) *Theorizing Masculinities*, Newbury Park, Cal.: Sage.

Brown, Wendy (1987) 'Where is the sex in political theory?', *Women and Politics* 6: 3–23.

Brown, Wendy (1988) *Manhood and Politics: A Feminist Reading in Political Theory*, Totowa, N.J.: Rowman & Littlefield.

Butler, Judith (1990) *Gender Trouble: Feminism and the Subversion of Identity*, London: Routledge.

Butler, Judith (1993) *Bodies that Matter: On the Discursive Limits of 'Sex'*, London: Routledge.

Coole, Diana H. (1992) *Women in Political Theory: From Ancient Misogyny to Contemporary Feminism*, 2nd edn, Brighton: Harvester/Wheatsheaf.

Dunn, John (ed.) (1992) *Democracy: The Unfinished Journey, 508BC to AD1993*, Cambridge: Cambridge University Press.

Evans, David T. (1993) *Sexual Citizenship: The Material Construction of Sexualities*, London: Routledge.

Gatens, Moira (1992) 'Power, bodies and difference', in M. Barrett and A. Phillips (eds), *Destabilizing Theory*, Cambridge: Polity Press, 120–37.

Haraway, Donna (1991) *Simians, Cyborgs, and Women: The Reinvention of Nature*, London: Free Association Books.

Hearn, Jeff (1992) *Men in the Public Eye: The Construction and Deconstruction of Public Men and Public Patriarchies*, London: Routledge.

Hearn, Jeff and Collinson, David (1994) 'Unities and differences between men and between masculinities', in H. Brod and M. Kaufmann, *Theorizing Masculinities*, Newbury Park, Cal.: Sage, 97–118.

Jones, Kathleen B. (1993) *Compassionate Authority*, New York: Routledge.

Locke, John (1988) *Two Treatises of Government*, ed. Peter Laslett, Cambridge: Cambridge University Press.

Mendus, Susan (1992) 'Losing the faith: feminism and democracy', in J. Dunn (ed.), *Democracy: The Unfinished Journey, 508BC to AD1993*, Cambridge: Cambridge University Press, 207–19.

Pateman, Carole (1988) *The Sexual Contract*, Cambridge: Polity Press.

Phillips, Anne (1991) *Engendering Democracy*, Cambridge: Polity Press.

Phillips, Anne (1992a) 'Universal pretensions in political thought', in M. Barrett and A. Phillips (eds) *Destabilizing Theory*, Cambridge: Polity Press, 10–30.

Phillips, Anne (1992b) 'Must feminists give up on liberal democracy?', *Political Studies* 40 (special issue on 'Prospects for Democracy'): 68–82.

Riley, Denise (1988) *'Am I that Name?': Feminism and the Category of 'Women' in History*, London: Macmillan.

Segal, Lynne (1990) *Slow Motion: Changing Masculinities, Changing Men*, London: Virago.

Seidler, Victor J. (ed.) (1991a) *The Achilles Heel Reader*, London: Routledge.

Seidler, Victor J. (1991b) *Recreating Sexual Politics*, London: Routledge.

Walby, Sylvia (1990) *Theorizing Patriarchy*, Oxford: Blackwell.

Weeks, Jeffrey (1985) *Sexuality and its Discontents: Meaning, Myths and Modern Sexualities*, London: Routledge & Kegan Paul.

Wolff, Robert Paul (1978) 'There's nobody here but us persons', in C.C. Gould and M.W. Wartofsky (eds), *Women and Philosophy: Toward a Theory of Liberation*, New York: George Putnam's Sons, 128–44.

Young, Iris Marion (1990) *Justice and the Politics of Difference*, Princeton, N.J.: Princeton University Press.

3 The state and the making of gender
Some historical legacies

Ursula Vogel

Introduction

Recent debates on the reform of the divorce law and the equally heated controversies about suitable educational policies to enhance the standing of the traditional marriage among school-children[1] are a good example of the close interrelationship between gender and the state. Neither of these terms figures explicitly in the rhetoric that characterises the debates. While the appeal to family values is generally couched in the gender-neutral language of responsible parenthood, on the one hand, and of individual selfishness, on the other, the main beneficiary of a reinvigorated family appears to be the stability and moral cohesion of society as a whole. It is not difficult to see, however, that public perceptions of 'the' family are shot through with assumptions about gender roles; and the seemingly unproblematic demands of society's common interest cover for what is in fact a highly contested political issue: that of the right and the capacity of the modern liberal state to enforce a particular order of private life.

For most of past history, in Europe as elsewhere, marriage has been the dominant site which has produced 'men' and 'women' through the meanings which the law prescribed – and enforced – in the status of husband and wife. This chapter examines European marriage laws of the nineteenth century in order to reconstruct some paradigmatic historical legacies that can illuminate the characteristic patterns of the modern state's involvement in the making of gender. (It should be clear from the outset that these legacies are taken to refer to the normative constructions of gender that we find embodied in the legal institution of marriage and in the discourses that served to interpret and legitimate it. I shall not be concerned with social experiences and practices and thus not with the question how the law affected men and women in the everyday dealings of married life.)[2]

I shall begin with some general reflections on the conceptual relationship between 'gender' and 'state' and on its place in feminist political theory. The main part of the chapter will use the French *Code civil* of 1804 as a case study to represent the conflicting demands of private freedom and public coercion that were the distinctive marks of the bourgeois legal order of the nineteenth century: as heir to a political revolution (the French Revolution of 1789) which had destroyed a social system rooted in hierarchical status ascriptions, the *Code civil* established a normative framework of individual liberty and formal equality which facilitated the pursuit of private interests, private property and market opportunities. As the custodian of the patriarchal marriage and of the authoritarian structures of the *gouvernement domestique*, on the other hand, the same code entrenched a quasi-feudal order of gender for more than a century to come. Attention to this constitutive division in modern legal systems challenges the commonly held view that nineteenth-century thinking identified marriage unambiguously with the normative principles of the private sphere, that is with a sphere left to the voluntary contractual arrangements of private individuals and free from the impositions of the state. Rather, in the heyday of liberalism, individualism and *laissez-faire* marriage was widely understood to entail a public, coercive status for both men and women. To put it differently, within the terrain of the private law – in which the public authority confines itself to supplying procedures and guarantees to the uncoerced transactions of private persons – marriage formed an enclave of relationships that were in virtually every respect determined by the state.

We shall see that the rights which a husband held over the person and property of his wife differed in two salient respects from the rights which pertained to individuals under the contractual and formally equal provisions of bourgeois private law. First, the status of husband and wife expressed a distinctly political relationship of rule and subordination (not, that is, one of merely social and economic inequality). Second, the status attributes of marriage belonged in the category of coercive law (*ius cogens*). They were enforced upon every marriage irrespective of the will or choice of the individuals concerned. Vestiges of the public status of marriage survived in all European legal systems until after the Second World War. The conclusion will consider the implications of these historical legacies for the present situation: a situation where, in western liberal societies at least, the state and its law are no longer involved in enforcing a particular order of gender and where, equally, such an order can no longer be claimed as a necessary component of the political order.

The meanings of both 'gender' and 'state' are open to numerous ambiguities which in turn will bear upon the ways in which we perceive the connections between them.[3] 'Gender' often serves as a general label for research which is primarily concerned with knowledge about women. Such focus will, of course, include men, masculinity and male power as ubiquitous reference-points, but it may not give adequate attention to the foundations and origins of the relationship that constitutes 'men' and 'women' in the first place. In the context of this chapter, it is not the legal condition of women that is of primary interest but the legal status and function ascribed to both sexes or, more precisely, the legal construction of the sexual division itself. We can say that it has been a central tenet of all legal systems to establish a sexual order by determining the distinction between male and female.[4] This order is wholly artificial in the sense that it derives from the authoritative pronouncements of the law-making power: the law transforms the indeterminate physical facts and relations of sexuality into obligatory norms. Thus, as we shall see throughout the chapter, the normative meanings of 'husband' and 'wife' have little to do with biological determinations (just as the legal definitions of 'father' and 'mother' may be largely independent of the actual conditions of fatherhood and motherhood). Understood as a construct of an 'institutional logic',[5] gender refers not to two entities, but to a tripartite relationship in which 'man' and 'woman', 'husband' and 'wife' are constituted by the normative power of the law.

Attempts to define or locate the state in relation to gender are beset by similar difficulties. Given the prolific range and the diversity of studies devoted to 'women/gender and politics', it is perhaps surprising that the state does not figure more prominently in the inventory of dominant themes. A cursory review of book titles and indexes, especially in the field of normative theory with which we are concerned here, will reveal relatively few instances of direct and explicit feminist engagement with the concept. We can speak of distinctive feminist conceptions of justice, authority, democracy and citizenship[6] and of the critical reassessment of the major paradigms of political argument.[7] It is more difficult to trace similarly numerous and distinctive feminist attempts at theorising the state.

Several reasons may account for the relative invisibility of the state. First, it is generally the case – and not a feature peculiar to feminist scholarship – that in the tradition of Anglo-American political theory the state has never played the key role attributed to it in the corresponding French, German and Italian disciplines. The disparity points to the specific historical contexts in which academic subjects such as jurisprudence, political science and political theory have evolved since the eighteenth and nineteenth centuries. And the peculiarities of this academic history reflect in turn upon significant differences of political culture. These include, for continental Europe, the long prevalence of absolutist government, the power and extent of centralised legal and bureaucratic systems, the late development of representative institutions and, enveloped in all this, a different relationship between the individual and the political authority. While these latter historical legacies have tended to put the state at centre-stage of political theorising, the rooted individualism characteristic of English and American political experience and the associationist traditions of a civil society independent of the state have made for more diffuse and decentred conceptions of politics.

A second and more specific reason for the seeming marginality of the state to the interests of feminist political theory relates to the main thrust of the feminist enterprise itself. As a radical critique of the premises that have traditionally constituted and delimited our discipline, feminism has aimed to disperse the meaning of politics, that is to take what we understand as 'political' beyond the institutions, formal processes and legal abstractions

of the public sphere. It has shifted attention to family arrangements, care relations, motherhood and sexuality as so many sites of political power where
gender is constructed and the subordination of women maintained. In opening up the allegedly private sphere of women's distinctive experiences and
activities to the scrutiny of political analysis, feminist theory has exposed
the practical inefficacy of the modern state to guarantee the necessary conditions of autonomy to all its members. As a consequence, there has been a
tendency to sideline the state and to move the relevant domains of politics
elsewhere. From this perspective it is, however, easy to lose sight of the
fact that the forms of 'political' power associated with the private sphere
have, by historical origin at least, been intimately connected with the legiti-
mating and coercive agency of the state.

As a means of locating the state, I begin with a loose version of the
Weberian definition.[8] It identifies the modern European state (since the end
of the sixteenth century) with that power which claims the supreme right
to make and enforce rules for all the inhabitants of a given territory.
Considered by its primary and common functions, the state serves to establish a legal order capable of enforcing the peaceful coexistence and co-
operation among individuals. What is missing from this definition, as from
many others of its kind, is the explicit recognition that one of the indispensable requirements of any legal order – and one as necessary to human
survival and well-being as the guarantee of peace – resides in those rules
which ensure the reproduction of society over time.

Reproduction belongs to the fundamental problems of politics because,
among humans, it involves something more than and different from the
mere physical continuation of the species. What is at stake, and what requires
the normative and coercive involvement of a public power, is orderly procreation. The natural, biological process of propagating offspring has to be
transformed into an artificial order which will identify parents (those with
responsibility to care for the young), legitimate children and heirs, and
thus rightful titles to property and family lineages. What is reproduced in
each generation, is 'not life itself but the legal organisation of life'.[9] Given
the need to guarantee the transmission of material and cultural goods by
creating stable links between successive generations, marriage will be the
core institution of any society and a central object of its laws. Marriage
singles out among all possible sexual unions those which society legitimises
as a means of perpetuating itself without endangering its structures: 'It is
through the institution of matrimony, through rules and the way those
rules are applied, that human societies control their future – even those
societies that claim and even believe to be the freest.'[10]

The French *Code civil* (from 1804 until 1814 '*Code Napoléon*'), to which
I shall now turn, was modern Europe's first comprehensive codification of
private law.[11] Although its marriage law exhibited some unique particularities, the basic normative patterns which constituted the relation of husband
and wife as a nexus of domination and subordination were sufficiently

similar to those of other European legal systems to allow for a generalised picture of the role of the modern state in the 'making of gender'. The phrase requires some explanation, for, taken by their outward forms, European marriage laws hardly changed from the late Middle Ages to the end of the nineteenth century. In this respect, marriage seemingly stood outside modern society and outside the regulating power of the state. What did change, however, were the meanings ascribed to those traditional rules and the legitimations required to re-affirm them. Mill's *Subjection of Women* – and its German translation as *Hörigkeit* (feudal servitude) – played on the scandal of historical anachronism. For the majority of legislators, jurists and judges of the nineteenth century, by contrast, marital authority was uniquely suited to the needs of modern society and indispensable to the stability of the public order. Among the numerous and diverse legitimations of gender hierarchy, the claim of the primarily public function of marriage and of its unique relationship with the state proved to be the most effective barrier to gender equality until well into the twentieth century.

The construction of gender in the marriage law of the *Code civil*

The French Revolution affected the institution of marriage above all through the separation of church and state. Centuries of struggle between the secular and the spiritual power over which was to wield supreme jurisdiction in this central domain of the social order came to an end in two momentous changes initiated by the revolutionary legislation: the enactment of the obligatory civil marriage (1791) and the introduction of divorce (1792).[12] The first brought the conditions and procedures required of a valid, publicly recognised union under the sole auspices of the state, thus relegating religious dogma and church ceremonies to a matter of private belief. The second act replaced the Catholic doctrine of the indissolubility of the marriage bond with the right of individuals to terminate the contract – not only on grounds of severe violations, such as adultery and desertion, but also by mutual consent of the partners. (As we shall see later, the controversies about the private or public status of marriage throughout the nineteenth century revolved around this issue of the consensual divorce.)

Civil marriage and divorce expanded the terrain of individual liberty and gave force to the idea of religious tolerance and neutrality of the state while at the same time enhancing the power of the state, which gained essential attributes of sovereign control over all its subjects. Both acts stood justified by the claim that marriage was essentially a civil contract and as such subject to the same rules as all other contractual exchanges between free and equal individuals under the private law: in the domain of private freedom the public power was to intervene only to enforce the formal conditions of valid contractual arrangements; it was not to prescribe the substance or direction of individual choice nor to regulate the conduct of the contracting parties beyond compelling adherence to certain procedures.[13]

However, as the family law of the *Code Napoléon* demonstrates and as was the case everywhere else, freedom of contract and choice did not extend to the internal space of marriage, that is to the relationship between husband and wife. To conclude a marriage contract meant, for both men and women, to enter a pre-established status within a hierarchical order whose structures were determined by the state and exempt from individual choice.

The *Code* defines the position of husband and wife in two general concepts which encapsulate and shape the whole ensemble of their particular rights and obligations: *puissance* and *incapacité*.[14] The former refers to a husband's extensive powers of command, control and discipline with regard to the person and property of the wife. He is the one to determine the place of residence, which means that as a matter of ultimate sanction he can call upon the courts and the police to enforce her presence. He has the right to watch over her friendships, social contacts and correspondence, to authorise her application for a passport or (in the twentieth century) a driving licence, to prevent her working outside the home. He acts for her in the public world of the market and the courts. In short, according to the letter of the law, a husband is able to control a wife's freedom of movement and action in virtually every respect. Napoleon, who took great pride in the achievements of his code and a particular interest in its family law, put the matter succinctly: 'The husband should have the right to say to his wife: "Madame, you will not go out today; Madame, you will not visit the theatre; Madame, you will not see this person; in short, Madame, you are mine with body and soul."'[15]

The incapacity of the married woman is the direct consequence of, and logically entailed in, the husband's *puissance*. She is incapable of performing legally valid actions in her own right, whether they be contracts, purchases, credit transactions, law suits. Unless she obtains the husband's permission in every single case – and the law explicitly rules out any blanket authorisation – her actions are null and void. Moreover, *puissance* and *incapacité* carry over to, and are sustained by, the regime of property.[16] The goods that a wife brings into marriage or acquires subsequently, as well as any earnings from independent work, become part of the common property (the *communauté des biens*) over which the husband has exclusive rights of administration and disposal. The wife is entitled to an equal share of the combined assets at the point when the marriage ends, but before then she is unable to act with regard to her own property. European regimes of matrimonial property displayed a great deal of regional and local variation and immense complexity.[17] Some systems organised the nominal ownership claims of husband and wife by separate rather than communal entitlements (English common law, Austria, many regions in Germany, the provinces of the *droit écrit* in France). But irrespective of these differences, most systems placed the wife's goods – those that nominally belonged to her – under the husband's control.

A detailed balance sheet, however extensive, of the particular rights, powers and incapacities on either side of the marriage equation cannot tell us much about the peculiar character of this relationship. This is why an exclusive attention to women's rights – and there are, interestingly, no substantive studies on the rights of husbands – tends to provide an incomplete picture from which some important elements are missing.[18] A wife's disabilities, considered by themselves and in isolation, will not reveal the assumptions that are at work in the construction of gender. The key points in this respect can be summarised as follows.

First, *puissance maritale* and *incapacité de la femme* (and the same applies to the *feme covert* of the common law and to the relation of guardian and ward in German legal language) are not to be understood as naturalistic categories. That is, they do not refer to natural differences between the sexes. In contrast with popular beliefs, the law itself did not assume that wives – as women – are physically or mentally incapable of legal agency, just as it did not assume that it is the superior strength of the male that constitutes the legal powers of a husband over the wife. Not only did single women enjoy civil rights (for example, rights of dealing with their property) largely on a par with men: even a wife, as we have seen, could with the permission or authorisation of her husband perform all those actions that she was otherwise deemed incapable of. What was required was that she act as his agent. It was because of his claims on her person that she lacked the capacity for agency, not because of any attributes inherent in herself. Moreover, most regimes of matrimonial property, in France as elsewhere, allowed for exceptions, usually in the form of prenuptial contracts, as a consequence of which a wife might take control over part of her property and exercise the full rights and responsibilities of ownership. Marginal though they might have been to the general pattern, these concessions illuminate the artificial, state-made order of 'husband' and 'wife': gender derives its normative meanings from the law itself, not from some independent essence, such as nature.

Second, marriage envelops both men and women in a web of mutual rights and obligations. We need to get a grip on this mutuality in order to understand how 'husband' and 'wife' relate to each other. As a husband, a man has not only extensive powers but also enduring obligations towards his wife, be it in the form of maintenance, of protection of her interests towards third parties, of liabilities for her debts or of provisions for the livelihood of the widow. Conversely, a wife is not merely the subject of power in the sense of having no protected rights; she has definite, enforceable claims on her husband's support and on his property. The point is, of course, that the pattern of mutuality is not symmetrical. It is structured by a prior norm which the key article of the *Code civil* states as 'the husband owes his wife protection, the wife owes her husband obedience' (Article 213, in force until 1938!).

Third, the correlation of *protection* and *obéissance* is inadequately described as a relation of inequality (although it involves it). The feudal connotations of the language in this and many other instances are obvious and significant: in the relation of husband and wife, gender is constructed as a form of *Herrschaft* (domination) akin to that which in pre-modern society expressed the protective and disciplinary power of a feudal lord, or *seigneur*, over his dependants of inferior social rank. The linguistic connection with medieval institutions is not peculiar to French law. It has its equivalent in other legal languages of the eighteenth and nineteenth centuries. Thus Blackstone's authoritative summary of the English common law speaks of 'baron and feme' and of the wife's legal person being incorporated into that of her 'lord'.[19] German texts and commentaries conceptualise the husband's power over the wife in the term sex guardianship (*Geschlechtsvormundschaft*), which embodies the elements of medieval trusteeship and, reaching further back still, of the Germanic *mundium* which denotes the quasi-political power that in the absence of a state the head of a sib exercised over all its members.[20]

Carole Pateman has rightly warned us against the fallacy of understanding patriarchal right as merely a remnant of pre-modern institutions and practices, rather than as a specifically modern assertion of male power.[21] But the feudal reference can be useful, if only as a first step, to unravel the specifically modern meanings of the husband's 'right in the person and property of the wife', which are otherwise difficult to explain. For by the nineteenth century a right of this kind no longer existed in any other legal relations outside marriage and the family. What does it entail? Briefly, medieval conceptions of *Herrschaft* display two characteristic elements: they do not separate rights of personal rule and of ownership (of *imperium* and *dominium*), and they do not draw a clear distinction between private and public power. Thus, the husband's control over the wife's property in our time is not a modern property right; it is not acquired by contract or gift. This is how the standard commentary on the Napoleonic code explained the arrangements of the community of goods: 'because the husband is the seigneur of the wife, he controls her property as if it were his own'.[22] That the husband's powers over the wife's property derive from quasi-proprietory rights in her person is clearly revealed in those provisions of the law which not only make him the owner of her earnings but also empower him to decide whether or not she may take up paid employment or set up a business of her own. As the Prussian Civil Code of 1794 put it, a married woman cannot enter into any commitments towards third parties that would 'impair [his] rights to her person'.[23] The power to veto the wife's occupation outside the home was still reaffirmed a hundred years later in the German Civil Code of 1900. She could not, in the words of one commentator, dispose of her own labour, 'just as a non-owner cannot dispose over another's property without the permission of the owner'.[24] Although fenced against abuse and probably not applied very much in practice, the rule was not abolished until the 1970s.

Another residue of meaning that attached to medieval *Herrschaft* is manifest in the quasi-political character of the marriage relation. Just as a *seigneur* exercised jurisdictional and disciplinary powers over his dependants in lieu of the state, so a husband acts, in the domain of the civil law, as the intermediary power between the state and his wife. Married women are not autonomous subjects of the law and, in this respect, not members of the state.

Fourth, while the historical link with pre-modern principles of social order can help us to identify the peculiar normative structure of marriage under modern law, it cannot shed light on what is the salient issue: namely, that these principles are reaffirmed by the modern state. To assume the undisrupted duration of older traditions makes no sense in the French case, given that the state of the early nineteenth century was heir to an antifeudal revolution. The claim of historical continuity between the pre-revolutionary, customary marriage law and the formulations of the *Code* was itself a potent ideological device which obscured the active role of the state in the very process of consolidating and affirming older traditions.

The deliberations about matrimonial property among the jurists who drafted the *Code* give us a glimpse of this entanglement of state interest and the order of gender in the making of the marriage law. At issue were the competing demands of the general principle of contractual freedom as the general norm of property arrangements, on the one hand, and the particular modes of ownership appropriate for marriage, on the other. The draftsmen affirmed that, as a matter of principle, matrimonial property arrangements, like any other property exchanges, belonged to the realm of contractual freedom: 'The law does not reign over marriage as far as the goods of property are concerned' (Article 1387). This meant in practice that couples could use the device of pre-nuptial contracts to settle their affairs according to their own preferences. They could choose arrangements other than the statutory regime of the community of goods (which would automatically come into force in the absence of any specific contracts). In opting, for example, for a separation of goods or for the dotal regime of Roman law origins, they were able to secure better protection for the wife's assets as well as provide her with some rights of independent administration and disposition. What were to be the permissible limits of such freedom? The seemingly technical question of whether a married woman should be entitled to alienate her landed property without her husband's consent sparked controversies about the ultimate implications of such independence: a world turned upside down where mutual agreement between the two partners would result in the wife's full control of her own and possibly even the husband's property and where, as an inevitable consequence, the *puissance maritale* would wither away. The lawgiver blocked the contractual options of private transactions at precisely the point where they threatened to subvert the *puissance*: 'The spouses cannot derogate the rights which are inherent in the husband's power over the person of wife and children and which pertain to him as chef' (that is, of the community of goods) (Article 1388). The prohibition was defended by invoking a categorical distinction between the private and public dimensions of marriage and by claiming the primacy of the latter over the former: while purely pecuniary affairs of marriage belonged in the sphere of legitimate private interests and as such were open to contractual choices, the husband's *puissance* was part of the public order itself and, like the latter, immutable and not at the disposal of private individuals.[25]

The example shows that the state asserted an interest of its own in enforcing the order of gender. It also shows that the meanings of gender and of the public order are locked into a circle of mutual substitution. One would look in vain for a definition of the public interest that does not already entail reference to the order of gender. That is, the question of what the public order is cannot be answered without referring to gender as a hierarchical order; and conversely, the latter cannot be understood without pointing to norms that are claimed to constitute the order of the state.

Gender and the public order

In France, as elsewhere, the core features of the marriage law remained unchanged throughout most of the nineteenth century. And despite the inroads made by the reforms of the married woman's property rights, substantial elements of the husband's prerogatives survived until much later. The hierarchical marriage withstood revolutions, reforms, constitutional struggles and the pervasive changes of economic and social modernisation. In this respect the normal indicators of political or economic progress have little to tell us. Republican America, liberal England, autocratic Germany – the different constitutional forms of the state and the different degrees of public liberty enjoyed by its citizens are not reflected in the constitution of marriage. The emergence of the women's movements, the passing of Married Women's Property Acts, the struggle for the suffrage entitle us to consider the nineteenth century as a period of improvement and of progressive advances towards women's emancipation. But this was also a century of reaction and of equality prevented. Two examples – the controversies about the divorce laws in the first half of the century, and the pressure for the reform of matrimonial property in the second – may serve to illustrate the powerful ideological trend to identify directly the institution of marriage with the order of the state.

Reactionary movements and ideologies in the first half of the century arose in response to the political disorder unleashed by the French Revolution and the Napoleonic wars; more generally and diffusely, they embodied resistance to the baneful consequences of a rapidly changing world: the weakening of traditional hierarchical social bonds under the impact of commercial expansion, the decline of Christian values, the political struggles for constitutional rights and mass participation. As is often the case, reactionary politics closed in on marriage as both the primary cause of the epochal crisis and the main vehicle of future regeneration. In Germany and France, the attempts to reverse the tide turned first and foremost against the liberal divorce provisions, especially divorce by mutual consent, which were the legacy of the Revolution and, in Prussia, of enlightened absolutism.[26] In that they restricted, or altogether barred, access to divorce, these policies affected both men and women equally. But as the incrimination of adultery and illegitimacy demonstrates, the specific sanctions deployed to enforce the sanctity of the indissoluble monogamous marriage targeted women in particular. For what was to be preserved was not only the permanence of the marriage bond but the order of gender which sustained it.

It cannot be my task here to give a detailed analysis of the different contexts which shaped policies on divorce in the French code, in the Prussian legislation of the 1830s and 1840s and the English Matrimonial Causes Act of 1857.[27] In all three cases the assertion, or reinstatement, of the double standard of adultery (which appended more severe consequences to the infidelity of the wife) and the new punitive measures imposed upon unwed mothers and their 'bastards' reveal comparable patterns of sexual politics. They attest to the increasing determination of the nineteenth-century state not only to police the borders of marriage (as the only legitimate sexual union) but also to entrench gender hierarchy in the very norms of sexual morality. Two points need to be stressed in this context. First, in comparison with the customs or statutes previously in force, the new measures extended and intensified the coercive sanctions which served to sustain women's place in the sexual order. In this as in so many other respects, the transition from the eighteenth to the nineteenth century details a process of regression. This process is reflected in discourses which forged inseparable links between the hierarchical meanings of gender and the specific injunctions of the public order: a woman's adultery weighed more heavily in the moral scale not only because it entailed the danger of another man's child usurping the husband's name, honour and property, and not only because it constituted an assault upon his proprietory rights in her person (the traditional reasons for the double standard). It rated in itself, and irrespective of those consequences, as a distinctly public offence. Nineteenth-century ideologies of gender complementarity re-described a wife's subordinate status as the locus of superior ethical purity which safeguarded the moral cohesion of the familial and the political community alike. To transgress the boundaries of that ethical realm was to destroy both the institution of the family and the state.

The reforms of the property laws in the second half of the nineteenth century offer a more ambivalent picture of the state's involvement in the making of gender.[28] The Married Women's Property Acts in England and America and the similar, if more limited, concessions enacted in Germany's Civil Code of 1900 and in French legislation (the *libre salaire* of 1907) did provide married women with an enclave of legal agency with regard to their separate property. Most importantly, they now had the right to dispose of their own earnings. It would seem then that the state (which made those concessions) had turned from an enforcer of women's subordination into an ally of their independence. However, the wife was released from the protective and commanding power of her husband only to the extent and within the limits of her separate property while he retained the prerogatives of ultimate say in all other affairs of the marriage.

Moreover, as closer scrutiny of legislative processes and of the implementation of the new laws by the courts can show, the reforms aimed at equity, not equality. They remedied particular grievances that arose from a wife's legal disabilities – especially those which had the effect of impeding commercial activities and the security of credit transactions. Legislators were also forced to recognise that in periods of economic instability a wife's earnings and savings were often crucial for the survival of the family and had to be protected against the consequences of a husband's misfortunes or negligence. In many respects, however, the reforms were a prevention of full equality rather than, as feminist campaigners envisaged, the first stage in an inexorable progression towards legal and political emancipation. Again, the debates that took place in legislative commissions, parliamentary assemblies and the wider public varied according to national and regional contexts. But everywhere the reforms were hedged by a strong apprehension that the independence of a wife as owner of her own property might spell the end to the unity of the marriage bond (the 'one flesh, one person, one property'). What constituted the unity of marriage was indistinguishable from the perception of gender as enshrined in the law of the husband's authority over the wife.

Many and diverse ideological beliefs were invoked on behalf of the essence of marriage as an indivisible community: ideals of sentimental love and the cult of domesticity, the elevation of motherhood into a quasi-political office, the benign separation of public and private spheres and, the most pervasive and effective of nineteenth-century fixations of gender, the notion of the essential difference and complementarity of male and female nature. None of these ideologies that exalted the dignity of marriage stood in opposition to the coercive norm of rule and subordination; on the contrary, they were predicated on that norm.

In the domain of legal discourse the most potent argument against gender equality derived from the re-conceptualisation of marriage as an 'institution' – as an objective order above and independent of the will of the individuals.[29] The concept signals a return to the sacramental status of the marriage bond in Christian doctrine, albeit in a modernised, secular form. It signals above all the polemical opposition to those legacies of Enlightenment rationalism and revolutionary individualism which had assimilated marriage to the normative paradigm of the civil contract. To understand marriage as an 'institution' was to claim its incommensurability to the norms of individual autonomy, formal equality and contractual obligation' which governed personal and property relationships among private individuals. In this formulation marriage came to occupy an extra-territorial space in the domain of private law which was subjected to special legal norms. Due to its unique constitution and its direct relevance to the foundations of the state, marriage barred comparison with other legal associations of the private sphere and was unassailable by the language of individual rights. Indeed, some jurists argued that because marriage and family relations were built on *Herrschaft*, that is on rights in other persons, they belonged properly in the province of the non-contractual, coercive relations of the public law.[30]

In the institution of marriage the political order and the order of gender were linked together in an inseparable nexus: one represented the other, neither stood on its own. It needs to be noted here that the institutionalist discourse was not a preserve of a conservative jurisprudence. Liberals and conservatives might have been deeply divided over the issue of the civil marriage and especially over divorce. As regards the 'inevitable rule of the husband'[31] in the institution of marriage, nineteenth-century liberalism was, with few exceptions, conservative. In the 1880s the German women's organisation petitioned the commission responsible for drafting Germany's new Civil Code with the demand to adopt a system of matrimonial property based on the strict separation of goods. The president of the commission – a jurist of respectable liberal credentials – conceded that this model was indeed the one most suited to ensure the independence of the married woman. But it contradicted the German-Christian understanding of the essence of marriage: the institution of marriage had to rank above the independence of the wife.

Conclusion

To return to the present situation sketched at the beginning of the chapter: the frequently voiced demands on the state to protect the institution of marriage against the waywardness of self-centred individuals speak a language which is still deeply implicated in the hierarchical construction of gender. In so far as it draws on assumptions of a stable, pre-established order of gender to guarantee the stability of marriage, this language is redundant. For in western liberal democracies the law no longer presumes and enforces a particular order of gender in the marriage relationship. What we are witnessing today, if only as a result of cumulative reforms since the 1970s and 1980s, is the retreat of the state from the authoritative determination of the roles and the behaviour of husband and wife.[32]

Many and diverse processes have contributed to this change: the increasing participation of women in the labour market and in the benefits of education; the availability of contraception and of divorce; political pressure to bring the law of marriage into line with the constitutional guarantees of equal rights and with the principles of democratic citizenship.

As far as the formal norms of the law are concerned, marriage now *is* a private relationship, that is, an association based on the recognition of the personal autonomy of the individual partners. 'Husband' and 'wife' have lost the connotations both of hierarchy and of public status. Indeed, as indicators of a normative division between men and women these categories have become obsolete to the extent that marriage has come to entail the same rights and obligations for women and men (a judgement which is of course quite compatible with enduring gender divisions as a fact of social experience). The unity of marriage which in the past was cemented by the state's endorsement of the husband's *Herrschaft* over the wife can now derive only from the agreement and co-operation between two partners who have the same status of independent legal agents.

To contrast past and present in this way is not to claim that gender has ceased to be a useful category of political analysis. On the contrary, the understanding of the historical legacies that have shaped the relationship between state, marriage and gender in the past points to the need as well as to the possibilities of reconceptualising this relationship. Reflection on the rights and obligations, the expectations and responsibilities of marriage under present conditions has to set out from the normative base-line of equality between women and men, on the one hand, and of their individual autonomy in relation to the state, on the other. This implies that we need to explore meanings encapsulated in partnership (and friendship) as an important element of gender and, equally, that we focus on the indeterminate, flexible and interchangeable attributes that will define 'men' and 'women' in a marriage that is no longer determined and circumscribed by the coercive power of the state.

Notes

1 *Guardian*, 28 October 1996: 1.
2 For the very different approach to the study of marriage taken by social historians, see O. Hufton, *The Prospect Before Her: A History of Women in Western Europe*, vol. I: *1500–1800*, London: HarperCollins, 1995, chs 2–4; G. Duby, *The Knight, the Lady, and the Priest: The Making of Modern Marriage in Medieval France*, translated from the French by B. Bray, Harmondsworth, Middx: Penguin Books, 1985.
3 Cf. J.W. Scott, 'Gender: a useful category of historical analysis', in Scott, *Gender and the Politics of History*, New York: Columbia University Press, 1988, 28–52.
4 See Y. Thomas, 'The division of the sexes in Roman law', in P. Schmitt Pantel (ed.), *A History of Women in the West*, vol. I, Cambridge, Mass., and London: 1992, 83–138.
5 Ibid., 85.
6 Cf. S.M. Okin, *Justice, Gender, and the Family*, New York: Basic Books, 1989; K.B. Jones, *Compassionate Authority*, London: Routledge, 1993; A. Phillips, *Engendering Democracy*, Cambridge: Polity Press, 1991; I.M. Young, 'Impartiality and the civic public', in S. Benhabib and D. Cornell (eds), *Feminism as Critique*, Oxford: Polity Press and Basil Blackwell, 1987, 56–76.
7 Cf. C. Pateman, *The Sexual Contract*, Cambridge: Polity Press, 1988.

8 Cf. D. Held, 'Introduction', in D. Held *et al.* (eds), *States and Societies*, Oxford: Basil Blackwell in association with the Open University, 1985, 1f.

9 Thomas, 'Division of the sexes', 86.

10 Duby, *Knight, Lady, Priest*, 18.

11 See E. Holthöfer, 'Frankreich', in H. Coing (ed.), *Handbuch der Quellen und Literatur der neueren europäischen Privatrechtsgeschichte*, vol. III(2), Munich: C.H. Beck, 1982, 883–960.

12 See P. Sagnac, *La Législation Civile de la Révolution Française (1789–1804)*, Paris: Librairie Hachette, 230–45.

13 See D. Grimm, 'Soziale, wirtschaftliche und politische Voraussetzungen der Vertragsfreiheit', in Grimm, *Recht und Staat der bürgerlichen Gesellschaft*, Frankfurt am Main: Suhrkamp Verlag, 1987, 165–91.

14 See J. Portemer, 'Le statut de la femme en France depuis la réformation des coutûmes jusqu'à la rédaction du code civil', *Recueils de la Société Jean Bodin* 12(2): 444–97.

15 Quoted in M. Ferid, *Das französische Privatrecht*, vol. III, 2nd edn, Heidelberg: Verlag Recht und Wirtschaft, 1987, 116.

16 See N. Arnaud Duc, 'Le droit et les comportements, la genèse du titre V du livre III du code civil: les régimes matrimoniaux', in I. Théry and C. Biet (eds), *La famille, la loi, l'état de la Révolution au Code civil*, Paris: Centre Georges Pompidou, 1989, 183–95.

17 See U. Vogel, 'Fictions of community: property relations in marriage in European legal systems of the nineteenth century', in W. Steinmetz (ed.), *Private Law and Social Inequality in the Industrial Age*, Oxford: Oxford University Press, forthcoming.

18 As an example, see L. Holcombe, *Wives and Property: Reform of the Married Woman's Property Law*, Toronto: Toronto University Press, 1983.

19 W. Blackstone, *Commentaries on the Laws of England*, Oxford, 1765, I: 430.

20 See U. Gerhard, *Gleichheit ohne Angleichung. Frauen im Recht*, Munich: C.H. Beck, 1990, 142–67.

21 Pateman, *Sexual Contract*, chs 1–2.

22 K.S. Zachariä, *Handbuch des französischen Zivilrechts*, Heidelberg, 1811, III: 214.

23 H. Hattenhauer (ed.), *Allgemeines Landrecht für die Preussischen Staaten von 1794*, Textausgabe, Frankfurt am Main and Berlin: Alfred Metzner, 1970, II.i. Art. 295.

24 W. Schubert, *Materialien zum BGB*, Frankfurt am Main: Suhrkamp Verlag, 1985 III: 301.

25 See *Conférence du Code civil avec la discussion particulière du Conseil d'Etat et du Tribunat, avant la rédaction definitive de chaque projet de loi*, par un jurisconsulte, Paris, 1805, V: 209–24.

26 See D. Blasius, 'Bürgerliche Rechtsgleichheit und die Ungleichheit der Geschlechter: Das Scheidungsrecht im historischen Vergleich', in U. Frevert (ed.), *Bürgerinnen und Bürger. Geschlechterverhältnisse im 19. Jahrhundert*, Göttingen: Vandenhoeck & Ruprecht, 1988, 62–84; I. Schwenzer, *Vom Status zur Realbeziehung. Familienrecht im Wandel*, Baden-Baden: Nomos Verlagsgesellschaft, 1987, 29–64.

27 See U. Vogel, 'Whose property? The double standard of adultery in nineteenth-century law', in C. Smart (ed.), *Regulating Womanhood: Historical Essays on Marriage, Motherhood and Sexuality*, London: Routledge, 1992, 147–65.

28 See for England: Holcombe, *Wives and Property*; M.L. Shanley, *Feminism, Marriage and the Law in Victorian England*, London: I.B. Tauris, 1989, chs 2 and 4; for the United States: N. Basch, *In the Eyes of the Law: Women, Marriage*

and Property in Nineteenth-century New York, Ithaca, N.Y.: Cornell University Press, 1982; for Germany: U. Gerhard, *Verhältnisse und Verhinderungen. Frauenarbeit, Familie und Rechte der Frauen im 19. Jahrhundert*, Frankfurt am Main: Suhrkamp Verlag, 1978; for France: B. Schnapper, 'Autorité domestique et partis politiques de Napoléon à de Gaulle', in H. Mohnhaupt (ed.), *Zur Geschichte des Familien- und Erbrechts*, Frankfurt am Main: Vittorio klostermann, 1987, 177–220.

29 See B. Harms-Ziegler, *Illegitimität und Ehe*, Berlin: Duncker & Humblot, 1990, 264–72.

30 See J.P. Schäfer, *Die Entstehung der Vorschriften des BGB über das persönliche Eherecht*, Frankfurt am Main: Peter Lang H.C.V., 1983, 221f.

31 C. von Rotteck, 'Familie/Familienrecht', in Cv. Rotteck and C. Welcker (eds), *Das Staats-Lexikon. Encyklopädie der sämtlichen Staatswissenschaften*, 2nd edn, Altona, 1846, IV: 598.

32 See Schwenzer, *Status*, 62–4.

4 Beyond liberalism?

Feminist theories of democracy

Kate Nash[1]

Introduction

This chapter is concerned with a central issue in contemporary feminist theory, the question of how to re-think the liberal state. It will compare aspects of three feminist theories of democracy which attempt to go beyond liberalism and specifically beyond the exclusion of the feminine on which it was premised: the theories of Iris Marion Young, Anne Phillips and Chantal Mouffe. All three are concerned with how to displace what has been the dominant legitimation of justice in modernity: the universal principles of liberalism in which the abstract individuals for whom justice may be claimed are essentially identical and therefore subject to identical principles and procedures. The critique of abstract individualism is now well established in feminist theory; the apparently gender-neutral individual is seen as actually masculine and the universal principles of liberalism as particular, applying only to persons with male attributes (Phillips 1993a). The liberal state is, on this reading, intrinsically biased towards men, even if the question of whether it is necessarily and monolithically patriarchal remains open. However, it is also recognised by feminist theorists that there is a danger in this critique of reproducing a binary opposition between the sexes, of essentialising sexual difference, which Young, Phillips and Mouffe are all concerned to avoid. The problem is how to take differences between the sexes into account without freezing them in their current forms and without denying the importance of other differences which may cut across that of sex: class, race, sexuality and so on. While it seems to be necessary to identify a specifically feminine political subject in whose name the masculine bias of the state may be challenged, it is acknowledged that such a subject is problematic in theory and elusive in practice. One of the criteria, then, on which these theories will be compared is how well each one deals with the problem of representing women without essentialising a given identity.

The other main point on which they will be compared is their notions of democracy. Both Young and Phillips are concerned with democratic representation in sites designated for 'politics'. This is a new departure for feminist theory, given the concern of second-wave feminism to extend the definition of politics beyond the institutions and practices of the liberal-democratic state. In my view, to think of democracy as tied to a specific site is extremely limiting for feminism, and, combined with the problems of essentialism that representing women as a group give rise to, a wider meaning of democracy than the representation of differences in the political arena is important. It is for this reason that I argue in the conclusion that Mouffe's theory is to be preferred. Although, *contra* Mouffe, some degree of essentialism is necessary to her version of radical democracy, the wider concept of democracy she uses and her defence of a particular reading of universalism which privileges the continual disruption of gender identities as the democratic ideal is to be preferred to models of democracy as the political represention of group differences.

Iris Marion Young's theory of group democracy

Iris Marion Young has explicitly drawn on the feminist critique of liberal universalism to develop a theory of group representation which is intended to allow for the democratic recognition of difference without essentialism. On Young's account, citizenship in contemporary liberal societies is premised on universality in two senses: (a) citizens are defined by what they have in common and in opposition to the particular characteristics of different groups; and (b) laws and rules are the same for all and are blind to particular individual and group differences (Young 1990b: 114). What this means is that universality of citizenship in the sense of the inclusion and participation of all is actually denied because, first, the general view of what all have in common excludes the views of those who do not conform to it, and, second, where there are differences between groups, adherence to an ideal of equal treatment as the same treatment perpetuates existing disadvantages (ibid.: 115). Young concludes that for a truly universal citizenship there must be mechanisms for representation of groups' differing experiences and perspectives in the political process. The ideal of democracy should no longer be that of the attainment of a general, impartial view of the common good transcending all particular interests, perspectives and experiences; rather it should be that of the participation of citizens speaking from their specific experiences and interests with rights to propose policies on the basis of those interests and to veto others that might affect them adversely (ibid.: 121–9). Furthermore, laws and rules should not attempt to treat all alike since such universal principles reproduce norms which privilege certain groups at the expense of others. The 'normal' should be denormalised and different groups should be treated appropriately according to their needs, values and capacities (ibid.: 129–35). Probably the paradigm case here for feminists is the rights that should be accorded pregnant, birthing and, Young states, breastfeeding mothers (ibid.: 131).

Young, then, opposes the universality of liberal-democracy to the 'true' universality of group differentiated citizenship rights. But how far does the institutionalisation of difference manage to avoid the problem of essentialism? She specifically states that a group should not be seen as an essence or nature with a specific, fixed set of attributes but rather as the historically specific product of social relations. It should be understood as fluid – groups form and fade away, contextual – they aren't effective in all circumstances, and made up of members with multiple identities who, as simultaneously members of other groups, cannot be exhaustively described in uniform terms (Young 1990b: 123). It is, however, difficult to see how groups can be posited in this anti-essentialist way if democracy is to involve institutionalised mechanisms of group representation. According to Young, which groups are to count as worthy of this representation is not something that can be decided outside the political process itself. But calling such a decision 'political' does not alter the fact that it would require the listing of a set of attributes as criteria for the inclusion of group members and the exclusion of non-members. Young suggests some possible criteria: group members should be disadvantaged in terms of their exploitation, marginalisation, powerlessness, cultural domination and/or experience of racial hatred (ibid.). These criteria are very abstract but she suggests that in the US the following at least would qualify: women, blacks, American Indians, Chicanos, Puerto Ricans and other Spanish-speaking Americans, Asian-Americans, gay men, lesbians, working-class people, poor people, old people, and mentally and physically disabled people (ibid.: 123–4). The members of each of these groups must, then, share a common set of characteristics which distinguishes them from other groups (though a member of one group may also be the member of another); far from solving the problem of essentialism which has so exercised feminists recently, Young's formulation seems to re-state it anew. She seems here to be supposing that there are some experiences, interests and values that *all* women (in the US at least) have in common, that women form a group which should be represented, when it is precisely this that has been brought into question under the name of anti-essentialism.

There are, in fact, two rather different, though interrelated problems that are named as 'essentialism' in contemporary feminist theory. In political terms it names the problem that black feminists in particular have insisted on: not all women share the same socio-economic positions, cultural backgrounds and political concerns, so that to speak of 'women' as if they were a homogeneous group of persons is to collude with the exclusion of certain women from representation. This problem is also theoretical to the extent that the same point can be made about theories which explain white women's oppression as if it were the oppression of all women (Carby 1982). However, a more thorough problematising of the theoretical category of women as essentialist comes from post-structuralist feminism. For post-structuralist feminists 'women' is a signifier without a necessary referent: the term 'women' does not designate in advance a group of actual embodied persons who share a certain set of characteristics; rather, it may construct its referent, a group who are identified with or identify themselves with the term as it is used in a particular context. This point links up with the previous problem: given the multiple contexts in which 'women' appears, including contexts of class, race, sexuality and so on, there is no aggregate of individuals who identify with all its uses and no single group of women with the same experiences, values and interests (Butler 1990). It is important to note that on the poststructuralist view an essentialist theorisation or description of women need not involve the presumption that women share a common set of characteristics and experiences rooted in biology, in their 'natural' differences from men; it may also involve the view that women share a common set of experiences by virtue of their shared social construction as women.

As Diana Fuss (1990) has pointed out, the significant distinction here is not between 'essentialism' and 'social constructionism', but between metaphysical and nominal essentialism: where the first presupposes that women have something fundamental prior to their description in language in common, the latter assumes that they have something, however minimal, in common as a result of living descriptions of themselves as such. The most significant difference between the two different criticisms of essentialism seems to be that they give rise to rather different political strategies. For those who criticise 'women' as an exclusionary category, the point would seem to be that those who find themselves currently under-represented in feminist political forums and in feminist theory should represent themselves, and also that diversity among women should be acknowledged and respected. For post-structuralists, on the other hand, the most important point is to deconstruct representations of women, to show their limitations and their subordination in relation to representations of men. For poststructuralist feminists the problem is not how women should best be represented – such a question is meaningless for them – but rather how to transgress and disrupt any and every representation of women; the imposition of identity on lived possibilities is the problem and it is not dealt with by further and more fully taking on that identity (Butler 1990; Riley 1988).

In what sense, then, is Young's theory of group representation a restatement of the essentialism she is concerned to avoid? The problem is that without the presupposition that women have something in common, there would seem to be no answer to the question of why women should be represented *as* women. Young appears to reject metaphysical essentialism (identity is fluid, contextual and multiple) only to reintroduce nominal essentialism (women all experience a socially determined exploitation, marginalisation, powerlessness, and so on). How important is this problem? First, it would seem to be important from the point of view of those who are marginalised by the dominant understanding of women as white women for precisely the reasons Young outlines in making her case for the representation of women as such: it would mean marginalising and disadvantaging those whose views and experiences were not dominant within that group. This is not to say that there is no possible construction of 'women' with which all embodied individuals identified as women could identify (though it's not easy to think of one), but such a homogeneous identification would be rare and would not justify setting up mechanisms by which the group 'women' could be democratically represented. And second, from a post-structuralist feminist perspective, if the institutionalisation of mechanisms to represent women as a group worked to construct the constituency they were set up to serve this would be counterproductive since it would then entrench further the limitations of sexed identity. Presumably this would not be the case if those within the group contested the very identity in the name of which they were grouped together as post-structuralists recommend; it is hard to see, however, how it could hold together at all in such a case, or what its purpose might be, since it would most emphatically not be to represent women.

Anne Phillips's theory of representative democracy

It is hard, then, to escape the conclusion that Young's theory of democracy as group representation deals with the injustice of liberal universalism only at the expense of essentialising identities and reifying differences between them. Anne Phillips explicitly distances her rethinking of liberal-democracy from Young's for such reasons (Phillips 1993b), but it is not clear that Phillips's own much less ambitious proposals are able to pick a secure path between too abstract universalism and too concrete essentialism. Phillips is ambivalent about liberal universalism. On the one hand she endorses the feminist critique of universalism as masculinist, particularly in the context of representative democracy with which she is concerned: if liberalism were adequate, if individuals were essentially identical and differences between them unimportant, political representation would reflect more faithfully the groups in contemporary society than it actually does, dominated as it is by white, middle-class men (Phillips 1991: 63). For this reason she favours quotas as a way of equalising participation in representative democracy, though not, it should be noted, as a way of representing women (we will return to this point).

Phillips's endorsement of the feminist critique of liberal universalism, at least in this context, does not, however, lead her to abandon it altogether. On the contrary, she argues for a modified version of universalism on anti-essentialist grounds. Phillips is concerned to avoid a pluralism in which groups are concerned only to fight their own corners, however idealistic those corners might be, and for this reason she breaks with the main body of feminist theory in advocating the public sphere as distinctively political. Feminists concerned with democratisation have generally argued for the empowering of citizens in civil society but for Phillips this is a dangerously sectarian view of politics; there is a distinctive shift, she suggests, between groups in civil society organising to achieve specific aims and the negotiations that must take place between those groups at the level of the state in order to promote understanding, allocate resources and so on (ibid.: 115–19).

Phillips, then, endorses the view that Young is specifically concerned to reject as contributing to the disadvantage of those groups already disadvantaged, that there is a general view on which all citizens can, and should, agree and it is at this level of the general that she locates politics. Phillips's definition of universalism is, however, somewhat different from that of Young. For Young the abstraction of universalism, of the impartial view from nowhere, not only results in the contingent exclusion of the views of the least powerful, in the sense that it allows for them legitimately to be ignored, it *necessarily* results in the exclusion of the concerns of those associated with attributes opposed to the reason which enables us to attain impartial understanding: the body, desire, feeling and so on (Young 1990a). Liberal universalism is for Young exclusive of certain concerns by definition. For Phillips, on the other hand, universalism can accommodate difference because it need not be premised on rationalism; it does not require the liberal definition of the individual as consisting of an essential core of rationality surrounded by the accidental peculiarities that make people different. Anti-essentialist universalism involves seeing that core of rationality as itself accidental, as one quality among others, a peculiarity of the dominant group in the modern, secular West. What anti-essentialism allows us to do, Phillips suggests, is to consider *all* those attributes we consider to be essential as accidental and so, rather than trying, as liberalism does, to find rules that are appropriate to all individuals in their underlying, rational, essence, we will try to understand others by identifying with their accidental features in order to establish what would *actually* be acceptable to all (Phillips 1991: 53–9). Universalism on this account is a matter of sympathetic identification with the other in order to reach agreement across differences rather than of simply denying or ignoring differences and applying the same standards to all.

But does this version of universalism really break with liberalism? And does it answer Young's fears? It is problematic, I think, because it is still substantially dependent on liberal individualism. For Phillips, good citizens in the public sphere must distance themselves from themselves and take as accidental those qualities which in other contexts they take to be crucially defining of themselves: 'Somehow or other, we have to be able to stand back from the things that are peculiar to us, whether it is our sex, our religion, our race or our political views, and try to think ourselves into another's place' (Phillips 1991: 57). This capacity for detachment does not seem so different from the essential quality of the liberal individual, the capacity for reason: although in Phillips's terms the former facilitates a sympathetic understanding of the other while the latter supposedly enables the transcendence of otherness, both require disengagement from the self as a first step. And if rationality is associated with the dominant group in contemporary society, the capacity for detachment is equivalent in this respect too: Phillips herself, following a discussion of the Salman Rushdie controversy, expresses the view that funda-mentalists are feared because they cannot detach themselves from their beliefs in this way (ibid.: 57); and since the question of women's participation in politics was seriously raised in the nineteenth century a frequent argument against it has been that women are too emotional, too involved, to see the larger picture (Hollis 1979: 305–6). Phillips's universalism may, then, con-tribute to the exclusion of specific differences which a feminist theory of democracy is especially concerned to include.

Phillips's theory of democracy does not, however, rest solely on her rethinking of universalism; she is also concerned, again like Young, with the mechanisms by which groups traditionally excluded from policy-making can make themselves heard. From an anti-essentialist perspective Phillips is critical of Young's proposals, arguing that they would serve to 'freeze' differences between identities (Phillips 1993b: 98) and that if each individual is the site of multiple identities there is no mechanism that can ensure the representation of any single one of those identities on any particu-lar occasion. (If a woman votes in a group of women, is she voting *as* a woman or as a complex of different identities or even as something altogether different, as a Christian, say, or a member of the green movement? (Phillips 1991: 77).) What she proposes instead is a system of quotas at the level of the selection of party candidates for election in order better to reflect the compo-sition of the population as made up of different groups, for the sake of equal-ity of participation in politics and because, although she explicitly says that women don't all share the same experiences, having women present in policy negotiation makes it possible for concerns specific to women which were not on the political agenda to be incorporated into policies as they are made (Phillips 1991: 149–56; Phillips 1995: 70–1).

Phillips's project aims, then, to allow for the recognition of difference in democracy, without essentialising contingent and mutable identities. Never-theless, from our discussion of Young's delineation of groups suitable for representation it is clear that the use of *any* criteria to isolate specific groups as requiring special treatment is at risk, first, of freezing identities which would otherwise be historically transient and which, arguably, should be resisted as limiting actual possibilities; and second, of giving undue weight to one aspect of multiple identities at the expense of those who do not define themselves, and who are not defined, in the terms of the dominant group. Given, then, that any delineation of groups risks this essentialism, the important question is whether the probable outcome of the proposed strategy is worth such a risk.

In the case of quotas this is very much open to question; first, as Phillips herself makes clear, although the presence of representatives of those groups currently marginalised in the democratic process *might* affect the terms in which policies are defined, given that women in parliament would not be there as representatives of women and need not represent *themselves* as women there either, there is no particular policy outcome to be expected from increasing their numbers in parliament; second, as she also points out, quota systems can achieve the aim of increasing numbers of women in parliament without social and economic revolution, as they have done in the Scandinavian countries (Phillips 1991: 78–91). Quota systems may not, then, have very much effect on the lives of women, other than those few elected to parliament, either at the beginning of the process of getting more women elected, or at the end, in policy-making. They would, however, in singling women out for special treatment, risk freezing, or even creating, a group identity of women in politics (possibly, as in other cases of affirmative action, as less competent, less committed and so on) and thus of hindering change in other areas. It may well be that the risk of essentialism is not worth taking in these circumstances.

Finally, Phillips's democratic theory is problematic because it defines democratic politics extremely narrowly. From holding a more conventional feminist view of the superiority of participatory democracy she has come to the conclusion that representative democracy is indispensable as the only means of ensuring that all perspectives – not just those of the unrepresentative few who regularly attend meetings – are considered and voted on (Phillips 1991: 145–6). She further contests another meaning that feminists have given democracy, the pursuit of equality in all social relations. Whilst not wanting to deny the importance of feminist demands for equal respect in all aspects of life, she is concerned to make a sharp distinction between this kind of activity and democratic politics which involve 'stand[ing] back a bit from ourselves' in the specifically political public sphere (Phillips 1991: 115–19, 161).

Phillips insists that a distinction between public and private must be drawn to take into account the difference between particular concerns and considerations of the general interest, but she is uncharacteristically unclear about exactly how or where this distinction is to be drawn. Is it a topographical distinction? Are certain areas – all those in which a vote is cast according to the procedures of representative democracy, presumably – to be seen as public, while other areas are to be seen as private? Does it conform to the traditional distinction of political theory between the state and civil society? Or is civil society itself seen as divided between public and private on this account (and where, then, is the domestic)? The problem is that because feminists have extended the notion of the political beyond the public sphere of formal democracy it now seems arbitrary and unnecessarily limiting to restrict the term to specific areas or activities. Even if, as Phillips recommends, feminists now give more attention to representative democracy as a way of revitalising the public sphere, we will still want to consider how issues and perspectives come to be considered there, how they are informed by positions and identities which are not represented in the processes of formal democracy – which may well, on Phillips's own admission, continue to be gender-blind – and how certain issues get excluded. There seems to be no good reason not to label such questions, and questions concerning social relations and practices which are not even debated in the public sphere or are not suitable to be resolved there, political in so far as they address inequalities of power, access to resources and so on. On the contrary, any feminist theory of democracy must surely equip us with the tools to consider precisely these questions, not just because of the way they affect the representation of women at the level of procedural democracy but also because of the feminist commitment to equality in all social relations, not just the formally political.

Chantal Mouffe's theory of radical democracy

Chantal Mouffe's theory of democracy does retain this wider definition of the term: democracy for her means both procedural representative democracy and also the equalising of unequal social relations. Like the other theorists we have looked at, Mouffe is concerned to construct a democratic theory that goes beyond liberal universalism to allow for the representation of differences without essentialising identities and to this end she argues for democratic citizenship as specifically political. But for Mouffe politics is not a topographical category, it does not refer to any pre-designated area of society; it is an activity that can take place anywhere. Democratic politics, on Mouffe's account, involves the contestation of relations of inequality and subordination using the principles of freedom and equality that are supposed to apply to all citizens of liberal-democracy, regardless of differences between them. The project of radical democracy she advocates involves the extension of these principles into more and more areas of the social and the institution of the maximum degree of liberty and equality for all that can be achieved in that particular context, as well as the – never realisable – aspiration towards complete freedom and equality for everyone (Laclau and Mouffe 1985: 176–93).

Although procedural democracy is important on Mouffe's account, in order to protect pluralism and individual liberty, it is not the privileged site of democratic politics as it is for both Young and Phillips in different ways. She specifically rejects Young's theory of democracy as group representation on the grounds of essentialism: democratic identities are constructed in the political process and cannot be posited in advance with pre-given interests which must be represented (Mouffe 1993a: 85–6). And although, like Phillips, she argues for the need for compromise and co-operation across differences, she does not see this as the attainment of a general point of view which the process of representative democracy is particularly well-designed to produce. For Mouffe politics is analogous to war and agreement across differences is the building of alliances, which always also means the construction of an opposition between friend and enemy; it necessarily means the exclusion of other differences which act as the constitutive outside of the friends' common identity (Mouffe 1993a: 114). On Mouffe's account, democratic politics is a good deal messier and combative, more partial and erratic, than either Young or Phillips allows.

Despite her emphasis on these agonistic features of democracy, however, Mouffe does not entirely reject universalism. She is concerned to go beyond liberal individualism, agreeing with the feminist critique that it has postulated a homogeneous citizenship along masculine lines which has relegated all differences to the margins to the detriment of women and other 'minorities' (Mouffe 1993a: 81). This is counter to the anti-essentialist view of the individual as nothing more than the site of convergence of multiple, shifting identities which she sees as vital to radical democracy, enabling as it does an appreciation of the contingency of identities and of the alliances between them and the possibility of making new links in order to carry out the project (Mouffe 1993a: 77–8). But according to Mouffe, universalism is necessary because there is no possible democracy without a certain homogeneity, an acceptance by the citizens of political principles that are held in common.

In contemporary liberal-democracy it is the universal principles of liberty and equality which provide the 'grammar' of citizenship, the identification that holds citizens together (Mouffe 1993a: 65) and it is these principles that are extended in radical democracy. The democratic grammar has been developed historically from the nineteenth-century articulation of liberalism and democracy, but on Mouffe's theory the form of its universalism is quite different from that of liberalism; first, because, unlike liberalism, post-colonial democratic universalism is aware of its own cultural specificity, of the way in which it necessarily excludes other forms of life: it is a univeralism aware of its particularity (Mouffe 1993a: 131–3); and second, because although like liberalism the grammar of democratic citizenship is universal only at the most abstract level, it does not necessarily ignore or exclude identities which are *a priori* incompatible with its definitions of the essential nature of the good citizen. It does not do so because the crucial aspect of the political principles of liberty and equality on Mouffe's theory is that they are used by citizens in political struggles so that citizens define these principles in their own terms, or rather, the definition of the principles is itself an important aspect of political struggle. As Mouffe (1993a: 71) puts it: 'To the idea that the exercise of citizenship consists in adopting a universal point of view . . . I am opposing the idea that it consists in identifying with the ethico-political principles of modern democracy and that there can be as many forms of citizenship as there are interpretations of those principles.' So while citizenship is homogeneous in so far as all citizens identify with the principles of equality and liberty, it is differentiated in so far as they use them in different ways, according to their own interpretations.

In theorising democratic citizenship as universal, Mouffe is opposing the feminist view, including that of Young and to a lesser extent Phillips, that in order to take social and/or natural differences between the sexes into account citizenship must itself be gendered. According to Mouffe, a gender-differentiated citizenship would be inappropriate because it would necessarily involve the essentialising of identities, the institution of a fixed definition of women that would preclude its articulation in different relations to other identities; it is the possibility of multiple and contextually sensitive links that is the precondition of a radical democratic politics (Mouffe 1993b).

On this point, however, I find Mouffe ambiguous; she does not sufficiently distinguish between democratic citizenship *tout court* and the radical democratic citizenship she advocates. Democratic citizenship in her terms undoubtedly is, and should be, universal and so gender-neutral, but the same is not true of radical democratic citizenship. We can analyse radical democracy as involving two aspects. First, it involves the mobilisation around and struggle over definitions of the political principles of democratic citizenship, in which alliances between different identities are forged into a common project which excludes certain interpretations of those principles and aims to institute its own. It is, then, far from universal in its self-conscious refusal of some possible interpretations of liberty and equality. And in its second aspect, the institution of its own definitions in social relations, including those regulated by the state, the radical democratic project is still more concrete and particular, still less abstract and universal. Although the institution of certain interpretations and the exclusion of others is always contestable, since the grammar of democratic citizenship remains available to all, the institutions of radical democracy embody a certain interpretation of those principles that is unashamedly particular. And in this respect they may not be gender-neutral. To return to Young's example, radical democracy might institute certain maternity rights for women in the name of sexual equality. It might institute certain rights which are not gender-neutral and, in so far as it thereby institutes a particular form or interpretation of citizenship, that citizenship would not be gender-neutral either.

There is a difference, then, between Mouffe's abstract conception of citizenship as universal and the concrete instantiations of citizenship – in this case radical democratic citizenship – which can not be universal and which, arguably, must differentiate between the sexes in some respects. This does indeed involve the risk of essentialism, of freezing those identities in their current forms but, on Mouffe's account, a certain degree of fixity of identities and their relations is inescapable in the concretisation of an interpretation of citizenship. The question must, therefore, surely be which essentialism to risk and for what ends, rather than how to avoid essentialism altogether.

Conclusion

In conclusion, then, each of the three theories of democracy we have looked at has attempted to think beyond liberalism, specifically to think beyond the 'false' universalism of liberal individualism in order to develop a universalism that would be genuinely universal, inclusive of all citizens of a democratic society and, in the case of Chantal Mouffe, self-conscious about the limits of that inclusiveness. In their adherence to universalism as an ideal their aim is not so much a break with the traditions of political liberalism as its realisation in a form which allows for the equal participation of all citizens. Within the terms of the theories we have looked at here it would seem that this realisation is impossible without essentialising differences to a greater or lesser degree.

This does not mean, however, that we should abandon the problematic of anti-essentialism: in a complex, pluralist and fast-changing world, the anti-essentialist description of identities as relational, multiple and historically and culturally specific are undoubtedly the most appropriate. It is for this reason that I have argued against Young's and Phillips's models of demo-cratic representation: given that, as both would readily agree, there could be no guarantee that such representation would achieve a greater degree of substantive equality for women (although Young's would necessarily achieve a greater degree of formal participation in the political process), these models propose running a risk of essentialism which cannot be justified by the prob-able outcome of the procedures they recommend. On the other hand, what Mouffe's attempt at an anti-essentialist citizenship for women indicates, I take it, is that a more egalitarian polity requires the institution and main-tenance of specific forms, including forms of gender identity, which feminists concerned with substantive equality for women should support. So while democracy requires a refusal of fixed, exclusionary identities in order to be genuinely open to all citizens, if the aim is genuinely to increase the participa-tion of all in the wider society then it may also require support for policies which institute relatively stable gender identities in the name of equality. Democracy itself should not be seen as *essentially* concerned with contesta-tion, disruption and refusal; given feminist concerns with the institution of social and political equality, on occasion it may require a commitment to policies which risk fixing an identity for women as citizens. Although 'women' is not a fixed category with a specific set of characteristics, it may be necessary sometimes to commit oneself to the fiction of 'women' in order to enable the social and political participation of those for whom this is a lived identity.

Note

1 I should like to thank Jelica Šumič-Riha and Simon Thompson for their suggestions on earlier versions of this chapter, and also Vicky Randall for editorial comments which helped me knock it into its current, much more refined, shape.

References

Butler, J. (1990) *Gender Trouble: Feminism and the Subversion of Identity*, London: Routledge.
Carby, H. (1982) 'White woman listen: black feminism and the boundaries of sister-hood' in Centre for Contemporary Cultural Studies (eds), *The Empire Strikes Back*, London: Hutchinson.

Fuss, D. (1990) *Essentially Speaking: Feminism, Nature and Difference*, London: Routledge.

Hollis, P. (1979) *Women in Private: Documents of the Victorian Women's Movement*, London: George Allen & Unwin.

Laclau, E. and Mouffe, C. (1985) *Hegemony and Socialist Strategy: Toward a Radical Democratic Politics*, London: Verso.

Mouffe, C. (1993a) *Return of the Political*, London: Verso.

Mouffe, C. (1993b) 'Feminism, citizenship and radical politics', in C. Mouffe, *Return of the Political*, London: Verso.

Phillips, A. (1991) *Engendering Democracy*, Cambridge: Polity Press.

Phillips, A. (1993a) 'Universal pretensions in political thought', in A. Phillips, *Democracy and Difference*, Cambridge: Polity Press.

Phillips, A. (1993b) 'Democracy and difference', in A. Phillips, *Democracy and Difference*, Cambridge: Polity Press.

Phillips, A. (1995) *The Politics of Presence*, Oxford: Clarendon Press.

Riley, D. (1988) *Am I That Name? Feminism and the Category of 'Women' in History*, London: Macmillan.

Young, I. (1990a) *Throwing Like a Girl and Other Essays in Feminist Philosophy and Social Theory*, Bloomington, Ind.: Indiana University Press.

Young, I. (1990b) 'Impartiality and the civic public: some implications of feminist critiques of moral and political theory', in I. Young *Throwing Like a Girl and Other Essays in Feminist Philosophy and Social Theory*, Bloomington, Ind.: Indiana University Press.

5 The state and the discursive construction of abortion

Barry Gilheany

Introduction

This chapter addresses the interplay between the state, gender and discourse in the area of abortion politics. It focuses on how the state mediates between competing discourses on abortion and on how fields of discursivity structure the abortion debate. It draws on the theoretical work of R.W. Connell on gender relations and that of Michel Foucault on discourse and the deployment of sexuality in order to specify state interests in abortion. Specifically it makes use of this corpus of theory in the case study based on the Republic of Ireland. The issue of abortion first appeared on the Irish political agenda in the early 1980s with a campaign to insert into its Constitution a clause which purported to guarantee the right to life of the unborn. After a bitterly intense debate, the Irish electorate duly voted in a national referendum in 1983 to amend the Constitution accordingly (Hesketh 1990). It then reappeared on the agenda after a sensational judicial interpretation of this clause in the landmark X-case in 1992 which declared that abortion was legal in Ireland in certain circumstances.

We shall argue that different organs of the state apparatus have different interests in sexuality and abortion. The state, because it is not a unitary actor nor coterminous with government nor constant from state to state, does not have *a priori*, fixed reducible interests in the regulation of human sexuality and, by extension, abortion. In so far as an overarching state interest in the abortion issue can be identified, it lies, in liberal democracies at any rate, in the construction of an appropriate regulatory framework wherein the medical procedure of induced abortion can be carried out. Foucault has shown how through biopolitics or the administration of life the state deploys sexuality to ensure an ordered and healthy population; in the nineteenth century, curbs on abortion were subsumed within legislation dealing with infanticide and child abandonment. In the twentieth century abortion is regulated within biopolitical, medicalised frameworks such as Britain's Abortion Act 1967 or judicial parameters as in the United States and Canada. In other contexts biopolitics assumes pronatalist and even racist connotations.

In the case of the political entity known successively as the Irish Free State, Eire and the Republic of Ireland, the state's agenda and span of control were historically and symbiotically interwoven with those of the dominant interest group, the Roman Catholic Church. Initially, the Irish state needed the Church in order to legitimate itself after the violence and instability of the Civil War period. It thus enlisted the Church as a force for stability and order and inserted much of its moral code into its legislation.[1] The homology between Church and state was especially apparent in the social and gender orders embodied in the 1937 Constitution which sanctified the right to private property and the role of woman as wife and mother, the legal bans on the sale and distribution of contraceptives and birth control information (encompassed within a whole array of censorship mechanisms) and the removal of married women from large sectors of the labour force. On abortion, the Irish state retained the British Offences Against the Person Act 1861 which made the practice of abortion unlawful.[2]

In the early 1980s the Irish political classes capitulated to the demand of a small but vocal lobby of conservative Catholic lawyers, medics and lay religious, the Pro-Life Amendment Campaign, for the aforesaid constitutional amendment which would copper-fasten this existing ban on abortion. The amendment with all its potential complications was easily passed because discourse and practice on socio-sexual matters had been traditionally limited by the moral monopoly of the Church, which caused it to be virtually impossible to make public statements in favour of a woman's right to choose an abortion. By the 1990s discursive shifts had made possible the utterance of such statements; the intervening decade had seen a legitimation crisis for the Church and the social formation which had dominated the state. The reality of Ireland's abortion problem was now being acknowledged within Irish discourse if not being fully acted upon by Irish decision-makers.

But before we consider the course of and contestation around Irish abortion politics in greater detail, we shall attempt to locate abortion within a general constellation of state, gender and discourse.

State and gender

First, what is the relationship between the state and the constitution of gender and how does it connect to the abortion issue? The most comprehensive conceptualisation of the interlinking of gender relations has been the work of R.W. Connell. He starts out with the view of gender as a 'property of collectivities, institutions and historical processes' and as 'practice organised in terms of, or in relation to, the socially reproductive division of people into male and female'. Connell theorises his constellation of state, gender and sexual politics as follows: the state consists of a set of governmental and para-governmental actors subject to co-ordination by an executive and directorate. Sexuality is part of the domain of human practice organised (in part) by gender relations and sexual politics is the contestation of issues of sexuality by the social interests constituted within gender relations. Gender politics is a broader term embracing the whole field of social struggle between such interests (Connell 1987: 125–32). The abortion conflict can thus be seen as an arena of contestation consisting of actors such as medical interests, religious authorities and pro-choice and pro-life social movements.

To examine Connell's analysis of the state in a little more detail, he sees it as an actor in sexual and gender politics in the following ways. State elites are the preserve of men; the administrative and coercive apparatuses of the state correspond to quite visible gender divisions in which judicial and military personnel are mostly male and those in the 'caring' education and social services departments are mostly female. The state arms men and disarms women. The diplomatic, colonial and military policy of major states is formed in the context of ideologies of masculinity that put a premium on toughness and force.

The state attempts to control sexuality by criminalising or decriminalising homosexuality and legislating on the age of consent, venereal disease and Aids. It intervenes in the sexual division of labour in ways ranging from subsidised immigration to equal opportunity policies. Accordingly, the state has been a major object of strategy in sexual politics. The main focus of groups like the Campaign for Homosexual Equality and the Abortion Law Reform Association in Britain has been legal reform through the lobbying of parliamentarians and bureaucrats. The American New Right in its turn has attempted to roll back the gains of feminism through control of courts and legislatures; a central objective of this campaign has been the reversal of the 1973 Supreme Court judgement in *Roe* v. *Wade* which legalised abortion throughout the United States.

Thus the state is deeply involved in the social relations of gender. Alain Touraine remarks that 'the state is . . . the agent of a concrete historical collectivity, situated in relation to other communities and to its own transformation'.[3] In trying to define this 'historical collectivity' in gender as well as class terms, Connell addresses four approaches to the gendered state: first, the liberal feminist theory that thinks the state is in principle a neutral arbiter between competing interest groups and proposes that the institutional sexism of the state be rectified by legal equality (suffrage, the Equal Rights Amendment and equal employment opportunity) and specific welfare entitlements (increased child benefits and paid maternity leave); second, the view presented by Jacques Donzelot's *The Policing of Families*, Michel Foucault's *History of Sexuality*, Volume 1, and by theorists of gay liberation such as Jeffrey Weeks of the state as part of a dispersed apparatus of social control working through dominant discourses as well as through force; third, the Freudian Left approach of Wilhelm Reich and Herbert Marcuse which views the state as a class state in which sexuality is either repressed or carefully ventilated according to the needs of capitalism; and fourth; the view of Catherine McKinnon, Carole Pateman and others that the state is *a priori* a patriarchal institution.

Connell synthesises these analyses to suggest that the state represents a distillation of different masculinities (the physical aggression of soldiers or police, the authoritative maleness of commanders and ministers of state and the calculative rationality of technicians, planners and scientists) and that there is no consistency between states in their processing of gender issues. Thus the state is neither monolithic, reducible to universal categories, nor inherently patriarchal. It is historically constructed as patriarchal in a political process whose outcome is open.

Through its management of institutions and relations such as marriage and motherhood the state plays a major part in not just the regulation but the constitution of the social categories of the gender order such as 'mothers' and 'homosexuals'. Through them the state plays a part in the constitution of the interests at play in sexual politics. Marriage is a legal relationship defined, regulated and enforced by the state. State concerns about the quality and supply of its labour force can impinge on birth control practices. The state at times even engages in direct and coercive ideological activity; for example, in the imposition of dress-codes on women such as the wearing of the *chador* in Iran and compulsory family limitation programmes in India and China.

The state, sexuality and abortion

How then does abortion pertain to gender relations and to sexuality and what are the state's interests in abortion? Feminist theorists themselves disagree on these questions. As a radical feminist Catherine McKinnon (1989: 184–94) has argued that the right to abortion frames the ways men arrange among themselves to control the reproductive consequences of intercourse. She claims that since Freud the social problem posed by sexuality has been understood as the problem of the innate desire for sexual pleasure being repressed by the constraints of civilisation. In her account civilisation's prerogatives fuse women's reproductivity with their attributed sexuality in its definition of what a woman is. Women are defined as women by the uses, sexual and reproductive, to which men wish to put them. Therefore, the right to abortion has been sought as freedom from the unequal reproductive consequences of sexual expression, with sexuality centred on heterosexual genital intercourse.

Rosalind Petchesky (1986) gives a rather less reductionist view of the relationship between abortion, sexuality and women's reproductive role. Drawing upon theoretical assumptions on sexuality derived from Michel Foucault, Jeffrey Weeks, Linda Gordon and others, which understand sexuality primarily in historical and cultural terms, Petchesky critiques the 'drive-reduction' model of sex as biological instinct formulated and adopted 'uncritically' by sex radicals like Wilhelm Reich, Herbert Marcuse and Havelock Ellis (Petchesky 1986: 3). In her model human sexuality exists always in a context of social relations from which it derives its meanings, both conscious and unconscious; it is mainly a social, not a biological, activity. The historical theory of sexuality thus calls into question the assumption of most feminists and sex radicals that control over sexuality – through the family, the Church, or the state – takes the simple form of 'repression', the flip-side of the 'instinctual drive' model.

Sexuality may be defined in relation to procreative ends in some cultures or periods but not in others, may be associated with pleasure in some and with danger and taboos in others (such as post-Famine Ireland), may be organised mainly across gender in some or within genders (homosocially) in others; there are no universal or transhistorical forms. Cautioning that the modern cultural meaning of sex as an assertion of self and individuality tends to be a male definition and that earlier feminist advocates of birth control such as Margaret Sanger, Emma Goldman and Marie Stopes did not see in it a means toward the sexual self-expression of women, Petchesky senses that larger issues about women's sexuality – its boundaries, subjects, forms and age limits – are being distilled into the abortion conflict without fully understanding why, or why now.

The specificity of abortion from the 1960s through to the 1990s lies in two features. First, on the level of ideology, the right to abortion has been connected, by some feminists, to the right of women to sexual self-determination. This is in contrast to the understanding of liberal and religious feminists who think of abortion as a matter of 'private conscience' rather than social and sexual need. Those who oppose abortion make the same connection in a negative sense: the rise in abortions represents promiscuity, immorality and hedonism. Second, on the level of popular practice, for Petchesky abortion has become in the United States a phenomenon predominantly of young unmarried white women, a large proportion of them teenagers living with their parents. Abortion – organised legal abortion – is associated with sex because it is seen to reveal sex; it is a signifier that helps make sex visible and therefore subject to scrutiny and an inevitable drawing of boundaries between the licit and the illicit. In the context of late twentieth-century US society, it helps identify and categorise a new sexual subject: the 'promiscuous' white teenage girl.

Abortion appears on the agenda through contestation around the sanctity of foetal life, the right to self-determined sexuality, medical control over reproduction and even the quality of national human resources; depending on the context, these sites of struggle may or may not be congruent with each other. State interventions in abortion and human reproduction range from coercive controls on women's reproductive behaviour such as the late President Nicolae Ceauşescu's decree in Romania that women bear at least four children and China's one child per family policy, to elective abortion in the Netherlands within the framework of fully state-subsidised sex education and family planning services to the medicalised and biopolitical framework within which the 1967 British Abortion Act is cast.

State interests in abortion vary over time and space: from a pronatalist interest in ensuring large populations as in Ceauşescu's Romania to placating key interest groups such as the medical profession. So far as a common state interest in abortion across western liberal democracies can be identified, then it is in the construction of appropriate regulatory frameworks within which the medical procedure of induced abortion can be regulated and abuses eradicated. Since the state represents the sedimentation at different levels of different discourses, particular state interests in abortion will reflect the discourse within which the abortion issue is framed. Consequently we need to understand something of the processes through which abortion is discursively constructed.

Discourses and abortion

Here our starting-point must be the work of Michel Foucault, specifically *History of Sexuality*, Volume I. As defined by Foucault, a discourse is an ensemble of meanings which produces knowledge and is at the same time a practice embodied in everyday life. A discourse includes both linguistic and material practices; it structures a given field so as to make possible certain statements while ruling out others.

According to Foucault, discourse can make possible opposing discourses, discourses of resistance. Pointing to the development of discourses around homosexuality, he asserts that the appearance of these in nineteenth-century medicine, jurisprudence and literature made possible the formation of a 'reverse discourse': homosexuality began to speak on its own behalf, using the same categories by which it was medically disqualified (Foucault 1990: 17–35). In the Irish Republic, the widely accepted subterfuge used in the prescription of the menstrual cycle regulator prior to the liberalisation of the laws on contraceptives was an example of how birth control spoke its name by using the discourse used to disallow it. The passing off of therapeutic abortions carried out in Irish hospitals as D&C operations is another example of a socially taboo subject speaking its name in code. (As will be shown later, the Irish abortion controversy largely originated within the medical profession through such discursive practices.)

Taking issue with the 'repressive hypothesis' of Wilhelm Reich, Herbert Marcuse and others about sex in the Victorian era, Foucault (1990: 35) argues that 'what is peculiar to modern societies, in fact is not that they consigned sex to a shadowy existence, but that they dedicated themselves to speaking of it ad infinitum, while exploiting it as the secret'. He suggests that discourses around sexuality emerged with modernisation; they were prompted by the new political concern with the welfare of the population taken as a totality, on the one hand, and of the individual, on the other. These overlapping poles of development he called respectively 'anatomo-politics and 'bio-politics' which together constituted the phenomenon known as 'bio-power'.

For Foucault, bio-power was an indispensable element in the development of capitalism. The emergence of the great instruments of the state, as institutions of power, ensured the maintenance of production relations by disciplining and socialising the population into the routines of the factory system and early modernisation processes. The rudiments of anatomo- and bio-politics created in the eighteenth century as techniques of power were present at every level of the social body and utilised by multifarious institutions (the family, army, schools, police, individual medicine and the administration of collective bodies) as well as operating in the sphere of economic processes. They also acted as factors of segregation and social stratification, exerting their influence on the respective forces of both these movements, guaranteeing relations of domination and effects of hegemony.

How does this analysis relate to the specific issue of abortion? In his genealogy of the abortion issue, Minson (1985) seeks to link the history of the rise of biopolitics to the concerns of the modern pro-life movement. The first way in which biopolitics pertains to the abortion question is through the fact that, for the first time, both the preservation and taking of human life become the subject of a variety of new types of moral and political decision-making (Minson 1985: 65–79). He argues that the prestige of the medical profession and its extra-medical prerogatives were a consequence of the rise of a complex of relations, powers and knowledge already both medical and social.

Particularly pertinent to abortion are the social consequences of the distinction between life and death. A salient feature of the clinical concept of death is its multifaceted character, which in turn leads to a systematic, scientifically grounded blurring of the distinction between life and death; the pro-life movement's 'foundationalist first principle' of the absolute sanctity of life ignores the fact that the concept of life is an historical event, for from its inception as a concept, 'life' has been an object of economic and political decision-making.

As stated before, biopolitics discovers the human body as a socio-economic and moral resource. The policing of abortion and infanticide in the eighteenth and nineteenth centuries accompanied administrative measures against child abandonment, wet-nursing and baby-farming along with the growth in the interventionist powers of health visitors and child welfare officers. The 'sanctity of human life' enunciated by the modern pro-life movement principle could not therefore have been articulated before this biopolitical threshold had been crossed. Thus the nineteenth-century attempt to criminalise abortion in Britain and the United States along with infanticide was not motivated by a religious imperative to respect the sanctity of life but rather by the imperative to prevent the squandering of valuable human labour. It was subsumed within an attempt to clean up infanticide, child-abandonment and neglect which are precisely those issues about which opponents of the pro-life movement accuse it of indifference. Indeed the 'discovery' of the sanctity of human life by religious authorities like the Roman

Catholic Church was also a consequence of greater understanding of the processes of conception and gestation. Thus the papal proclamation of the dogma of the Immaculate Conception of Mary in 1854 and application of the penalty of excommunication to 'include the abortion of any embryo' in 1869 were intimately related to the discovery of the joint action of spermatozoon and the ovum in generation.

Since much of the debate around abortion in our case study in the Republic of Ireland revolves around the 'sanctity of human life' principle frequently invoked by the Catholic Church, to which 96 per cent of the Republic's population belong, it is worth paying brief attention to the particularity of Church doctrine on abortion. In drawing a distinction between 'detached' and 'derivative' opposition to abortion, Dworkin (1993: 39) observes that the Church's condemnation of abortion throughout its history has relied 'not on the derivative claim that a foetus is a person with a right not to be killed, but on the different, detached view that abortion is wrong because it insults God's creative gift of life'.

For substantial periods in its history, it was held within the Church hierarchy that a foetus became a person not at conception but only at a later stage of pregnancy, later than the stage at which almost all abortions take place. The early denunciations of abortion by St Augustine and St Jerome did not presuppose foetal ensoulment: that a foetus had been granted a soul by God at the moment of conception.

The thirteenth-century philosopher-saint, Thomas Aquinas, held firmly that a foetus does not have an intellectual or rational soul at conception but acquires one only at some later time – forty days in the case of a male foetus and later in the case of a female; he rejected Plato's view that a human soul can exist in a wholly independent and disembodied way or can be combined with any sort of substance. Catholic philosophers are presently engaged in a vigorous debate as to whether Aquinas would have modified his views of foetal ensoulment (Dworkin 1993: 41–2) had he been aware of the nineteenth-century biological discoveries concerning the spermatozoon and ovum.

The increasingly absolute papal proclamations of the nineteenth and twentieth centuries on abortion were to come down on the side of the view that the foetus has a full human soul at conception. This shift to the doctrine of immediate ensoulment helped to unify abortion with other Church concerns around sexuality and procreation; namely, the use of artificial contraception and masturbation. It further enabled the Church to advance derivative secular claims of right on behalf of unborn children throughout a secularising western world in which it is intellectually difficult to deploy religious-based arguments. However, it also puts a great distance between Church dogma and the opinions and practices of most Catholics. Opinion polls in Britain, the US and Ireland have found significant pluralities of Catholic respondents advocating the availability of abortion in a variety of circumstances.[4] As the statistics for abortions performed on Irish women in Britain indicate,

Catholic women are little less inclined to resort to abortions than any other group.[5] Thus it may be argued that the historical inconsistencies of the Catholic position on abortion show that the real concerns of clerical authorities on abortion are more the policing of extra-marital sexual activity than the primacy of individual human life, be it pre-natal or post-natal (Dworkin 1993: 30–50).

Ireland

We can now turn to our case study of abortion politics in the Republic of Ireland. From the early 1980s the issue has been high on the Irish political agenda. In 1983 after a national referendum the Eighth Amendment or Article 40.3.3 was written into the Irish Constitution stating that:

> The State recognises the right to life of the unborn child and guarantees in its laws, as far as practicable, to uphold and vindicate that right with due regard to the equal right to life of the mother.

Later in the 1980s the Irish courts interpreted this clause as outlawing information and assistance to women seeking abortions outside Irish jurisdiction, mainly in Britain (*Attorney General (at the relation of SPUC, Ireland)* v. *Open Door* and v. *Dublin Well Woman Centre*, and also *Attorney General* v. *Grogan* and *Attorney General* v. *Coogan*). As a result these pregnancy counselling agencies and student welfare organisations had to suppress any mention of abortion in their publicity literature and were perpetually restrained from giving any advice to their clients about the availability of abortion services outside Ireland (O'Reilly 1992; Smyth 1992). Both sets of litigation later entered European jurisprudence; the European Court of Human Rights ruled that in the *Open Door* and *Well Woman* cases the ban on information constituted a breach of human rights covenants while in the student cases the European Court of Justice ruled that abortion clinics constituted an economic service within the terms of the Treaty of Rome; it did not overturn the original injunction; the Supreme Court eventually removed it in March 1997.

A separate judicial development in 1992 put abortion firmly back on the Irish political agenda. In that year the Supreme Court in a landmark judgment (*Attorney General* v. *Ms X*) found abortion to be a legal medical procedure in Ireland if carried out in circumstances where the life of the mother was held to be in imminent danger through the risk of suicide. The defendant in the X case, a pregnant, fourteen-year-old rape victim, had been the subject of judicial restraint by the Republic's Attorney-General after he had learned of her intention to have an abortion in Britain. His injunction was upheld by the High Court but, after national and international outcry and after hearing expert clinical psychological evidence as to the girl's suicidal intentions, the Supreme Court overturned the injunction.

The court found that the Eighth or Pro-life Amendment passed a decade earlier actually permitted legal abortion despite the protestations of its sponsors that it would permanently foreclose such an outcome. The Irish government was thus obliged to devise a framework within which abortion would be regulated; it attempted to do this by coming up with a constitutional amendment proposal to permit abortion in cases where 'there was a grave risk to the life of the mother; that risk not being one of self-destruction'. What would have been the Twelfth Amendment to the Constitution was rejected by the electorate after opposition from pro-life and pro-choice opinion (Girvin 1994). In that year also, travel and information rights were guaranteed by two other constitutional amendments; an Information Act in 1995 was to give legislative effect to the latter.

It is necessary to place events in a wider historical context in order to understand the difficulties that the abortion issue has posed for Irish governments in the 1990s (they have never given legislative effect to Article 40.3.3 or to the X case judgment); why it is a particularly divisive issue in the Irish body politic, and why the pressure group, the Pro-Life Amendment Campaign (PLAC), which lobbied for the original anti-abortion constitutional clause in 1983, scored such a spectacular success. As stated earlier, the Catholic Church has been historically the dominant interest group in the Republic of Ireland. It emerged as a power bloc in Irish society in the course of the economic and social transformation which occurred in the country after the Great Famine in the 1840s. By acquiring physical control of much of Ireland's health, education and social service infrastructure and psychic control of the Irish people through its devotional culture of religious practice, the Church was able effectively to interpolate itself among the populace and historically to limit Irish discourse and practice. Meaning systems around sexuality and human reproduction in Ireland tended to be produced by a particularly austere version of Church teaching on sex and the nature of the human person. The Pro-Life Amendment Campaign, was thus able to give a coherent narrative on the evils of abortion because an alternative idiom, an alternative explanation of reality, was not available. Communicative competence on sex and on the morality of abortion had not emerged by and large in Ireland by this stage (Inglis 1987: 14–17). Even in the 1990s, when such a language had developed, liberals horrified by the course of the X case tended to preface their sympathy for abortion rights by stating: 'I am opposed to abortion.'

However, the institutional dominance of the Church is not in itself a sufficient explanation for the taboos in Ireland which have surrounded sexuality generally and abortion especially. For a fuller reasoning we must look more closely at the course of Irish societal development, or what Inglis terms first-wave modernisation, since the Famine.

The Famine, which occurred because of the mass failure of the potato crop, the staple diet of most of the labouring and landless classes of the time, led to the halving of Ireland's population, from 8 million to 4 million through death and emigration. It also led to fundamental economic changes in the country-side and consequently to changes in the social structure. There was a switch from the subsistence mode of agriculture production, prevalent in pre-Famine times due to the high yields to be gained from the potato, to a more commercialised small-holding system for which the overwhelming rationale was the avoidance of subdivision, felt to be the major cause of the Famine. A *de facto* mode of kinship organisation known as the stem-family system emerged in which the need to preserve inheritance intact was paramount and in which marriage was only possible on production of a dowry by brides. Those unable to inherit faced the prospects of celibacy, postponed marriage or exile.[6] Sex was consequently subversive of this new economic order in rural Ireland and of the material interests of the class which became hegemonic: that class of tenant farmers, identified by Larkin (1975), who owned thirty acres or more. This class and its kindred merchant classes in the towns and cities emerged after the relaxation of the disabilities suffered by the majority Catholic population, known as the Penal Laws, in the mid-eighteenth century; they largely survived the ravages of the Famine and later would purchase their farms outright from the Anglo-Irish landlords through the Wyndham Land Acts of 1903. The tenant farming classes became the backbone of successive Irish nationalist movements from Daniel O'Connell's Repeal movement in the 1840s, the Home Rule Party of the 1880s to Sinn Fein in the early twentieth century.

The tenant farmers also constituted the backbone of the Church in that recruits for the priesthood came disproportionately from their ranks and aided the physical expansion of it through capital in the form of bequests for Church buildings. The Church as an organisation had become centralised under the leadership of Paul Cullen who served as Cardinal or Primate of All Ireland from 1850 to 1878. Cullen orientated it towards an ultramontanist (or pro-Vatican) theology and set about eradicating abuses prevalent in pre-Famine times such as drunkenness and the illicit sexual liaisons of the clergy. As a political actor, Cullen succeeded in gaining clerical control of education and a wide array of health and social welfare institutions, from hospitals to orphanages to reformatories. Austere, Augustinian doctrines on sex and gender inculcated into novices in seminaries in Ireland and abroad were transmitted throughout these institutions and to the population at large through the Church's array of printing and publication outlets in an age of growing mass literacy. The tenant farming classes were particularly receptive to these doctrines as they connected with their perception of the consequences of feckless sexual behaviour, that is subdivision, and their ambitions to further their standard of living. They thus adopted enthusiastically symbols of the 'Devotional Revolution' imported into Ireland from Europe, such as the saying of the Rosary and the cult of the Virgin Mary, and internalised sexually repressive attitudes to a virtually unprecedented degree.

A triptych of familism, Catholicism and nationalism was thus to structure Irish discourse and practice for virtually a century after the Famine. Farmers, tradesmen and priests as groups of men dominated the political and social thinking of the new independent Irish state which came into existence in 1921. In the words of Terence Brown (1985): 'their economic prudence, their necessarily puritanical, repressive sexual mores and nationalistic conservatism encouraged by a priesthood and Hierarchy drawn considerably from their number, largely determined the kind of country which emerged in the first decades of independence'. The defining features and architecture of the Irish state had largely been in place since 1886 through an informal concordat between the Catholic episcopacy and the Irish Home Rule Party led by Charles Stuart Parnell (Larkin 1975). In return for the party's support for the bishops' demand for a denominational education system, the bishops not only endorsed the party's lead on the Home Rule question and tenant purchase of land but also established their individual right to be consulted about the suitability of parliamentary candidates within their episcopal jurisdiction. In the new Free State this constitutional division of labour was broadened to include all that was essentially political and economic within the remit of the state, while the Church expanded its acknowledged prerogative in education into other social areas.

The gender order that was constructed in post-independence Ireland rested on two ideological pillars: Catholic social teaching and English common law. It reflected the needs of a peasant and patriarchal property-owning political community. At the apex of the gender order was Bunreacht na hEireann, or the Irish Constitution, of 1937 which was drawn up by the Prime Minister of the time, Eamonn de Valera, in extensive consultation with the Catholic Archbishop of Dublin, John McQuaid (O'Dowd 1987).

The social role of women was prescribed in Article 41.2.1 which specifically laid down that 'the State recognises that by her life within the home, woman gives to the State a support without which the common good cannot be achieved'. Therefore the State in 41.2.2 would 'endeavour to ensure that mothers shall not be obliged by economic necessity to engage in labour to the neglect of their duties in the home'. Article 41.1 recognised the family as the natural primary and fundamental unit group of society and as a moral institution possessing inalienable and imprescriptible rights, antecedent and superior to all positive law. In Article 41.2 'the State therefore guarantees to protect the Family in its constitution and authority, as the necessary basis of social order and as indispensable to the welfare of the Nation and the State'. Article 45.4.2 promised that the State would 'endeavour to ensure that the inadequate strength of women and the tender age of children shall not be abused' and that women and children would 'not be forced by economic necessity to enter vocations unsuited to their sex, age or strength'. Finally, Article 41.3.3 stipulated that 'no law shall be passed permitting the dissolution of marriage'; a clause which was only removed by referendum in November 1995.

Women's participation in the public sphere was further rolled back by marriage bars on women civil servants and teachers, the Juries Act of 1927 and the Conditions of Employment Act 1935. But it was the system of socio-sexual controls imposed at the behest of the clergy and lay lobbies which most symbolises the repressive nature of Ireland's gender order. Following episcopal fulminations against the 'bad book', 'immodest' female dress, 'Californication' and sensuous dancing, to mention just a few alien evils of the time, the Censorship of Publications Act of 1929 and the Criminal Law Amendment Act of 1935 were passed. The former Act, which arose out of the recommendations of the Committee on Evil Literature of 1926, established a Censorship Board with virtually unlimited powers to ban any 'obscene' or 'indecent' publication; the word 'indecent' was construed 'as including suggestive of, or inciting to sexual immorality or unnatural vice or likely in any other way to corrupt or deprave'. Part III of the Act laid down that it was unlawful to publish any 'indecent matter' or any medical, surgical or physiological details in relation to judicial proceedings which 'would be calculated to injure public morals'. Under Part IV it was also an offence to publish, sell, offer or distribute any book or periodical 'which advocates or which might reasonably be supposed to advocate the unnatural prevention of conception or the procurement of abortion or miscarriage or any method, treatment or appliance to be used for the purpose of such prevention or such procurement'.

A catalogue of the works examined by the Committee on Evil Literature and an inventory of the books prohibited by the Censorship Board would reveal the extent of the sexual knowledge being accumulated in secret in Ireland at the time; sex and particularly birth control was thus speaking its name and being scrutinised in a manner Foucault would recognise. However, this does not negate a repressive hypothesis about the construction of sexuality in post-independence Ireland.

Section 17 of the Criminal Law Amendment Act read: 'It shall not be lawful for any person to sell, or expose, offer, advertise or keep for sale or to import or attempt to import into Saorstat Eireann for sale, any contraceptive'. It is to be noted that the contraceptive ban was subsumed in the full title of the Act under other matters of social and moral hygiene as 'the protection of young girls and the suppression of brothels and prostitution'. The passing of this Act followed the deliberations of the Carrigan Commission set up to inquire into the law relating to sexual offences; the findings of this commission were never published and the terms of the Act were thrashed out in what the Minister of Justice called 'an informal Committee of the Dail' (*Seanad Debates*, vol. 19, col. 794, 12 December 1934) rather than on the floor of the House. Members of Parliament were not even allowed to see the Bill; some felt that it was 'not a pleasant subject to discuss in public' (Colonel Moore, *Seanad Debates*, op. cit.). Another example of the secret surveillance of sexuality in Ireland at this time, of a category speaking its name while forbidden, was a report on juvenile prostitution submitted to the Department of Justice in August 1931.

For almost the first four decades of the Irish state's existence there was a virtual symbiosis between Church and state; both shared a common vision of Ireland as a rural nation of farmers and small property-holders. The interests of the two began to diverge from the early 1960s as the Republic of Ireland underwent second-wave modernisation. As the state looked for external capital investment in a newly open economy and sought to join international associations such as the European Community, so it required new referents such as Brussels and multinational capital instead of the Church. With growing affluence being created through urbanisation and industrialisation and expanded career opportunities through free secondary and tertiary education so the repressive socio-sexual controls of the past began to be loosened and eventually removed, and a growing media network in Dublin began to operate as an alternative power centre to Church and state.

On matters pertaining to sex and gender, the state no longer felt obliged automatically to take the Church on board as it had in the notorious 'Mother and Child' affair in 1951, when free medical care for mothers of children under sixteen years of age was scrapped after episcopal objections. The Church hierarchy also began to accept that legislators had a duty to legislate regardless of the teachings of their Church. New surfaces of emergence had appeared in the form of women's self-help groups such as the Dublin Well Woman Centre, and pregnancy counselling agencies like Open Door and the Irish Family Planning Association which provided contraception and abortion information to clients regardless of the legal situation. In 1973 the Supreme Court in *McGee* v. *Attorney-General* found the 1935 legislation prohibiting the sale and importation of contraceptives unconstitutional, a judgment which had a seismic impact at the time and which was the culmination of a decade of radical judicial activism in Ireland.

However, the backlash was at hand. The *McGee* judgment caused intense disquiet among conservative lawyers who feared that, just as the Supreme Court had read off from US jurisprudence a right to privacy to justify the legalisation of contraception, so it could find abortion on demand to be legal in Ireland as the US Supreme Court had done in its *Roe* v. *Wade* judgment in 1973. A host of lay Catholic and pro-family groups sprang up throughout the 1970s to counteract the burgeoning women's movement in Ireland and to demand action to curb the alleged abortion referral activities of the Well Woman Centre and others. Within the medical profession horror was expressed by gynaecologists at the high abortion rates throughout western Europe and discontent at practices within Irish medicine such as prescription of the menstrual cycle regulator (it was not until 1985 that contraception became legally available to single persons over the age of 18). The Pro-Life Amendment Campaign, a loose association of fourteen lay, medical and legal groups, was formed in 1981 to harness this discontent and lobby for an amendment to the Irish Constitution which would prevent the legalisation of abortion. By May of that year it had secured the commitment of the leaders of Ireland's three major political parties, Fine Gael, Fianna Fail and Labour, to hold a referendum to insert such a clause into the Constitution (there was virtually no consultation with the respective parties' rank and file).

Over the next two years the Irish political system was to suffer unprecedented blood-letting over the Eighth Amendment. The Labour Party, smaller left-wing parties, women's groups, liberal professionals and representatives of the minority Protestant churches coalesced into the Anti-Amendment Campaign (AAC) to oppose a constitutional proposal which was increasingly perceived as sectarian in its wording and as having potentially serious consequences for women's health. The text of the amendment became a political football as Fine Gael and Fianna Fail came up with rival wordings. (The former under its then leader Dr Garret Fitzgerald was forced to renege on its original commitment to PLAC after discovering legal problems with the text which was eventually ratified by the electorate.) Virtually every interest group was split asunder over it and the letter columns of the newspapers and the postbags of parliamentary deputies opposed to the measure revealed appalling levels of bigotry and intolerance. Eventually, on 8 September 1983, the Amendment was passed in the referendum by a two-thirds majority of the 53 per cent of the electorate who voted.

The anti-abortionists were able to score with such devastating success in the early 1980s because of the residual strength of tradition in the political culture, despite the rapid social change of the previous two decades. As mentioned earlier, political mobilisation in Ireland in the nineteenth and twentieth centuries occurred around a petit-bourgeois nationalism and Church demands for denominational education. The Church along with another influential association, the medical profession, had acquired a moral monopoly of knowledge around sex and ethics (Inglis 1987). The political style of the new Irish state reflected the traits of family and community: localistic, authoritarian and patrimonial with little real toleration of opposing views. Secrecy and taboo pervaded the legislative process concerning issues such as censorship in the 1920s and the Mother and Child Bill in 1951. The dynamic of tradition remained unacknowledged and therefore unchallenged until the 1980s. A public sphere in which alternative conceptions of the good could compete with Catholic orthodoxy and in which there were consensual norms around the morality of abortion had simply not developed. The anti-abortion forces had also struck at a moment of systemic crisis for the state in the early 1980s when these were spiralling inflationary pressures in the economy, overspill from the conflict and prison hunger-strikes in Northern Ireland and growing conservative anxiety at the perceived tide of permissiveness sweeping Ireland. The pro-life movement was to tap into the latter sentiment with great effect as it had access to traditionalist discourse that its opponents could never have. The strategic necessity for the Anti-Amendment Campaign to deny publicly a pro-choice position meant that it was campaigning on terms set by PLAC; their arguments were ultimately blunted. At the grass-roots, PLAC was able to utilise the parish infrastructure of the Church to devastating effect. The lack of a public language with which to conceptualise the relationship between woman and foetus was especially apparent in the excessively legalistic judgments which the Irish courts were later to hand down in the cases which came before them through litigation by the Society for the Protection of the Unborn Child (SPUC). In granting virtually unequivocal rights to the foetus and in criminalising abortion information services, the courts denied any sort of agency and autonomy to women in connection with pregnancy.

The aura of secrecy thus prevalent in Irish public life was to cloud discourse and praxis around abortion in Ireland in the 1980s and 1990s. The political parties initially agreed to the amendment proposal with virtually no internal discussion. It is not known which state official drafted the wording of the Eighth Amendment in 1983. The identity of the persons who drafted Protocol No. 17 to the Maastricht Treaty on European Union in 1991, which promised that the application of the Eighth Amendment would not be affected by Ireland's membership of the European Union, remains unknown and the Protocol was appended without any discussion in the Irish cabinet.

However despite the overt triumphs of the Catholic Right in the 1980s (a proposal to remove the constitutional ban on divorce in 1986 was overwhelmingly defeated in a referendum), other undercurrents of change in Irish society were occurring which would determine a different outcome to the conflict between liberals and conservatives over abortion in the 1990s. In 1990 Mary Robinson, a feminist lawyer with a radical track record on family law, contraception and opposition to the 1983 anti-abortion clause, was elected to the hugely symbolic position of President of Ireland. The results of feminist campaigns around rape, domestic violence and family law reform were percolating through the state bureaucracy. A new cosmopolitan Irish identity was being fashioned around new tastes in popular culture, the arts and new political alignments. Above all, the figures for Irish women seeking abortions across the Irish Sea (at a conservative estimate, running at 4,000 a year), was evidence that Ireland had an abortion problem just like any other late twentieth-century western society.

Thus when abortion reappeared on the political agenda with the X case ruling, the anti-abortion lobby was put on the defensive as the Irish polity and society was forced to address the consequences of the decision to give into their demands in the early 1980s. For just as legal experts had warned, the Eighth Amendment had led to court injunctions being served on women and also to the legalisation of abortion in circumstances wider than anyone had imagined. In taking into account the clinically suicidal state of the defendant, the Supreme Court justices in considering 'as far as practicable the equal right to life of the mother' had introduced mental health criteria for abortion decision-making, something which pro-life movements everywhere strive to oppose. It now became possible to articulate a pro-choice position, as was done in parliament and outside it by groups such as the Alliance for Choice and Repeal the Eighth Amendment (REAC) which sought the removal of the anti-abortion clause from the Constitution, legislation at least in conformity with the X case judgment and the restoration of travel and information rights for Irish citizens that had been called into question by the jurisprudence which had developed around abortion (Girvin 1994; Kennelly and Ward 1993).

The immediate response of political elites to the abortion crisis was to seek consensus around a redefinition of the issue, a pattern familiar in abortion policy-making elsewhere. To this end the Fianna Fail/Progressive Democrat coalition government sought a renegotiation of Protocol No. 17 from its European Community partners so that a forthcoming referendum to ratify the Maastricht Treaty would not become entangled with the abortion issue and any future abortion legislation would not fall foul of European law. It failed to secure a reopening of the Protocol but did obtain from the EC Council of Ministers a Solemn Declaration that the Irish government and the other EC member states would not be bound by the terms of the Protocol. After brushing aside demands from the Pro-Life Campaign (formed out of the remnants of PLAC) for a fresh referendum to re-establish their meaning of Article 40.3.3 prior to the Maastricht Treaty, the Irish government set up a Cabinet subcommittee to examine and resolve the issues arising out of the X case. This committee came up with three referendum proposals dealing with travel and information rights and the 'substantive issue' of abortion itself.[7] As stated earlier, the latter proposal was defeated in the triple referendums held on 25 November 1992 (in conjunction with the general election poll) while the constitutional amendment proposals relating to travel and information were passed (Girvin 1994; Kennelly and Ward 1993).

There has been academic debate around how to interpret the rejection of the government wording of the 'substantive issue' amendment.[8] It is possible to read it as rejection of legal abortion in any form, as a rejection of abortion laws which did not incorporate the Supreme Court suicide criteria or the outcome of genuine confusion on the part of some of the electorate as to what they were being asked to vote upon. Taken in conjunction with the 'Yes' votes on travel and information and with opinion poll evidence (see below), it is however apparent that there was developing a pro-choice constituency in Ireland (Sinnott *et al.* 1995; Kennelly and Ward 1993).

The discursive shifts since 1983 were also visible in the manner in which the politicians handled the abortion issue this time. No advance promises were made to the anti-abortion lobby and the Church hierarchy was pointedly not consulted before the formulation of the Referendum bill; the first time in the history of the state that its views had not been sought prior to a major item of social legislation. There was a consensus amongst all the parties in the Irish parliament that the wording suggested by anti-abortion groups for the abortion referendum, which would only have permitted 'indirect' abortions permitted by Catholic Church teaching, be rejected. This time it was the women's and pro-choice groups which took a proactive stance and it was the pro-life groups who were put on the defensive as their strategy of a decade previous was widely seen to have imploded.

Yet peculiarly Irish pathologies were visible in the events proceeding the X case. Rather than substantial legislation to effect the Supreme Court judgment, the government came up with a highly legalistic referendum proposal which in its callous distinction between life and health as criteria for abortion aroused widespread revulsion among women parliamentarians and women's groups. The wording itself was believed to have been pushed through the Cabinet sub-committee by Fianna Fail over Progressive Democrat objections because of the need to placate backbenchers in Fianna Fail who were felt to be susceptible to pro-life lobbying. The Fianna Fail/Labour coalition government which was formed after the general election of November 1992 promised legislation on abortion 'in accordance with the sensitivities of the community' but never came forward with it; proposals drawn up by the Labour Minister of Health, Brendan Howlin, were jettisoned by Fianna Fail members of the Cabinet (Girvin 1996). The administration which succeeded it, after Labour withdrew its support due to a scandal involving a delay in the extradition of a paedophile priest to Northern Ireland, came up with an Information Act which allows health professionals and voluntary agencies to give the names and addresses of abortion clinics outside Ireland to clients but not to directly refer them to such clinics. But it did not come up with a legislative framework for the medical procedure of induced abortion; John Bruton, the leader of the largest coalition party, Fine Gael, and incumbent Prime Minister, has stated that if his party is in a position to form a government after the general election, it does not plan to legislate on abortion.[9]

Thus abortion in the Republic of Ireland remains technically legal under the conditions of *Attorney-General* v. *X* 1992, notwithstanding any future Supreme Court interpretation of Article 40.3.3 and the 1861 Offences Against the Person Act, ss. 58 and 59. The medical profession in Ireland, however, forbids its members under its Code of Ethics to perform therapeutic abortions, and the pro-life movement is still lobbying for a fresh referendum to restore their meaning of Article 40.3.3, seemingly oblivious of Supreme Court and electoral verdicts on it.[10]

Conclusion

This chapter has shown how, through Foucault's analysis of biopolitics and the deployment of sexuality, a discourse around abortion can be structured upon the imperative of social hygiene and the figure of the Malthusian couple. The problematisation of women's bodies is arguably another field of discursivity relevant to abortion. In nineteenth-century Ireland, as elsewhere in Europe, there was an explosion of sexual discourse. Through its hegemonic role in the civilising and socialisation of the Irish people, the Roman Catholic Church developed a monopoly of sexual knowledge in the confessional box and in its carceral archipelago of schools, orphanages and hospitals. At the apex of the power alliance of Church, family and community was that between priest and the Irish mother; the latter was interrogated about her sexual feelings and desires in the confessional box and made to feel guilty about her body. In turn she internalised the gendered morality of priest and nun and became responsible for inculcating body discipline into her children. In this way the stem-family practices of the Irish analogue to the Malthusian couple – the three-generational family of the peasant smallholder – were sanctified. The Irish people were thus disciplined and socialised into the routines of first-wave modernisation and the Irish social formation was to reproduce itself accordingly. A way of life and morality which later traditionalists were to postulate as a universal was in reality a particularity of the post-Famine economic order in Ireland and its deployment of alliance mode.

Earlier, we argued that the state's interests in the abortion issue would depend on the discourse within which it was framed and that a fairly constant state interest across most liberal democracies was the construction of an appropriate medical framework within which a termination of pregnancy procedure could be carried out without the law being brought into disrepute. With the onset of independence, the Irish state had an administrative interest in clarifying British Victorian legislation on abortion and on the legality of birth control information. This it achieved through the *kulturkampf* of censorship and criminal justice legislation in the 1920s and 1930s. The former defined information and publicity relating to birth control and abortion as obscene and the latter criminalised the sale, importation and supply of contraceptives. The Offences Against the Person Act 1861 was simply retained on the statute books, where it remains to this day. In this way sexuality was deployed to uphold the placement of alliance in rural Ireland.

The last three decades have witnessed a sexualisation of the Irish body by a competing power bloc to the traditional Catholic religious regime: the media and the emergence of new sexual discourses told by the women's and gay movements. These narratives include abortion and, when articulated, tend to press buttons in the culture. The Irish abortion debate was not just a theological account of the sanctity of unborn human life but about Ireland's relationship to the external world and the nature of modernisation in Irish society. It was a fulcrum for a dialogue between modernity and tradition. It had become possible in the 1990s to articulate pro-choice positions (albeit within discursive rules relating to the sanctity of life). Abortion everywhere is essentially a contested issue and nowhere more so than in the Republic of Ireland, where either through residual deference towards traditional values or lazy, *laissez-faire* policy-making style no government has ever put an abortion law on the statute books.

Notes

1 See O'Dowd (1987) for further elaboration.
2 Offences Against the Person Act 1861:

> s. 58 Every Woman, being with Child, who, with Intent to procure her own Miscarriage, shall unlawfully use an Instrument or other Means whatsoever with the like Intent, and whosoever, with intent to procure the Miscarriage of any Woman, whether she be or not with Child, shall unlawfully administer to her or cause to be taken by her any Poison or noxious Thing, or shall unlawfully use any Instrument or other Means whatsoever with like Intent, shall be guilty of Felony, and being convicted thereof shall be liable, at the Discretion of the Court, to be kept in Penal Servitude for life, or any Term, not less than Three Years – or to be imprisoned for any Term not exceeding Two Years, with or without Hard Labour, and with or without Solitary Confinement.

> s. 59 Whosoever shall unlawfully supply or procure any Poison or noxious Thing, or any Instrument or Thing whatsoever, knowing that the same is intended to be unlawfully used or employed with Intent to procure the Miscarriage of any Woman, whether she be or not with child, shall be guilty of a Misdemeanour, and being convicted thereof shall be liable, at the Discretion of the Court, to be kept in Penal Servitude for the Term of Three Years, or to be imprisoned for any term not exceeding Two years, with or without Hard Labour.

3 See Alain Touraine, *The Voice and the Eye: An Analysis of Social Movements*, Cambridge: Cambridge University Press, 1981; quoted in Connell (1987: 176–7).
4 For example, in 1992 a Gallup poll reported that 52 per cent of American Catholics thought that abortion should be legal in 'many or all' circumstances; a further 33 per cent in 'some' circumstances; and only 13 per cent under no circumstances. It also reported that 15 per cent of Catholics believe that abortion is morally acceptable, 41 per cent in some circumstances, and only 13 per cent in none.

   A National Opinion Poll (NOP) carried out in Britain in 1997 which showed over 70 per cent support for the 1967 Abortion Act also found that 50 per cent of Catholics backed it.

   An *Irish Times*/Market Research Bureau of Ireland (MRBI) poll taken in May 1992 at the height of the X case abortion crisis found that 46 per cent of respondents believed that abortion should be available in special circumstances, while a further 19 per cent thought it should be available when the mother's life was threatened.
5 In 1995, 4,532 abortions were carried out in England and Wales on women resident in the Republic of Ireland. Since many Irish women presenting themselves for terminations of pregnancy in Britain do not reveal their addresses, the true annual figure for abortions performed in Britain on Irish women is probably nearer 7,000 (Office of Population, Censuses and Surveys, *Abortion Statistics, 1995: Abortions to Non-resident Women from Elsewhere in the British Isles*, London, HMSO).
6 The notion of the stem family is said to derive from the work of French sociologist, royalist and clericalist Frederic Le Ploy (1806–82). It was a three-generational structure which functioned to retain its original location (land and/or house) by means of dispersing most of the younger members while preserving the main family stem by a principle of single inheritance through the male line. Le Ploy and his fellow royalist and clericalist writers saw the rural family as a source of stability and a potential bulwark against the increasing

power of the central state and other social institutions hostile to the Church. Contemporary Irish nationalists validated the 'moral economy' of the 'peasant community' in similar terms.

There is a literature around the stem family system in Ireland: the three-generational system is fully elaborated by the anthropologists Arensberg and Kimball in County Clare in the 1930s; after the dispersal of sons and daughters unable to inherit to the emigrant ships, to service in the towns and to the convents there was the establishing of a new paterfamilias and his wife, the accommodating of their predecessors and the producing of a new generation (C.M. Arensberg and S.T. Kimball, *Family and Community in Ireland*, 2nd edn, Cambridge Mass.: Harvard University Press, 1968; see also P. Gibbon and C. Curtin, 'The stem family in Ireland', *Comparative Studies in Society and History*, 20 (1978): 429–53; D. Fitzpatrick, 'Irish families before the First World War', *Comparative Studies in Society and History*, 25(2) (1983): 339–74.

7 The three proposed amendments were as follows:

1   *Abortion issue* 'It shall be unlawful to terminate the life of an unborn child unless such termination is necessary to save the life, as distinct from the health, of the mother, where there is an illness or disorder of the mother giving rise to a real or substantive risk to her life, not being a risk of self-destruction.'

2   *Travel* 'Subsection 3 of the section [Article 40.3.3] shall not limit freedom to travel between the State and another state.'

3   *Information* 'Subsection 3 of this section shall not limit freedom to obtain or make available, in the State, subject to such conditions as may be laid down by law, information relating to services lawfully available in another state.'

8 See Kennelly and Ward (1993) and Sinnott *et al.* (1995). These studies of the 1992 abortion referendums reveal three distinct electoral pluralities: a 'conservative' or 'traditional Catholic' segment of 40 per cent which voted No to all three amendment proposals (right to life, travel and information); a 'liberal' segment which rejected the right to life or 'substantive issue' proposal but favoured the other two; and a 'conservative pragmatist' or 'moderate Catholic' segment, some of whom voted Yes to right to life but favoured travel and information rights.

9 Mr Bruton's government lost power in the General Election of June 1997 to a minority coalition of Fianna Fail and the Progressive Democrats headed by the current Taoiseach, Bertie Ahern. Like his predecessor, Mr Ahern has stated that no abortion legislation will be forthcoming. Instead, a fresh referendum will be held, probably in 1999, based on a Green Paper to be produced by a commission staffed by prominent anti-abortion figures.

10 Throughout early 1995 and again in 1997, pro-life groups lobbied district and county councils throughout the Republic to pass motions calling for a referendum to insert into the Constitution a clause forbidding all abortions except those 'indirect abortions' permitted by the 'double effect' doctrine enunciated by St Augustine.

References

Brown, Terence (1985) *Ireland: A Social and Cultural History 1922–1985*, Glasgow: Fontana.

Connell, R.W. (1987) *Gender and Power: Society, the Person and Sexual Politics*, London: Polity Press.

Donzelot, Jacques (1980) *The Policing of Families*, trs. Robert Hurley, London: Hutchinson.

Dworkin, Ronald (1993) *Life's Dominion: An Argument about Abortion and Euthanasia*, London: HarperCollins.

Foucault, Michel (1990) *The History of Sexuality*, vol. I: *An Introduction*, Harmondsworth, Middx: Penguin.

Girvin, Brian (1994) 'Moral politics and the Irish abortion referendums 1992', *Parliamentary Affairs* 47(2): 203–21.

Girvin, Brian (1996) 'Church, state and the Irish constitution: the secularisation of Irish politics', *Parliamentary Affairs* 49(4): 599–615.

Hesketh, Tom (1990) *The Second Partitioning of Ireland: The Abortion Referendum of 1983*, Dunleary, County Dublin: Brandsma Books.

Inglis, Tom (1987) *Moral Monopoly: The Catholic Church in Modern Irish Society*, Dublin: Gill & Macmillan.

Kennelly, Brendan and Ward, Eilis (1993) 'The abortion referendums', in Michael Gallagher and Michael Laver (eds), *How Ireland Voted 1992*, Dublin: Political Studies Association of Ireland Press, Folens, 115–34.

Larkin, Emmet (1975) 'Church, state and nation in Ireland', *American Historical Review* 80(5): 1244–77.

MacKinnon, Catherine (1989) *Towards a Feminist Theory of the State*, Cambridge, Mass.: Harvard University Press.

Minson, J. (1985) *Nietzsche, Foucault, Donzelot and the Eccentricity of Ethics*, London: Macmillan.

O'Dowd, Liam (1987) 'Church, state and women: the aftermath of partition', in Chris Curtin, Pauline Jackson and Barbara O'Connor (eds) *Gender in Irish Society*, Studies in Irish Society III, Galway: Galway University Press, 3–36.

O'Reilly, Emily (1992) *Masterminds of the Right*, Dublin: Attic Press.

Petchesky, Rosalind Pollack (1986) *Abortion and Woman's Choice: The State, Sexuality and Reproductive Freedom*, Boston, Mass.: Northeastern University Press.

Sinnott, R., Walsh, B.M. and Whelan, B.J. (1995) 'Conservatives, liberals and pragmatists: disaggregating the results of the Irish abortion referendums of 1992', *Economic and Social Review* 26(2): 207–19.

Smyth, Ailbhe (ed.) (1992) *The Abortion Papers Ireland*, Dublin: Attic Press.

6 Policing prostitution
Gender, the state and community politics

Barbara Gwinnett

Introduction

> Samantha works evenings at her house in Cheddar Road and rents the room out for £60 a day to girls who do the afternoon shift. At 32, she is in her fifth year of doing the windows and her 14th on the game. Depending on how many punters she has seen, she'll stay in the window from 7 pm to 4 am. Like some of her prostitute neighbours, she employs a sitter, who acts as a safeguard against difficult punters.
>
> (Boyle 1995: 144)

> Many street girls prefer working outdoors, as they can generally choose their working hours, view a client before agreeing to business and refuse to provide services they consider offensive. However, they have no anonymity, are more likely to be arrested, are vulnerable to violence from pimps and punters, and open to abuse from the public.
>
> (Boyle 1995: 135)

These two brief descriptions of prostitution capture something of the reality of prostitution from the women's perspective. However, this is just one perspective – and the particular forms of prostitution described above – 'working the windows' (that is, working from terraced houses) and working the streets – are generally situated in inner-city, 'red light' districts. These localities are shared with other residents, workers and visitors and prostitution is not usually welcome as a part of the local community.

By analysing the policing of prostitution in the 'red light' district of Birmingham, this chapter will explore the community politics which have developed around the control and regulation of prostitution in a 'red light' area. This involves untangling the complex interactions of different groups with differing perspectives on prostitution. Through this analysis the chapter will demonstrate how the state, acting primarily through the police, produces and maintains gender differences and gender inequalities. In effect, the policing of prostitution provides a case study which throws light on the complexity of issues raised by intersecting gender, politics and the state.

Classical definitions of the state emphasise its 'monopoly of the . . . use of force' (Weber 1991: 78) and its capacity to raise taxes and exercise authority (Engels 1978). Giddens (1985: 29) suggests it is a '"political community" within which citizenship rights may be realised'. Feminist writers (for example, MacKinnon 1989) have argued that the state acts in the interests of the dominant class, and that the dominant class is men: that the state acts in the interests of men and is therefore patriarchal. These definitions imply a monolithic, homogeneous model of the state. As the empirical evidence and subsequent analysis in this chapter will demonstrate, the state is altogether more complex. It operates at governmental and local levels and through policing of prostitution reaches deep into community politics. Nor do state controls of prostitution impartially uphold citizenship rights. This chapter will argue that prostitution is an example of gendered differences and inequalities inherent in the law and implicit in policing strategies.

The feminist model of a patriarchal state is connected with the feminist understanding of gender. The apparent biological differences between women and men are defined as sex differences, the socially constructed differences between women and men are defined as gender. Thus gender is a product of society and culture. At a commonsense level, gendered attributes expressed as femininity and masculinity are naturalised and essentialised – that is, seen as properties of individual women and men and rooted in their biological differences. Feminist social scientists have sought to uncouple the link between biology and society and argue that gender is an organising principle in the social structuring of relationships between women and men. It can be argued that this occurs at all levels in society and particularly in relation to the state. If the state is the arbiter of individual rights and freedoms *vis-à-vis* the individual and society, then in relation to gender Pateman (1994) argues that the state constitutes the individual subject as male. To be a civil individual is to be male, and women are brought into civil society through their contractual relationship to men. A patriarchal state is one in which civil freedom includes the right of men to subordinate women. This chapter, in analysing the research evidence, will argue that the state is not just an arena of gendered differences, but also of gendered inequalities, which privilege the interests of men over women. It will also discuss different forms of patriarchal control of women in a community.

In this chapter the state and gender intersect in the analysis of community politics. If politics is defined as the ways in which different groups present and represent their particular interests, then this chapter is an analysis of local struggles of competing, and at times conflicting, interest groups in the 'red light' district of Birmingham. The ways in which prostitution is a major political issue in Balsall Heath, Birmingham (Britain's second largest city) will be elaborated later in the chapter. However, it is in this community politicking that many of the taken-for-granted assumptions about gender and sexuality in relation to prostitution are reproduced and perpetuated. It is also in this community context that state policies from both the national level (through government) and local level (through the city council and local state agents and agencies such as the police) are worked out and contested.

Prostitution in Balsall Heath has been a highly contentious issue for many years, yet there is little more than commonsense understanding of prostitution by those engaged in the community politics. Shrage (1994: 100) defines prostitution as women's participation 'in relatively impersonal, non marital sexual activities where some type of material recompense is expected'. Shrage discusses the ways in which prostitution changes over time and in different cultural and social settings. It should also be pointed out that the sale of sexual services is not confined to women as vendors and men as consumers.[1] Prostitution can also be defined as a social practice – that is, an activity which has its own norms and structures – or what Shrage (1994: 12) refers to as 'hierarchies of social power and codes of conduct'. It operates in the informal economy and is subject to economic laws of supply and demand like any other economic activity. Prostitution is also an activity in which gender is differentially represented. Women and men do not participate in prostitution on similar or equal terms. Most notably, more men are involved in prostitution – in a variety of ways – as clients, pimps, landlords, and so on, than women. Research in Birmingham (Kinnell 1989) suggests that between 12 per cent and 20 per cent of the adult male population use prostitutes. Yet prostitution is generally perceived as a female activity; something women do.

For the purposes of this chapter, and given its empirical base, the particular form of prostitution analysed is the sale of sexual services on the streets or from houses by women in an inner-city location. By analysing both the policing of prostitution and the politics of policing prostitution in Birmingham's 'red light' district, this chapter will identify the specific ways in which the state, through its agents, regulates prostitution and thereby maintains and reproduces the gender differences and inequalities embedded in legal controls and policing strategies.

Feminist perspectives on prostitution

In order to elaborate the specific ways in which a study of the policing of prostitution can highlight the gendered differences and inequalities of patriarchal state controls, an examination of feminist research and scholarship is helpful. Until the contemporary women's movement influenced the social sciences, the literature on prostitution tended to locate it within the study of deviancy and crime. With their women-centred approach, feminist social scientists have contributed to our understanding of prostitution as a social practice by carrying out ethnographic research (see, for example, Hoigard and Finstad 1992; Jaget 1980; McLeod 1982) and by theorising and conceptualising prostitution. This section of the chapter considers the contribution of feminist research and writing to our understanding of prostitution.

However, it is important to note that feminists are not united in their perspectives on prostitution. The response of many feminists in the contemporary women's movement in the early 1970s was summed up as follows: 'However nicely our meetings begin, there always comes a crunch point where feminists cannot accept women providing sex for men' (Buckingham, quoted by McIntosh 1994: 1). According to Shrage (1994: 123), prostitution has raised two key moral and social questions for feminists: What is wrong with it? and Why should a woman want to do it? Given feminism's commitment to liberating action, to that can be added the question: What should be done about it? These questions have framed much of the debate within feminism, shifting the discussion from a simple argument that prostitution 'epitomises and reinforces men's oppression of women. Sex appears as something that men desire and women can supply or withhold, but women's own desires are irrelevant' (McIntosh1994: 4); to more complex feminist positions. Shrage (1994: 88) elaborates on this:

> Significantly, the division between women on the issue of prostitution does not divide neatly into feminist political leaders and feminist prostitute advocates, just as it does not divide into women who see themselves as feminists and those who do not. For some prostitute advocates, many of whom are former prostitutes, oppose prostitution, and some feminist spokespersons seem to want to tolerate it.

There are clearly problems in utilising a feminist approach to analysing prostitution which relate back to the earlier point that there is no unitary feminist perspective. The debates about what prostitution represents and how feminists should regard it mean that there is no single explanatory theory which can be applied to analysing empirical research. This chapter draws mainly on the conception of the state as a patriarchal state which privileges men's interests over women's interests. Prostitution provides examples of how this privileging works in practice. Although the analysis of law and policing owes much to liberal feminist perspectives on sexuality and gendered inequalities, the chapter uses those insights to argue that the state can be construed as patriarchal. The chapter also implies that an understanding of the economic and material basis of prostitution – both for the women involved and for the economy of the 'red light' district – is essential in making sense of prostitution as a social practice and the kind of conflicts and community politics which arise in such a locality. Despite the differences between feminist perspectives, their research can illustrate the ways in which gendered differences and gendered inequalities are produced and reproduced in relation to prostitution. Three areas relevant to this chapter will now be outlined.

The first area of feminist research is that which focuses on the material and economic basis of prostitution. Such an analysis highlights the economic advantages to women of working in the sex industry. The high rates of pay (relative to other kinds of work available for women with few skills and/or qualifications) supplements family incomes from other low-paid work or state benefits. In contemporary society the increased participation of women in the sex industry can be connected to the increasing feminisation of poverty during the 1980s and 1990s. According to Lewis and Piachaud (1992), the post-war period has seen a shift in the causes of poverty amongst women. Before the Second World War women's poverty was attributed to their financial dependence on husbands, low wages and large families. In the last 15–20 years there has been a shift to women's increasing dependence on state benefits. This has been exacerbated during the 1980s as general levels of poverty in Britain have increased, and there are many groups of young people (female and male) who are particularly vulnerable to poverty, and therefore to turning to prostitution to alleviate their poverty.

McLeod's (1982) research in Birmingham in the early 1980s found that it was economic necessity which first drove women into prostitution. O'Neill (1992: 15), in her research amongst prostitutes in Nottingham, also found that: 'For all the women I have spoken to, who are involved, or who were involved in sex work, *economic need*, sometimes together with peer group support, was the central reason for entering prostitution.' McKeganey and Barnard (1996: 26), in their research in Glasgow's 'red light' district, support the economic argument. They write:

> Stated in its broadest terms, women prostitute to make money. That is why women go to the streets to sell sex. Prostitution offers a means of earning a good income where otherwise employment opportunities might be considered limited and low wages the norm.

This economic analysis highlights gendered inequalities in wider society in which working-class women in particular are disadvantaged in the labour market in terms of pay and conditions and further disadvantaged by childcare responsibilities which can restrict the hours they are available for work. Prostitution, particularly as it operates currently in the informal street work location, provides work which is comparatively well paid, with flexible working hours which can fit in with family responsibilities and a level of autonomy which is not enjoyed by women working in other low-paid jobs. However, this is a limited economic analysis. The research for this chapter will show that there are wider implications for the local community and its economic activity, which may bring into conflict competing interest groups.

The second area of feminist research is that of human sexuality and how that relates to prostitution. Underlying prostitution in contemporary society is a commonsense assumption of its inevitability – its description as 'the oldest profession' informs such thinking. This is the case in the research analysed in this chapter where there was an underlying acceptance of prostitution as an activity.[2] It is assumed that prostitution is a 'necessary evil'. Shrage (1994: 120) challenges this notion, arguing that it is unlikely that early human societies exchanged bodies for goods. She suggests it is more a case of projecting 'our modern values back into the past'. Pateman (1988, cited in Shrage 1994: 205) argues that the idea of 'the oldest profession' is based on the 'assumption that prostitution originates in men's natural sexual urges'. This assumption is in turn predicated on the notion of the male sex drive as one which must be relieved. McLeod (1982: 65) writes:

> One of the main ideas is that of the primacy of men's sexual urges, i.e. that they are stronger and require more immediate satisfaction than women's urges. The corollary of this is that it is appropriate, or not so surprising, that men should find outlets purely for the sake of relieving those urges.

Weeks (1989) argues that the differentiation between male and female sexuality has its origins in Victorian moral values. The emerging middle classes in Victorian society had a moral 'double standard' which they sought to impose on society as a whole. This double standard was based on chastity for women and sexual freedom for men. It was linked to both the ideal of bourgeois family life and the economics of bourgeois family life. The requirements of respectability and the legitimacy of sons and heirs was paramount. However, middle-class female chastity and the sexual freedom of unmarried men could only be guaranteed by the availability of female servants and prostitutes. Thus there was both a clear differentiation in Victorian perceptions of male and female sexuality and moral crusades which sought to impose middle-class values on working-class women.

McIntosh (1978) argues that these commonsense ideas about human sexuality become naturalised. The view is that men are sexually active and therefore use a prostitute when other outlets are not available. To enjoy their right to sexual freedom is therefore tolerated. On the other hand, women are assumed to be sexually passive. In the nineteenth century, according to Edwards (1981: 23), women were seen to be 'totally devoid of sexual feelings, desires or needs'. In order to maintain the double standard of chastity for women, their sexuality is more closely controlled. As McIntosh argues, men have sexual acts, women have sexual relations. Thus this ideology of the naturalness of the male sex drive legitimates prostitution. Prostitution in turn reinforces the ideology of naturalness in two ways (McIntosh 1978: 64). One is that prostitution reinforces the idea of men as subjects – 'havers of sex'; women as objects – 'givers of sexual satisfaction'. Another is that society, not nature, produces 'socially scripted behaviour' and there are different scripts for men and women. Prostitution reinforces patterns of sexual behaviour to which men and women conform. But these patterns of sexual behaviour are based on ideas of difference between male and female sex drives. These perceived differences are just one example of gendered differences reproduced in prostitution.

If there is an ideological view of female sexual passivity and moral virtue based on chastity for women, how does society view women who sell their bodies for sexual services? Feminists point out how the double standard of human sexuality acts to divide women into 'good' women (wives and virgins) and 'bad' women (prostitutes). Edwards (1981) argues that the assumption of female sexual passivity effectively 'desexualises women' – ignorance of sexual matters is seen as a virtue. This ideology of female virtue is maintained by stigmatising women who do not conform to this standard. Women who work as prostitutes are seen as 'abnormal' women. This is partly because they are assumed to have sexual knowledge and partly because they are assumed to have, perhaps abnormally, voracious sexual desires.[3] Chadwick and Little (1987) argue that women who conform to social norms as wives and mothers receive social approval, whilst women who sell sexual services are regarded as 'fallen' women who have 'deviated from the dominant images and stereotypes of women as passive, submissive and feminine' (Chadwick and Little 1987: 264).

The problem with this division amongst women is twofold. On the one hand, there is the social construction of a category 'prostitute' which is based on stereotypical ideologies of female sexuality. On the other hand, it also ignores the fact that many prostitutes themselves are wives (or in long-term relationships) and/or mothers. Nevertheless, it could be argued from a feminist perspective that in a patriarchal society a 'divide and rule' strategy effectively means that women are set against each other where prostitution is an issue. This point will be developed further in discussing the empirical evidence of this chapter, where residents opposing prostitution clearly reinforced the dichotomy between 'good' and 'bad' women.

The third and final area where feminist research and analysis has contributed to our understanding of prostitution is in the area of legal controls, policing and the criminal justice system. It is here that the state becomes a more visible force. Not only do legal controls and policing strategies reflect and reproduce gendered inequalities, they are also illustrative of the themes discussed earlier in relation to gender and the state.

According to Weeks (1989), it was during the nineteenth century in England that the state first began to control and regulate sexuality, and this was achieved partly through the regulation of prostitution. State intervention reflected moral anxieties about the double standard. Moral crusaders campaigned for a single moral standard of sexual propriety for men and women. The laws which were enacted actually reinforced the double standard, because they regulated prostitution in the public sphere and left moral issues to the private sphere. However, the state did not do this in a gender-blind or gender-neutral way. Laws which were introduced were clearly targeted at women and at regulating their sexuality and reinforcing the prescribed sexual role of women. For example, the Contagious Diseases Acts of the 1860s (McHugh 1980) were meant to control the spread of venereal diseases amongst soldiers and sailors. They did this by giving local police and magistrates the power to subject to medical examination women suspected of working as prostitutes. If found to have a venereal disease, a woman could be forcibly detained for three months. Edwards (1981) argues that these Acts were based on the legal concept of 'precipitation' by women; in other words, women's involvement in prostitution contributed to their becoming the object of law. She writes that the 'Contagious Diseases Acts of 1864 and 1866 are explicit legal statements of the belief in the precipitating sexuality of certain women' (Edwards 1981: 57).

The gendered inequalities in the Acts were explicit in their focus on women, rather than men, spreading venereal disease. The ideological implications of the Contagious Diseases Acts, their focus on women rather than men, were reproduced in later legislation. In 1885 the Criminal Law Amendment Act sought to ban brothels and raise the age of consent to sexual activity for girls to sixteen years. According to Weeks (1989) the social concern behind this Act was child prostitution, but it ignored the social and economic conditions which drove young working-class girls into prostitution. One unintended consequence of this legislation was to move girls out of brothels and increase street soliciting and pimping. As Smart (1995: 67) points out: 'any area of law reform raises the possibility of perpetuating the cause of the problem by ameliorating its symptoms'.

The state clearly saw women's sexuality as the problem: their virtue was at risk and that became the focus of legal controls. By ignoring men's sexual behaviour the state reinforced the double standard, viewing their sexuality as something which either could not be controlled or was not desirable to control. Weeks (1989: 91) argues that by the 1900s the state had stopped formal control of prostitution, regarding it as 'an inevitable evil'. Instead, the state had adopted a policy of regulating public decency and ignoring private morality.

In the twentieth century the main contemporary law relating to prostitution resulted from the Report of the Wolfenden Committee on Homosexual Offences and Prostitution (1957). Driven by concerns about public indecency relating to increased soliciting in London in particular, Wolfenden adopted a utilitarian approach (Weeks, 1989). The law should maintain public decency and prevent exploitation of the weak. It was not the role of the law to determine the moral behaviour of individuals. Wolfenden recommended increased penalties for public indecency. In relation to prostitution, this led to the control of public offences by targeting women working on the streets, as they were the visible sign of prostitution. This was enacted in the Street Offences Act 1959. Just as the closure of brothels under the Criminal Law Amendment Act of 1885 increased street work, so the Street Offences Act inadvertently led to increased commercialisation of prostitution through clubs, call girls and so on. In this instance the law marked a shift from the nineteenth-century moral crusades, which sought a single moral standard, to more clearly emphasising the distinction between the public and the private. By applying the law to public decency and nuisance, women working as prostitutes have increasingly been criminalised. The implicit gender bias in the operation of the law was remarked on by the recent Parliamentary Group on Prostitution (Benson and Matthews 1996: 40). Their report recommended 'greater equity and consistency in the law' and noted a 'number of discrepancies in the ways in which the law treats those females and males who are involved in prostitution'.

The application of the law through policing strategies continues to reproduce gendered inequalities. The Street Offences Act makes soliciting illegal, and it is this law which is used by the police to tackle street prostitution. Women working on the streets are the object of police operations. According to Matthews (1986: 189), the Act has streamlined

> the process of apprehension and conviction of offenders by removing the formal need to prove annoyance and by increasing police discretion through the introduction of the cautioning system. Through this system the women entered the court as a 'common prostitute' whose guilt was assumed in advance and who could be safely convicted on police evidence alone.

The legislation which allows potential prosecutions for kerb crawling, the 1985 Sexual Offences Act, requires evidence of 'persistent' soliciting or causing a nuisance. The difference in evidential requirements of these two pieces of legislation means that in practice it is much easier for police to arrest women working on the streets than their male clients. For similar reasons of evidence, pimps and landlords are seldom prosecuted for living off immoral earnings. Furthermore, prostitution itself is not a crime, and soliciting is a victimless crime: this means that there is no complainant. For these reasons the police enforce the law against women working on the streets. Yet, as was pointed out earlier, women working in prostitution are only a small part of the commercial sex industry. Far more men are involved in different ways. Thus the application of the law through policing leads to gender inequalities, with women bearing the brunt of arrests and prosecutions.

When they go to court, women are further stigmatised by the label 'common prostitute'. Chadwick and Little (1987) argue that the criminal justice system applies the double standard by criminalising women but not criminalising men's participation in prostitution as clients or pimps. Nor does the law act to protect women: violence is viewed as a risk of the job, prostitutes who make allegations of rape are treated differently to women who are not prostitutes. Edwards (1981: 62) argues that 'it is very unlikely that a man would be convicted of rape on a woman known to be a prostitute . . . When a prostitute alleges that she has been raped, the social construction of promiscuity is set in motion.'

Thus the laws, their operationalisation through particular policing strategies and the criminal justice system exemplify the ways in which the state reproduces gender differences and inequalities. The research for this chapter is an example of such gender differences and inequalities. How these work out in practice in a particular urban locality, and the kind of community politics which develops, is the focus of the remainder of the chapter.

Prostitution in Balsall Heath[4]

Prostitution has been located in Balsall Heath for over sixty years and the main forms of activity are street work and 'working the windows'. Research in the area (McLeod 1982; Kinnell 1989) indicates that the boundary between these forms of sex working are indistinct. Women working as prostitutes may solicit on the streets and take clients to flats, houses, car parks and public open spaces. Alternatively they may work from houses located primarily in one street. Prostitution is actually concentrated in a very small area of Balsall Heath. The number of women involved in prostitution in that area is difficult to estimate – Kinnell's (1989) research suggests as many as 1000 women working in the red light district.[5]

As a social practice, prostitution is a complex economic activity in Balsall Heath. Women who work from houses pay high rentals for rooms from landlords. Police crackdowns on car drivers' kerb crawling mean clients switch to minicabs to go into the 'red light' area. Local corner shops and take-aways benefit from the trade through extra customers coming into the area. The connections with drug dealing adds another dimension to the economy. The police also have an economic interest, in so far as police resources are linked to the volume and type of crime in the sub-division. These various economic interests impact on the local politics of prostitution. Residents have what could be termed a social and moral interest in removing prostitution from the locality and there are groups who have an economic interest in maintaining prostitution. Thus prostitution needs to be understood as a complex social and economic practice which involves many people and groups in the locality and beyond.

However, it is the very nature of street working and working from houses – its public and visible nature – which causes prostitution to be an issue in the community and in particular for residents. In the 1960s Lambert (1970: 76) described the activities and nuisance very graphically:

> In the . . . area, prostitutes and clients use rooms in the houses and solicit from windows, doors or in the street. The road is busy with customers day and night who arrive by car, lorry, bus or on foot: some arrive drunk, and assault or accost any woman in sight or knock on doors of houses unoccupied by the girls. Many of the houses in the streets in the area are occupied by immigrant families and their children, who have to live amid the throng and bustle of the prostitutes and their clients.

Residents and people working in the area today claim they face a situation similar in certain respects to that described above. For example, in an interview for this research in 1991 a local community education worker stated:

> A number of prostitutes hang about the school gates, and the kids then have to walk past. And there is rubbish in the play grounds [i.e. used condoms]. People have fights outside houses a few yards down the road, you know. And cars constantly up and down accosting all sorts of women who obviously didn't want that at all.
>
> (Gwinnett 1993: 295)

The situation developed a more threatening aspect in the early 1990s. The sale of drugs locally had become entwined with prostitution in several ways. First, a proportion of prostitutes were also injecting drug users (25 per cent according to Kinnell's (1989) research). They were more inclined to engage in higher-risk sexual activities[6] and work longer hours than non-drug-using prostitutes. The majority of these drug-using prostitutes were also partners of injecting drug users and so had an even stronger motivation for working to support their own habits and their partners'. Second, some of the prostitutes were working for pimps who were drug users. They were forced to work long hours to pay for their pimps' habits. Third, some of the pimps were also drug dealers and could be violent towards both prostitutes and their clients. The local police superintendent stated: 'It's not just prostitution, it's the allied things surrounding it – drugs, violence. It's a problem . . . because of the propensity to sporadic violent disorder there' (Gwinnett 1993: 294).

This created a rather intimidating climate for residents. One local man stated in interview that residents who complained to the police experienced harassment:

> Now we have some very bitter residents in the area. They feel that they are being threatened because the moment that they go and report what is happening with prostitutes, somehow they get a backlash. Either telephone calls very late at night, harassment and all this sort of thing . . . from the prostitutes, pimps and so on. Because you know they seem to be an organised group of people and they have some hangers-on that carry out these sort of things.
>
> (Gwinnett 1993: 297)

Other residents interviewed for this research were clearly adamant that they had had enough of prostitution in their locality. A typical comment was: 'the people of Balsall Heath would certainly wish to see the back of them . . . we just don't care where they go providing the people of Balsall Heath don't have them here' (ibid.: 297).

It is in these perceptions and comments that commonsense ideas about prostitution and the women who work on the streets and in houses are reproduced. There is an implicit dichotomising of women into 'good' women (the respectable residents) and 'bad' women (the prostitutes). This links back to the earlier points about Victorian middle-class moral values and perceptions of sexuality. Balsall Heath is an inner city location of working-class housing. Yet the respectable residents are those who are presented as having adopted middle-class values. By articulating their concerns and campaigning about prostitution, such moral values are reinforced. By focusing their campaigns on the women who work as prostitutes, the gendered issues of human sexuality are also reinforced: it is the activities of women which are the object of the campaigns, and their clients, pimps and landlords remain shadowy figures.

Residents and similarly interested parties in Balsall Heath have campaigned for many years to move prostitution from the neighbourhood. They have used a variety of forums to express their concerns: residents associations, police liaison and consultation groups. Community groups have also campaigned through public meetings and local media to remove prostitution. It would be true to state that prostitution can be described as *the* political issue in Balsall Heath. This campaigning and politicising of prostitution has at times brought them into conflict with residents of adjoining areas when police activity in Balsall Heath has displaced prostitution to the more middle-class suburbs of Moseley and Selly Park.

However, a crude dichotomising between residents and prostitutes would not give the whole picture. There are also groups working with prostitutes[7] and they generally shun the political forums and concentrate on provision of services. The other voices which are missing from community politics are those of the prostitutes themselves. They have no effective representation on the various forums and their views are seldom sought by state agents (that is, police, council, community workers) or the media. Nor are residents' representatives agreed on what they want or what should be done, so local meetings can be guaranteed to produce heated debates.

The community politics of prostitution is complex and the police are key agents in this. The policing of prostitution in Balsall Heath illustrates how agents of the local state both implement the law and respond to public concerns. The police use a variety of strategies. In the late 1980s a series of high-profile raids was launched[8] – operations which targeted women working on the streets. Arresting street prostitutes offered an easy option for the police. By using the Street Offences Act, with its requirement of the evidence of a police officer alone to obtain a successful prosecution, the police were reproducing the gender inequalities inherent in the law. This also had the effect of building up public confidence in terms of arrest rates and visible police presence on the streets and appeared to respond to residents' demands. Yet the nature of street work and work from houses is such that it is highly unlikely to be eliminated. Instead, police operations generally displace prostitution to surrounding areas and thus set one group of residents against another.

The police also targeted kerb crawlers in the early 1990s. This was partly in response to residents' demands, but also reflected policing strategies elsewhere (for example, Nottinghamshire police also focused on clients' activities). Kerb crawling is one issue about which residents complain; they argue that potential clients are indiscriminate in their approaches to women and girls in Balsall Heath and that being approached in this way is offensive and intimidating to those not involved in prostitution. According to Home Office statistics (cited by Boyle 1995), this is a less effective strategy in terms of arrest and conviction, and therefore deterrence, than targeting women. In both these strategies the police use legal control which reproduces gender differences and inequalities. The women working in Balsall Heath are criminalised, whilst their clients and pimps are only marginally deterred.

The role of the police as key agents in politicising prostitution also works through the way in which they publicise the issue of prostitution and raise moral panics in the area. Senior officers co-operate with the local media to ensure that raids and operations are given maximum publicity. The police use publicity to amplify the potential, rather than the actual, nuisance and problems of street prostitution and thereby legitimise their operations. However, it is also apparent that the policy of highly publicised operations against street prostitution created its own problems in terms of resources. One senior officer stated: 'a lot of our resources and time are actually pushed into that particular area – probably at the expense of policing other parts of the sub-division' (Gwinnett 1993: 294). Publicising the operations raises expectations amongst local residents that the police will act, yet it is not actually seen by the police to be effective. Thus they are drawn into increasingly expensive operations at the risk of being unable to fulfil their obligations elsewhere in the sub-division.

Another way in which the police are active in the politics of prostitution in the 'red light' area is through the local community liaison and consultation groups, where they meet to discuss issues with residents' representatives. In particular the police use the local police consultative committee.[9] The Balsall Heath committee was characterised by the large number of residents' representatives who attended meetings. Prostitution was clearly a major issue: although not a formal agenda item, it was discussed at every meeting observed for this research. Through this forum the residents' representatives from Balsall Heath and the surrounding areas have been instrumental in encouraging police operations against prostitution.

Discussions of prostitution at police consultative committee meetings reproduce some of the commonsense understandings discussed earlier. There is an underlying acceptance of the inevitability of prostitution, of it being a 'necessary evil'. There is also a lack of understanding of the complexity of prostitution as a social and economic activity. This is accompanied by a resistance to prostitution in 'our area'. This polarises representatives of residents groups from the women working on the streets – the women are the visible face of prostitution and therefore the immediate object of residents' campaigns and police operations.

The relationship between the police and residents is a dynamic one: the residents make demands on the police for effective action against the visible form of prostitution in the neighbourhood. The police respond to these demands and are able to legitimise their operations. In this way police and residents are bound together in a cycle of demand and response. However, running parallel to this is the relationship between police and prostitution. Policing of prostitution seems to have more to do with control than elimination. The police are able to use the issue of prostitution to obtain additional resources for the division and thus reinforce their economic interest in maintaining prostitution. Furthermore, policing prostitution is a relatively easy policing option – it produces reassuringly high arrest rates and demonstrates to the public and residents that the police are actively fighting crime. If prostitution is dispersed through a city, then it is harder to police, so it is in the interests of the police to contain prostitution in one locality.

This cycle of demand and response, control and containment could have carried on indefinitely without any noticeable effect on prostitution but for two recent developments. First, Birmingham City Council took up the issue of prostitution under their multi-agency crime prevention policy.[10] In 1990 a Community Safety Strategy was drawn up and in 1991 the issue of prostitution was included in the first *Community Safety Annual Report*. A recommendation from this report was that an investigation should be made into the nature and extent of prostitution in Birmingham. In 1992 a confidential report, *Street Prostitution in Residential Areas*, was discussed by the community affairs subcommittee of the city council.

One proposal from this report, and one promoted by councillors and reported widely in the press, was the establishing of a 'zone of tolerance', based on the Utrecht model.[11] This proposal was publicly debated and initially was supported by Labour councillors and residents. However, it was not supported by the police[12] or the Home Office. By 1995 the city council had also dropped the idea of a zone of tolerance and was advocating a wider range of strategies. The Community Safety Strategy had drawn the local state into the politics of prostitution. As an activity, prostitution occurs in many forms and localities in the city of Birmingham, yet the council report focused on street work in Balsall Heath. The reason why this happened is not transparent, but it may have been that that was the contentious area where residents (council tax payers) had been most vociferous.

While the council was vacillating on a strategic approach to prostitution, the second development occurred. In the summer of 1994 an alliance of local residents took the initiative and organised street patrols in Balsall Heath to move prostitution away from the area. Pickets with posters warning off kerb crawlers were set up at street corners and operated from 10 a.m. to 4 a.m. Car registration numbers of possible kerb crawlers were taken and passed on to the police. Local meetings were held and press statements issued. Organisers claimed that around 500 local people were involved in picketing rotas. In the national media it was projected as an Asian initiative – in particular a Muslim-led movement.[13] Evidence from local media coverage (television and press) suggests initially a broader base of support from local residents and a local campaign group. These street pickets have been maintained and leaders claim they have driven prostitution out of Balsall Heath. In 1995 the Home Office formally recognised the pickets under the status of their Street Watch scheme – an extension of Neighbourhood Watch. Here we can see the state acting to incorporate a community-based initiative into more formal state structures. In this instance the state is controlling prostitution without recourse to the law or policing.

However, the campaign's claim of success in dealing with prostitution through community action has to be treated with some caution. Not all groups in the community support this kind of activity. For example, many church leaders are cautious and express concern over this kind of vigilante action. Some residents argue that the pickets are intimidating local people – women alone on the streets are assumed to be soliciting and men are assumed to be clients.[14] Prostitutes and representatives of the English Collective of Prostitutes complain in the media that women working in the area have been harassed and forced to move out of houses and on to the streets. Their dispersal to surrounding areas makes their work potentially more dangerous as they are isolated from other women working the streets. Displacement has also concerned the police, who argue that prostitution has not stopped in Birmingham, only in Balsall Heath, and that they still have to police prostitution.

These two actions – that of the local state acting through the city council and that of the community pickets – broaden the politics of prostitution. The council's community safety strategy brings prostitution into a wider public arena and attempts to encourage council departments to work together to address the issues raised during consultation with local residents and community groups. This is not an easy role for the council. A report from the Planning Department (Birmingham City Council 1993) was highly critical of the failure of various council departments to co-ordinate their respective roles in relation to prostitution. Changes of leadership of council committees has also meant that some strategies were promoted over others and then dropped when leadership changed. Although the Community Safety Strategy did initially attempt to overcome implied gender differences in perceptions of crime and address community-led issues, the focusing on street prostitution has eventually resulted in gendered differences being perpetuated. The community-based pickets are taking over the residents' representatives in mobilising around the issue of street prostitution. Although the pickets' leader claims to be targeting kerb crawlers, in fact it is mostly women who have been driven from the streets of Balsall Heath. However, far from eliminating public nuisance, they are creating a climate of fear and intimidation for local people, some of whom are just as afraid to walk the streets of Balsall Heath as they were when prostitutes and clients were soliciting.

The complexity of community politics discussed in this chapter highlights the social structuring and positioning within communities. Ostensibly aiming to clear the streets and make them safe for local women, the pickets have arguably asserted male control over all women in Balsall Heath. Before the pickets were active, residents complained of harassment, offence and intimidation by clients and kerb crawlers. Now women, irrespective of whether they work as prostitutes or not, appear to be barred from the streets of Balsall Heath at night. The state's compliance in this male activity – through the tacit support of the local police and Home Office official incorporation of the pickets – is a further example of the state privileging a male agenda in the local community. This is a reconfiguration of the politics of prostitution. It has been taken out of the hands of one patriarchal group (the police) and put into the hands of an alliance of residents led by Muslim men. Neither the police nor the original groupings of residents and their representatives are key players in this community action. Ultimately, however, the streets and the women who work in them and on them are still under a form of patriarchal control.

Conclusions

This final section draws together the relevant points from this case study of the policing of prostitution and links them to the theoretical concepts of gender, politics and the state discussed earlier. The fundamental approach of this chapter has been that of the feminist argument that the state produces and maintains gender differences and gender inequalities. This chapter has shown how this happens in a variety of ways.

The analysis of the policing of prostitution has shown how gender differences and inequalities are reinforced and reproduced through community politics. The double standard of women's supposed sexual passivity and men's sexual activity and their right to sexual freedom is reflected in the attitudes and actions of key actors and groups. Despite thirty years of women's supposed liberation in Britain, including their sexual liberation, prostitution as a social practice remains resolutely imbued with notions of gender differences in male and female sexuality. State action turns these ideological differences into inequalities through law enforcement in both policing and the courts. The law is contradictory. It does not act to promote women's passivity or to protect the weak. From the analysis in this chapter it is clear that women's sexual activity is the target of policing, and thus patriarchal control is established. Despite a far greater proportion of the male population being involved in prostitution in different ways, compared to women's participation in prostitution, it is generally women who remain the central target of policing and prosecution. Women are labelled, stigmatised and criminalised by working in the sex industry. Their activities on the streets are controlled by the police and the pickets. Gendered bias in the law and in its application is used to control women's participation in prostitution while maintaining men's access to prostitutes.

The gendered inequalities which underpin law and policing are further reinforced through the community politics and action. Women are polarised because the residents of Balsall Heath are divided into 'good' women (residents) and 'bad' women (prostitutes). The fact that women working in the sex industry may also be part of the community – they may live in the area, send their children to local schools, spend their money in local shops – is overlooked. The contribution of prostitution as an economic activity in the locality is also ignored. A crude dichotomising into 'good' and 'bad', 'moral' and 'immoral' ignores the complexity of women's lives and the reality of prostitution as work: a way of surviving in a society which subordinates women's needs to those of men.

The analysis of the policing of prostitution also demonstrates the complexity of community politics. As different, and at times competing, interest groups seek to represent their interests they take up entrenched positions. These configurations can be displaced when new social actors engage with the political issues in a pragmatic way. The emergence of well-organised pickets at first seemed to displace police power on the streets. However, their subsequent incorporation into the state reinforces the argument that the state privileges men's interests through an alliance of older campaigning groups, state agents (the police) and the pickets.

Finally, the chapter demonstrates the problem of trying to capture 'the state' as a single entity. The state operates at different levels (national and local). Each of these levels is complex and the levels themselves interact – as is demonstrated by a Home Office directive being interpreted as a Community Safety Strategy in one city. It is state agencies and actors like the police and the local council who interpret state policies and enforce state laws. This chapter has shown how, in enforcing the law, the police as key agents of the state reproduce and reinforce gender inequalities. This feminist analysis of the policing of prostitution has unmasked the state's supposed 'neutrality'. The state may have the 'monopoly of the use of force', and this chapter has given evidence of that through its account of the policing of prostitution, but it does not use force in a way which protects the rights of citizens equally. Thus the chapter has demonstrated how the state is itself gendered and can therefore be construed as patriarchal.

Notes

1 Prostitution is not a static activity. In modern, capitalist societies like Britain it operates in a variety of locations: on the streets, in houses/brothels, through escort agencies, sauna and massage parlours, hotels, through telephone call cards and so on. Prostitutes work alone or through pimps. Both women and men work as prostitutes, usually for men, but also for women. Clients come from all classes, occupational groups and social and ethnic backgrounds. The point is that it is a complex activity, and this chapter concentrates on a very particular aspect of prostitution – street work and work from houses, both in Birmingham's 'red light' district of Balsall Heath.

2 The following quotes from people in Balsall Heath interviewed for this research are typical: 'One can argue that you'll never get rid of it, all you can do to some degree is control it and try and make the environment as pleasant as possible for the people that live here' (police superintendent); 'You wouldn't get rid of it. I mean, you could try to control it, but again all it does is die down for a little while and then it's back' (resident); 'A city the size of Birmingham is going to have prostitution . . . you'll never get rid of it' (resident/businessman).

3 Ethnographic studies of prostitutes indicate that women do not derive sexual pleasure from their work. In fact they adopt a variety of strategies to distance themselves from sexual pleasure or desire when they are with clients.

4 This empirical section is based on research which began in Balsall Heath in 1990 and is ongoing.

5 The estimation by Kinnell of the numbers of women working in Balsall Heath is based on field interviews of women themselves, court statistics of women appearing on charges of soliciting, and police crime statistics. Because of the nature of the work these are estimates and it is recognised that reliable figures are extremely difficult to obtain.

6 'High risk' in terms of both increased exposure on the streets and the risk of arrest, and high risk in terms of willingness to have unprotected sex with clients and thereby contract a sexually transmitted disease.

7 For example, the SAFE Project gives health advice and free needle exchanges and is sponsored by the health authority; the Sisters of Charity is a Christian organisation which works with prostitutes in Balsall Heath.

8 In particular this was related to the appointment of a new superintendent in charge of the subdivision in 1989.

9 Police consultative committees were established following the recommendations of the Scarman Inquiry into the Brixton riots of 1981. Meetings of the Balsall Heath police consultative committee were attended from January 1991 to October 1992 as part of the research on which this chapter is based.

10 In 1984 Home Office Circular 8/84 recommended a multiagency approach to crime prevention involving the police, probation service, local authorities, the voluntary sector and the private sector. In 1987, as a response to this, Birmingham City Council issued a joint policy statement with West Midlands Probation Service and West Midlands Police outlining a multi-agency approach to crime reduction. A Community Safety Team was set up within the Council and in 1990 they produced a paper outlining a Community Safety Strategy. This emphasised community development approaches which included involving and consulting local communities and groups. The remit of the strategy was wider-ranging than the typical police-led crime prevention programmes and included, for example, domestic violence, child abuse, racial harassment and personal safety. A council officers' strategy group was appointed to oversee the implementation of the strategy. This was in turn devolved to 12 area community safety panels, so that specific local issues could be addressed at local level.

11 In Utrecht, Holland, in 1986 the municipal authority designated part of an industrial estate as an area in which street prostitution could operate without police interference. Medical, counselling and social work facilities are available through the Huiskamer Aanloop Prostituees project which supervises the zone.

12 At a meeting of the Balsall Heath police consultative committee in September 1992, shortly after the report's proposal for a zone of tolerance had been made public, a local police inspector expressed vehement opposition to a zone. During 1993 a clergyman from the Birmingham diocese met with the Chief Constable, who expressed his opposition to a zone of tolerance. A zone of tolerance can only work under current law if the police are prepared to 'turn a blind eye' to soliciting, which is a criminal offence. Police opposition to a zone is understandable in view of its potential to compromise the maintenance of law and order.

13 For example, the *Guardian* headline on 20 July 1994 read: 'Angry Muslims picket city's red light streets'.

14 This information was given in a confidential interview with a woman living in Balsall Heath. She also supplied, again in confidence, unpublished records of local meetings and correspondence of people concerned about the pickets. As this material was given in confidence and is not in the public domain, it is not possible to quote directly.

References

Benson, C. and Matthews, R. (1996) *Report of the Parliamentary Group on Prostitution*, London: Middlesex University.

Birmingham City Council (1992) *Street Prostitution in Residential Areas*, Report commissioned by the Community Safety Unit of Birmingham City Council.

Birmingham City Council (1993) *Community Safety: Balsall Heath Design Guide*, Birmingham: Birmingham City Council's Planning Department.

Boyle, S. (1995) *Working Girls and Their Men*, London: Smith Gryphon.

Chadwick, K. and Little, C. (1987) 'The criminalization of women' in P. Scraton (ed.), *Law, Order and the Authoritarian State*, Milton Keynes: Open University Press.

Edwards, S. (1981) *Female Sexuality and the Law*, Oxford: Martin Robertson.

Engels, F. (1978) 'The origin of the family, private property, and the state', in R.C. Tucker (ed.), *The Marx–Engels Reader*, New York: W.W. Norton.

Giddens, A. (1985) *The Nation-State and Violence*, Cambridge: Polity Press.

Gwinnett, B. (1993) 'A sociological analysis of four police consultative committees in Birmingham', unpublished PhD thesis, University of Aston.

Hoigard, C. and Finstad, L. (1992) *Backstreets*, Cambridge: Polity Press.

Home Office (1984) *Crime Prevention*, Circular 8/1984, London: Home Office.

Jaget, C. (ed.) (1980) *Prostitutes: Our Life*, Bristol: Falling Wall Press.

Kinnell, H. (1989) 'Prostitutes, their clients and the risk of HIV infection', Occasional Paper, Birmingham: Department of Public Health Medicine, Central Birmingham Health Authority.

Lambert, J. (1970) *Crime, Police and Race Relations: A Study in Birmingham*, London: Institute of Race Relations.

Lewis, J. and Piachaud, D. (1992) 'Women and poverty in the twentieth century', in C. Glendenning and J. Millar (eds), *Women and Poverty*, London: Harvester Wheatsheaf.

MacKinnon, C. (1989) *Towards a Feminist Theory of the State*, Cambridge: Harvard University Press.

Matthews, R. (1986) 'Beyond Wolfenden? Prostitution, politics and the law', in R. Matthews and J. Young (eds), *Confronting Crime*, London: Sage.

McHugh, P. (1980) *Prostitution and Victorian Social Reform*, London: Croom Helm.

McIntosh, M. (1978) 'Who needs prostitutes?', in C. Smart and B. Smart (eds), *Women, Sexuality and Social Control*, London: Routledge & Kegan Paul.

McIntosh, M. (1994) 'The feminist debate on prostitution', paper to the British Sociological Association Annual Conference, University of Central Lancashire.

McKeganey, N. and Barnard, M. (1996) *Sex Work on the Streets*, Buckingham: Open University Press.

McLeod, E. (1982) *Women Working: Prostitution Now*, London: Croom Helm.

O'Neill, M. (1992) 'Prostitution, ideology and the structuration of gender relations: towards a critical feminist praxis', paper to the British Sociological Association Annual Conference.

Pateman, C. (1994) 'The sexual contract: the end of the story?', in M. Evans (ed.), *The Woman Question*, London: Sage.

Shrage, L. (1994) *Moral Dilemmas of Feminism*, London: Routledge.

Smart, C. (1995) *Law, Crime and Sexuality*, London: Sage.

Weber, M. (1991) 'Politics as a vocation', in H.H. Gerth and C. Wright Mills (eds), *From Max Weber: Essays in Sociology*, London: Routledge.

Weeks, J. (1989) *Sex, Politics and Society*, London: Longman.

7 Remasculinisation and the neoliberal state in Latin America

Nikki Craske

Introduction

The purpose of this chapter is to examine the gendered implications of shifting political space accompanying the transition to and consolidation of democracy as it interacts with neoliberalism in Latin America. The social movements which emerged during the 1970s and 1980s, and which came to challenge authoritarian governments, shifted the locus of political activity from institutions to the community. In part this was necessary since military governments in the region closed off traditional political spaces; however, it was also due to the new agendas developing in defence of human rights and to protest the austerity programmes, and was not confined to military regimes. The dynamism and widespread nature of these movements meant that the whole of what constituted 'politics' was in a state of flux with new actors and issues receiving prominence.

Despite the return to civilian rule and the emphasis on the respect for human rights and good governance, many citizens find their socio-economic situation unchanged. New governments are reconstructing political space as they defend and promote the neoliberal state which, in many cases, was established by preceding authoritarian regimes. Social movements find their political presence has diminished in critical areas as key demands are sidelined. Many civilian governments have deepened the structural adjustment programmes (SAPs) undertaken by authoritarian governments and the high expectations which accompanied the transitions to democracy have not been realised. This radical neoliberal restructuring requires careful management of socio-political demands which Latin American governments have allowed through the implementation of poverty alleviation projects (PAPs) and the rewriting of political discourses, specifically the public–private, Left–Right, social–political, which serve to separate and contain political activity. Poverty alleviation programmes are of particular importance since they depoliticise service provision by removing issues from campaigning politics and relocate them to the bureaucratic political arena.

I argue that whilst the policies enacted by contemporary governments are not necessarily designed to have a direct, negative impact on women's political activity, they are gendered because of the different histories of political activity which women and men have.[1] Despite this 'remasculinisation', I do not wish to suggest that the political arena has returned to the conditions of the 1960s and 1970s; important gains have been made by women such as quotas in political parties, quotas for congressional representation (Argentina), the establishment of women's ministries, changes in laws regarding divorce, child custody, domestic violence and other issues with specific relevance for women. But we are witnessing a form of backlash; it is still difficult for women to acknowledge publicly their feminist identity and the antagonism towards the term 'gender' demonstrated at the pre-Beijing meetings shows the degree to which other forces are massing and the failure of the state to defend and promote women's interests in their multiple forms. Indeed, in many countries women's representation in Congress has barely changed over the past thirty years. Grassroots political experience has not translated into legislative representation. Grassroots women activists' energies are channelled through the bureaucratised PAPs rather than party politics.

In common with many northern countries, Latin America is witnessing the emergence of a deregulated and reduced state in the economic sphere, but regulation is maintained in other areas, particularly in the more private and intimate aspects to control sexuality and 'alternative lifestyles', frequently reinforced by the Vatican.

The chapter begins with an analysis of the major foci of women's political activity in challenging authoritarianism. This is followed by a discussion of the neoliberal economic state engaged in restructuring and poverty alleviation programmes, and how these have an impact on grassroots political organisation. The (re-)emergence of key political discourses and how these construct suitable political actors and spaces in the neoliberal state will also be discussed. Although women have made important gains over the past decades, these have been mediated by class and ethnicity and need to be defended from the depoliticisation strategies of 'democrac(ies) without citizenship' (Cammack 1994: 193).

Authoritarianism and the struggle for democracy in Latin America

The twentieth century has presented Latin America with many vicissitudes, leaving observers with a range of conclusions. Some focus on Latin America's 'authoritarian culture' to explain the region's difficulties, whilst others point to the dynamism of social movements spear-heading the anti-authoritarian struggles as the basis of a paradigmatic civil society. These observations are often more a reflection of the researchers' interests and foci than a clear analysis of events. In the twentieth century Latin American governments have been largely exclusionary, reaching their apotheosis under the military-led national security states of the 1960s and 1970s,[2] but even the 'model' democracies of Colombia and Venezuela were highly elitist. A characteristic of many countries was rapid regime change; Argentina has only experienced the exchange of presidents through elections twice: 1989 and 1995 (when Carlos Menem was re-elected). Until the late 1960s both elected and military governments tended to follow a state-led development project which often relied on populism and corporatism to keep social peace. This model began to be dismantled as economic crisis, precipitated in many instances by the hike in oil prices in the 1970s, exposed the structural weaknesses in the economies. The shift to neoliberalism and export-led development was promoted to varying degrees by the military governments, most enthusiastically by the deeply authoritarian regime of General Pinochet in Chile. A key element of the national security states' economic project was the suppression of popular political activity; effectively politics was suspended since it was deemed to be destabilising and an obstacle in the path of economic restructuring. State withdrawal from economic development had a massive impact on standards of living, exacerbating the impact of the crisis itself. Social order was maintained through state terror in many countries. The combination of human rights abuses and a dramatic fall in standards of living as the economic policies bit hard led to the rise of popular protest organisations throughout the region.[3]

The role of women in the social movements was key, reflecting the direct impact that government policies had on their lives and the way in which the political terrain was mutating under the extreme conditions. The initial stage of social movements was to protest against the results of authoritarianism, but they came to challenge the governments themselves. There were a number of principal outcomes of the rise of social movements and their popular protest activities. First, they broke the fear which underpinned the authoritarian governments and created an alternative avenue of political activity in the absence of political parties, trade unions, women's groups, student organisations and the like. Second, they introduced new actors on to the political scene, particularly women who were generally antipathetic towards institutional politics. Third, they challenged traditional distinctions between the political and social and between public and private which had reinforced women's exclusion from political life. There was also a challenge to the institutional arena as *the* place for conducting politics; and since the social movements often rejected political parties, the Left–Right distinction was undermined.

For women, the crucial element of the anti-authoritarian struggle came from the centrality of 'domestic' issues to the political struggle, the clear demonstration of the links between social, political and economic policies, and in highlighting the centrality of politics to their daily lives and their own importance to the political arena. As a result of their participation in social movements women's political identity developed; initially motherhood played an important role, given the emphasis on the domestic arena. The centrality of motherhood in the development of women's political activity is, perhaps, epitomised by the human rights organisations, but is also demonstrated in the issues coming out of neighbourhood organisations (Logan 1989; Alvarez 1990; Craske 1993; Fisher 1993; Chuchryk 1994; Jaquette 1994a; Puar 1996). But this did not remain static and the result of the 'politicisation of motherhood' was also varied. Some women were led to question gendered power relations, not only in the political and economic arenas, but also in private, domestic relationships, whilst others did not develop their political involvement, demonstrating 'an unconscious resistance' (Perelli 1994). Many women also analysed their discriminated position in the labour force and the way in which 'mainstream' unions ignored or marginalised their demands (Staudt 1987). This gendered consciousness and empowerment cannot necessarily be equated with feminism, which is often seen as 'imported' and frequently rejected in Latin America for its class and ethnocentric biases. There has been, however, an attempt to develop 'popular' feminism which integrates a class analysis with a discussion of gender issues based on the experiences of the women concerned (Stephen 1996).

Despite the importance and dynamism of these social movements, they have found it very difficult to maintain political influence with the return of civilian governments (Taylor 1996; Waylen 1993, 1994). The economic policies against which many social movements were protesting in their anti-austerity mobilisations have not been reversed. Indeed, all Latin American countries, including Cuba, are now embarked on some kind of externally oriented economic restructuring programme, many of which serve to deepen and consolidate the policies of the authoritarian governments which went before them; Latin America has embraced neoliberalism. The other major area of popular protest, human rights organisations, have also been sidelined and few prosecutions against the perpetrators of abuses have been realised. Argentina's experience shows us that even when prosecution is successful, the actions of governments might undo the good work: the Argentinian generals were given an amnesty by President Menem (its formal revocation in March 1998 had little practical impact). Many human rights organisations are now considered a distraction and the famous Madres split, rather acrimoniously, into two groups.

The neoliberal state

For feminists the role of the state has always been a matter for dispute; some see it as a useful tool in the furthering of women's rights and quality of life, whilst others see it as an essential element in the development and maintenance of patriarchy and therefore of no use to women. Inevitably, the role of the state in shaping gender relations and the advancement of women is not so clear cut; it has both helped and hindered women in their search for social justice and political representation. In northern countries there has been a long-standing debate about the role of the welfare state in providing an important political space for women and reshaping gender relations (Pringle and Watson 1992). Similarly, in the Third World there has been discussion of the spaces which state-led development offered women through positions in administration and as clients of programmes (Goetz 1992; Rai 1996; Waylen 1996). The state is a key factor in shaping gender relations in all countries (Pringle and Watson 1992: 64); equally the economic system influences the negotiation of public and private boundaries with the subsequent impact on gender relations (Brodie 1994: 55). This shift from state-led development to export-led neoliberalism has highlighted some of the complexities of the state and demonstrated its character as contested space where competing interests vie for influence over policy decision-making and the gaining of concessions. The neoliberal state in Latin America has favoured private, particularly international, capital.

Although neoliberalism was often instigated by authoritarian regimes where little attention was paid to social justice or to promoting women's (or anybody else's) welfare, the deepening of neoliberalism has occurred with transitions to democracy and offers certain unique opportunities to governments, allowing them to recast politics in terms of rights and responsibilities. The high degree of popular mobilisation during the process of transition is similar to the conditions which resulted in the coups in the 1960s and 1970s.[4] Despite the difficulties and on-going economic strictures, there is still goodwill towards the civilian governments and fear of a return to military rule (not shared universally); consequently opposition groups are still wary of demonstrating against government policy for fear of encouraging military intervention.[5] Furthermore, few of the major opposition parties are offering an alternative to neoliberalism; Peru's Fujimori campaigned on an alternative package in 1990 but reneged on his plans whilst still president elect. Similarly in Venezuela, Caldera's attempts to avoid restructuring have not been very successful.

The neoliberal state has two main facets: the withdrawal of the state from the economy, reversing the development model followed by most of Latin America in the middle part of the century; and the promotion of the political individual with rights and responsibilities. Many feminists have pointed out that this individual is effectively male and women's reproductive role is largely ignored (Brodie 1994; Pringle and Watson 1992). First, we will concentrate on the economic implications of neoliberalism in a Latin American context. In most countries it is synonymous with structural adjustment packages (SAPs). The collapse of state-led development was partly due to the bottleneck created by the failure to produce capital goods domestically, which meant that countries still had to import many goods, but with weak export records a balance of payments crisis ensued. This crisis was exacerbated by a fiscal crisis. Sparr (1994: 7) identifies four main components of SAPs: a currency devaluation to curb imports and make exports more competitive; a reduction in government spending, particularly through a reduction in subsidies (often in basic foodstuffs and basic services), public welfare provision and making public employees redundant; the removal of any restrictions on interest rates to discourage borrowing, curb inflation and help stop capital flight; and the abolition of price controls and the introduction of wage restraints in some cases. There is also the removal of tariff barriers as part of the 'opening-up' of the economy. It is important to note that SAPs were promoted and often forced on to governments by external agencies with few alternatives discussed. It is acknowledged by many that SAPs have a disproportionate impact on the more vulnerable in society and that they are gendered. Most Latin American governments have introduced poverty alleviation programmes (PAPs) to ameliorate the negative fall-out of SAPs and to contain social discontent. The political impact of PAPs is significant, given the importance of social movements, and has particular repercussions for women, as we shall see below.

With regard to individual rights and responsibilities, there is a great emphasis on self-help strategies for combating poverty and providing welfare at the local level. An important change noticeable in contemporary politics is the encouragement of participation in the political arena, which is generally constrained within the boundaries of 'responsible' participation in the electoral arena. This means making few demands regarding social justice and accepting the need to have economic growth before distribution. One of the results has been a widening of the gap between the rich and the poor. Camp (1995) has pointed out in his study of Mexican politics that elite politicians are becoming more homogeneously middle class rather than incorporating the working classes who formed the majority of popular protest organisations.

Although the perceived wisdom is that the neoliberal state is less susceptible to populist political stratagems on the part of politicians since the role of the state is reduced, limiting possibilities for co-opting the electorate, Roberts (1995) demonstrates the way in which Peru's Fujimori has succeeded in blending populism with neoliberal economics and suggests that similar arguments could be made for Mexico and Argentina. His argument is based, in part, on the way in which poverty alleviation programmes are used to ameliorate the excesses of structural adjustment and also contain social discontent and are used for electoral advantage (for Mexico, see also Craske 1994; Dresser 1991; Varley 1996; Molinar Horcasitas and Weldon 1994).[6] However, even where populism remains a dominant feature, Roberts (1995) suggests that there still is a shifting of the political terrain as institutions are reformulated to contain popular demands, a task which is heightened by the neoliberal agenda. Economic and political agendas are de-linked in an attempt to undermine social movements. Similarly, Brodie (1994: 56) argues that the effect of structural adjustment is 'to depoliticise the economic by representing it as self-regulating and directive'. She also suggests that the gendered implications of neoliberal restructuring are not incidental but intentional (ibid.: 51).

Generally, the literature focuses on the impact of neoliberal economic strategies on women's involvement in the productive sphere. Here, however, I concentrate on the impact on women's political participation. There are three ways in which neoliberal economics affects women's political participation: first, the whole project is gender-blind and makes assumptions about citizens and individuals which indicate a conceptualisation which is masculine and ignores women's unpaid labour, which is essential for the reproduction of the productive labour force and which underpins SAPs (Brodie 1994; cf. Pringle and Watson 1992). By ignoring the particular constraints which women face, the project does not acknowledge the different possibilities for women and men regarding their participation in politics, particularly regarding time, dependants and workplace location. Second, in the case of Latin America and most other developing countries, it promotes a comparative advantage based on a cheap labour force with, generally, the push towards the casualisation of production mirroring many of the practices characteristic of female employment in the region. In one of the growth industries in Latin America, assembly plants in the textile and electronic industries particularly in Mexico, it is women who traditionally formed the majority of the workers and who accepted the conditions demanded by export-led development.[7] With wage competition coming from such countries as Indonesia and Malaysia where labour costs are half those of Latin America, there is not much scope for improvements. At the same time, restructuring has resulted in massive privatisation leading to redundancies in traditional industries and increasing male unemployment, although there has been a greater impact on wages than employment rates (Lustig 1994), forcing greater female participation in waged labour. Furthermore, it must be remembered that structural adjustment came after economic recession which had already significantly reduced living standards, and even during the economic 'miracles' in the region in the 1960s and 1970s the benefits had not reached the poorest. The new regime of accumulation has increased women's participation in waged labour as well as increasing the importance of the informal sphere; however, since women's wages generally remain lower than men's there is a need for women to work longer hours to maintain family incomes, and conditions are often worse as well. Furthermore, the type of work available under export-led development tends to be short-term contract and the informal sector, neither of which offer much potential for workplace political activity.[8] These shifts in work patterns often have an impact on gender relations in the home not always to the benefit of women.

Finally, the impact of SAPs on developing (and other) countries has been to reduce social spending; those social welfare programmes which do exist are based on notions of co-responsibility which require participation in payment or in kind from the 'clients' of the projects and which are underpinned by their own gendered assumptions (see below). Goetz (1992: 15) suggests: 'Women have been the first to suffer, and to bear the cost, of conservative pro-market and anti-bureaucratic strategies which have sought to reprivatize the costs of reproduction, both within and outside of bureaucracies.'[9] It is this latter issue which I believe encourages a remasculinisation of politics in the region.

Remasculinisation and poverty alleviation programmes

The results of poverty alleviation programmes are mixed but they maintain their popularity with governments since they remove some responsibility from the state and emphasise public initiative in combating poverty. The aim is to offset the worst excesses of economic adjustment, but there are different approaches. Some programmes target the poorest who are suffering from the long-term structural poverty endemic in the region, whilst others concentrate on the 'new poor', those who have been displaced by structural adjustment.[10] In Latin America the more successful programmes have been those of Chile, Bolivia and Mexico; Peru, in particular, has been criticised for failing to address the problems generated by SAPs or long-term poverty. Most PAPs are demand-based projects mediated through local agencies, frequently non-governmental organisations (NGOs) and local social movements (Graham 1994; cf. Raczynski and Serrano 1992); given the constraints of the neoliberal project, the response can only be partial.[11] They tend to be separated into two main areas: service provision (basic services and employment) and targeted subsidies (for example, through food coupons) (Graham 1994: 5). Many programmes have 'women's projects' which tend to focus either on local income-generation projects frequently emphasising 'feminine' characteristics such as needlework or cooking, or on service provision which can reinforce gender stereotypes around women's domestic role (Gideon 1995; cf. Montaño 1992).[12] Furthermore, by having specific women's projects there is the potential for sidelining women and reinforcing ideas of discrete 'women's interests'; Kabeer (1995: 109) points out that the existence of women's projects can exaggerate their visibility at the rhetorical level without a similar commitment in terms of resources. But the existence of women's projects demonstrates the shifts in discourses around women's social, economic and political contributions and the seriousness with which states view this, especially those seeking international aid. However, as with most issues, if public spending is required, the projects will be seriously constrained. Also, more conservative elements may block programmes which challenge 'traditional' female roles.

There are a number of political implications resulting from PAPs. Here we will concentrate on the following: co-responsibility; bureaucracy; and empowerment. PAPs are underpinned by notions of co-responsibility between the state and the recipients of services and promote self-help strategies. Co-responsibility is an acknowledgement by the state that it has difficulties in responding to popular demands, particularly in providing basic infrastructure services, and that these will remain in the foreseeable future.[13] The model used by many governments reflects the organisation of social movements in their localised nature and self-reliance; many seek to incorporate the grassroots organisations (Raczynski and Serrano 1992). In many cases, however, the PAPs have undermined and marginalised autonomous organisation (Roberts 1995; Craske 1994; Montaño 1992). By using structures similar to the social movements and NGOs, it is hoped that people will identify with the political system by becoming stakeholders in the governments' socio-economic policies.[14] Co-responsibility requires the recognition of gender differences amongst participants, but to date this appears to have been ignored. In many programmes participants' contributions are in kind; since much of the work is physical (building schools, laying roads and so on) this can exclude women from participating since they have neither the skills nor the freedom to participate.[15] If contributions are financial this can exclude female-headed households which are disproportionately represented in the lower-income groups.

The demand-based element of PAPs means that the target community decides what services it wants, but there are difficulties in achieving agreement on this, and 'participants' may not know where and how to participate (Raczynski and Serrano 1992).[16] Grassroots opposition organisations tended to have very localised and small meetings and some groups deliberately encouraged women to take on roles which challenged stereotypes (Craske 1993). Although they could not completely escape the influence of clientelism and *caudillismo* there was an attempt to develop new ways of 'doing politics' which did facilitate women's participation. Many PAPs attempt to mirror the localised decision-making structures and take advantage of the self-help culture which has emerged. In order to attract support from international organisations, the PAPs emphasise the development of 'civic culture' and democratic credentials as recipients decide for themselves what service priorities they have.[17] The problem here is that the dynamics of public meetings do not favour the visibility and airing of women's views

The bureaucratisation of poverty alleviation programmes has both material and political implications for women. Bureaucratisation can have an impact on the structure and timing of meetings which may constrain women's involvement. The literature of social movements highlights the way in which these organisations helped women to break some of the constraints placed on their political activity. For many women involvement in grassroots organisations gave them a political education they did not receive in other arenas, but the bureaucratisation, whether through NGOs or state-sponsored agencies, takes away the negotiation and campaigning element of local participation.[18] To date we have few analyses which address the question of social movement leadership as the process has become more bureaucratised. It is clear, however, that parties have failed to endorse women active in community politics as candidates at the national level (Craske 1998). Bureaucratisation also has the effect of co-opting social movements into structures which would inhibit them from engaging in oppositional political activities where they posed the greatest challenge to the post-authoritarian settlement.[19]

In recent years empowerment has been a key concept in development and gender studies (see, for example, Kabeer 1995).[20] Kathleen Logan (1989) and Kathleen Staudt (1987) have shown that the degree of empowerment is often limited and partial. Staudt in particular has analysed different types of empowerment from political participation, and argues that even when women have attended courses at an 'organization committed to women's empowerment' (ibid.: 157), they rarely move beyond personal empowerment. Despite the centrality of empowerment to the discourses of political agencies and NGOs, it is doubtful that the activities of PAPs will engender empowerment amongst the clients/participants. Indeed, as Graham (1994) points out, many of the PAPs are subject to accusations of clientelism, precisely the political practice which limits the possibilities for citizenship with its foundations of favour trading rather than the realisation of rights (cf. Gideon 1995; Roberts 1995; Barrig 1992); empowerment in these circumstances is difficult. The insertion of women into such projects often reinforces stereotypical ideas of women's role in socio-economic development and the political process. Barrig (1992) notes that Peruvian women have frequently changed from being participants to mere collaborators in service provision. Clearly, PAPs do not automatically aid the development of citizen rights and transparency since they are often the mechanism through which clientelism is maintained in the neoliberal era (Roberts 1995; Cornelius *et al.* 1994; Raczynski and Serrano 1992).[21]

Reconstructing politics in a non-authoritarian context

The key to tackling the causes of social movements whilst maintaining political stability rests on the reassertion of delineated arenas to contain and control political activity. Both the struggle against authoritarianism and the impact of SAPs have led to social fragmentation, resulting in increased demands on the state which are extremely difficult to meet. Consequently, the reconstruction of politics has required setting the limits to issues which can be addressed and to where and how citizens can pursue their claims. The general goodwill towards the new democratic regimes has given the civilian governments considerable room for manoeuvre, but there are still significant challenges. There are two main issues to be discussed here: the re-emergence of parties as central to political activity and the reassertion of the public–private divide.

Party politics

Parties have returned to their pre-eminent position as *the* terrain of political action, displacing social movements, and questions of social justice have been relegated to a bureaucratic arena where they can be acknowledged as

legitimate issues to be addressed when economically feasible. Thus responsible citizens put the need of the nation (that is, the economy) before personal
demands (that is, social justice). Few parties are advocating alternatives to the
neoliberal paradigm which prioritises economic growth over wealth distribution in countries where the gap between the rich few and the poor majority is
already considerable. The emphasis on the responsible, self-reliant individual
undermines notions of universal rights, particularly regarding social welfare.
This prejudices women-dominated organisations which have mobilised
around these issues (Brodie 1994).[22] Although electoral politics is democratic
there is a tendency for 'the inequalities of civil society [to be] transmitted to
the political domain' (Beetham, in Pankhurst and Pearce 1996: 43), and in
the Third World electoral politics has been grafted on to very unequal
social structures where women are often marginalised – although not always
because they are women (ibid.: 1996: 44). Furthermore, the largely federal
states of Latin America have numerous elections, leading some to talk of
voter fatigue.

Another remasculinising element of the return to the electoral arena is that
women's issues often cut across party lines. This can lead to problems in
which women legislators and activists have to choose between party and
gender loyalties and developing cross-party support for issues can be difficult. There have been examples in many countries of multiparty co-operation
between female deputies and senators; but even in the case of Chile, where
there are only nine women deputies and an active women's ministry, it is
rare that all agree on issues and strategies. Since women's issues are not
seen as central to party platforms, they often disappear from the political
terrain altogether. The antipathy towards 'women's issues' is found on
both the Left and the Right. A notable feature throughout the region is the
inability of social movements to establish themselves in the institutional political arena and the lack of crossover between social movement actors and
political parties (Taylor 1996). A major exception is the Workers' Party
(PT) in Brazil where party activists are expected to maintain a dual militancy,
participating in both the party and grassroots political organisations. It is
perhaps not coincidental that the PT is the only party to have a black
woman in elected office. However, generally the elected politicians who
have emerged in the post-authoritarian period have been from the traditional
political elites and not the alternative political actors who had emerged
through social movements.

The centrality of the electoral political arena has strengthened the distinction between political and social. The struggle against authoritarianism
emerged, in part, around the politicisation of social issues, thus blurring
the distinction. The separation is effected by reserving the political arena
for elections and addressing social issues through a bureaucratic-political
response, designed to take the campaigning-oppositional element of service
provision. The bureaucratisation of service provision may seem to contradict
the neoliberal state project by giving an increased role for the state, but in

many countries the bureaucratisation can be represented as a *rationalisation* of service provision by removing it from populist party politicking. Also, by providing a rational-bureaucratic framework for dealing with popular demands, governments can argue that the problems are being dealt with fairly and without being subject to political (in this case, read negative) decision-making. NGOs are frequently used as a conduit for such service provision. Gideon (1995: 25) argues that one of the arguments for employing NGOs, which are seen as apolitical in party terms, in service provision helps encourage a 'civic culture'; a point which González (1992) reinforces in his discussion of NGOs, women and social welfare in Chile.[23] Since the governments in question are civilian ones which embrace multiparty competition, participation in politics is encouraged since this is the clear distinction between these governments and the authoritarian politics which preceded them. However as Centeno (1994) argues in the case of Mexico, it is democracy within reason which is the key to neoliberal state. What we are witnessing is political citizenship, acted out in the electoral arena, which is not extended to the socio-economic arena that was the focus of social movements; in these circumstances the role of parties is key to the remasculinisation of politics. Whilst some countries, such as Chile and Uruguay, have competitive party traditions, others, like Mexico and Brazil, do not. Women have long had a greater antipathy towards party politics, generally joining in smaller numbers and certainly making up a far smaller percentage of activists and candidates, so women are not necessarily concerned with the removal of service provision from the party political arena.[24] Separating social and political arenas encouraged women to return to their 'natural' habitat of home and community.[25] Whilst the main aim of the civilian governments may have been to depoliticise the potentially destabilising social movements, they have also depoliticised women to a greater degree than men.

The public–private distinction

The reassertion of the public–private dichotomy is occurring at both the micro and macro level, which are often mutually reinforcing. At the macro level, the renewed separation of political and social is complemented by the reinforcement of the public–private distinction which, I suggest, has a more deliberately gendered subtext. The SAPs which are central to all government economic projects are largely about the separation of public and private spheres. This separation is essential since it removes responsibility for labour force reproduction from the state. However, there is a contradictory element since the state views workers as degendered individuals who compete on the same terms for work, but it relies on women's domestic role both to reduce the costs of reproduction and, by retaining the domestic sphere as women's central responsibility, it maintains the myth about women's secondary role in the labour force to provide wage competition.

In order to do this successfully, certain status at the rhetorical level at least has to be given to the family and consequently to the traditional domestic role of women.[26] The mutually reinforcing discourses on private, family domains and social, but apolitical, spheres of action have marginalised women's political involvement once again.

Privatisation is also a feature of the rationalisation of social welfare provision with neoliberalism (Raczynski and Serrano 1992). The use of NGOs to facilitate state service provision is, as Arellano-López and Petras (1994) point out, another feature of the distinction between public and private spheres. The public arena is shunned in favour of more efficient responses from localised private organisations which include the community in the decision-making process, but which leaves the issue of accountability largely unanswered. However, in their analysis they leave aside the question of gender (Arellano-López and Petras 1994; cf. Roberts 1995; Graham 1994). In a similar fashion, Graham (1994) ignores the gender issues when discussing the depoliticisation of popular organisation, but studies of development NGOs in other countries demonstrate that development of social welfare often reinforces traditional gender roles and potential for empowerment is limited (Gideon 1995; Kabeer 1995; Montaño 1992). But the broader political implications of the gender-aware analyses are largely ignored other than by vague references to empowerment. Kabeer (1995) suggests that even when 'gender-sensitive' programmes are promoted within NGOs, they often fail to have an impact on institutional structures even at a local level, and her emphasis still remains one of empowerment within the socio-economic arena rather than on the political terrain (cf. Goetz 1992; Logan 1989).

NGOs are often favoured by both development practitioners and states alike for their flexibility and localised structures. They are decentralised, help to empower people through self-help strategies and to engender a civic culture (Gideon 1995; Kabeer 1995; Reilly 1995; Arellano-López and Petras 1994; Graham, 1994). But although they are public organisations their position in Latin America is compromised by their links with the state, on whose behalf they act as agents of welfare provision. Social movements have often jealously guarded their independence from the institutional arena and can be suspicious of such NGOs, although commentators illustrate the need for compromise if gains are to be made (Foweraker 1990; Munck 1990; Jaquette 1994a). National and international NGOs have also been swept along by the PAPs and have had some success in providing services and in developing more egalitarian political practices (González 1992). They have also, however, been key in the depoliticisation of popular protest by contributing to the demobilisation of social movements. A major problem for, especially international, NGOs is that their legality and right to organise depends to a large degree on the host state. This leaves projects with political implications, such as empowerment strategies, in a difficult position which limits their activities. The role of NGOs in the rationalisation of social welfare provision has aided the recasting of the political terrain into social–political and public–private, contributing to the marginalisation of women-dominated political activity.

Despite the fact that neoliberalism emphasises state withdrawal from economic decision-making, there is much more intervention on social issues. A common theme is the emphasis on 'family values' and the prioritising of women's domestic role in the reproduction of the labour force. This has been accompanied by some attention to 'women's issues'.[27] However, whilst governments may have different, and multiple, ways of viewing women's 'natural' role in national development, there are other agents participating in the ideological struggle around the conceptualisation of gender. There is considerable concern about the erosion of 'traditional feminine' roles for women and the backlash is coming from churches, particularly the conservative wing of the Catholic Church and supported by the Pope.[28] Despite the shift away from military governments, which stressed the interlinking of Christianity with patriotism and in the process marginalised what they perceived to be alien discourses, specifically communism and feminism, civilian governments engage in much of the same rhetoric. This concern, particularly over the term 'gender', was brought into sharp relief in the discussions leading up to the Fourth World Conference on Women in Beijing in 1995. The social conservatism which has characterised large parts of Latin America for decades was reinforced in heated debates over access to abortion and the fear that endorsing the term gender would somehow encourage 'unwelcome' practices such as homosexuality, extra-marital sex and the erosion of the family, considered the basic unit of society. These debates echo those which have taken place in northern democracies such as the US and Great Britain, which demonstrate a fear of the challenge that a reconceptualisation of gender poses for the social ordering of society, and which cannot have gone unnoticed by Latin American feminists. The continued socio-political subordination of women appears to be central to the neoliberal state project, espousing the sanctity of the ungendered individual but, at the same time, embracing and reinforcing gender constructions which allow women limited political, social and economic autonomy.

Conclusions: remasculinisation or feminisation of power?

The contemporary state in Latin America, be it industrialised Argentina, rural Bolivia or semi-authoritarian Mexico, is one which embraces neoliberalism: even Cuba has embarked on externally oriented economic reform. This may be to prioritise economic development following the model endorsed by the IMF and World Bank, but it has its socio-political complement. In this chapter I have argued that the consolidation of electoral politics in Latin America has resulted in the remasculinisation of politics in the region. Whilst many of the debates and practices reflect those of northern democracies which have also undergone economic restructuring, it has to be seen in a different political context. Latin American political development has recently witnessed particularly dynamic political activity spearheaded by women of all classes in the search for a wide-reaching democracy which challenged deeply repressive regimes. The narrowing of the political debate I have identified here is largely a result of an aggressive form of capitalist accumulation, but the threat of military intervention and state-sponsored paramilitary activity remains fresh in the minds of many, particularly in those countries with recent militarised pasts, which also restrains political activity. The neoliberal project depends on women retaining their 'traditional' family-oriented identities without undermining their availability for the labour market to provide low-wage competition. The remasculinisation of politics results from the interaction of poverty alleviation programmes, pro-family rhetoric, the rigours of the neoliberal economics and the threat of the military. PAPs under democracy depoliticise social movements, the focus of women's political action, through the bureaucratisation of service provision, and the official rhetoric which eulogises the role of the family (reflecting the discourse of many military governments) is congruent with the social rather than the political emphasis of service provision. The rigours of the labour market allow little time for political activity, and the fear of a return to military regimes and other repressive governments makes any kind of mobilisation for socio-political justice seem destabilising; under such conditions no one wants to be accused of rocking the boat. There is also the problem of mobilisation fatigue: how long can people who already work long hours in the reproductive and productive arenas be expected to engage in grassroots political activity in their 'spare time'? This has been the triple burden to befall women over the past decades. It is possible that what we are witnessing at present are the steps backwards after a period of transition and instability.

However, any assessment of the reconstruction of political space with democratisation has to acknowledge the gains that women have made. Remasculinisation is partly a reflection of the elevated expectations which the social movements engendered, particularly in the 1980s. Despite the generalised depoliticisation of social movements and its gendered repercussions, there have been advances made which have the potential to create greater political visibility for women. Many of these have been at the institutional level in the shape of women's ministries, women's sections within political parties, changes in the legal terrain particularly in social legislation on such issues as divorce, childcare and health services.[29] There has also been greater (rhetorical) attention paid to increasing the number of women representatives at all levels of politics with many parties having internal quotas to encourage greater numbers of female candidates; Argentina has gone further with a national quota law written into its electoral code. In many countries it is accepted that women have the same rights as men to participate in party political arenas, but there is a difference in the social status of the women and men involved in such activities. These advantages, however, are strongly mediated through class and location, with middle-class urban women more able to take advantage of them. The conceptualisation of the female political actor and her interests still rests on assumptions that her role in the private sphere is paramount, pushing her political activities into a distant second or third place. Where women's ministries do exist (almost all countries have some kind of women's department), they tend to concentrate on women's role in the economic or social spheres, rather than promoting the development of an inclusive citizenship or encouraging women's political involvement.

Women made many gains in the transition to democracy and many thought that with the re-institution of civilian governments they could again focus on their usual arenas, the battle won; after all, most had never intended to become political actors in the first place. Whether they choose to remain there is another matter. Whilst political parties may be reticent about promoting women as candidates, they still acknowledge their importance in Latin America today, and women are much more disposed to demand their rights as women, as well as mothers and so on. The pressure emerging from international organisations, such as the UN, have helped to keep the different needs and demands of women in the spotlight. Despite the difficulties, there have been positive changes, some of which only become apparent as new theorising undermines some of the traditional feminist assumptions about where Latin America women's political activity should be heading. Many grassroots organisations have returned to the neighbourhood to develop new agendas and think about demands they can make on the state, even under the constraints of the neoliberal state.

Notes

1 Brodie (1994: 51), however, maintains that the unequal gender impacts are 'integral to the current round of restructuring'.
2 In the late 1970s eight out of ten South American countries were governed by generals: Argentina, Bolivia, Brazil, Chile, Ecuador, Paraguay, Peru and Uruguay. Central American governments have been dominated by dictatorships and Mexico has been controlled by one party, the PRI, since 1929 which has relied on a mixture of clientelism, electoral fraud and coercion to stay in power.
3 There is a considerable body of literature on social movements and popular protest in Latin America, some with a specifically gendered focus; for example Escobar and Alvarez (1992); Foweraker and Craig (1990); Radcliffe and Westwood (1993); Jaquette (1994b); Eckstein (1989).
4 For the conditions leading to the coups in this period, see O'Donnell 1979.
5 The military is still active in most Latin American countries; there have been a number of thwarted rebellions in Argentina (resulting in amnesties and an end to legal proceedings against the military), Pinochet has flexed the military's muscles more than once in Chile, and the military is a key player in the politics of Peru and Colombia.
6 It must also be remembered that there has been considerable criticism of privatisation programmes which are not transparent or accountable and allow for favour trading and clientelism, albeit within the elite.

7 Women dominated the early *maquiladoras*, but there are indications that this pattern is changing, and certainly men always dominated the supervisory positions. See Pearson (1992) for a critique of the reasons behind women's domination in these industries based on stereotypical views of women's attributes. However, as ever, the picture is mixed; Roldán (1993: 50) comments that the economic restructuring has had a strongly negative impact on women's paid labour: 'If things continue as they are, women will become even more confined to peripheral activities and peripheral firms.' But Kandiyoti (in Rai 1996: 31) also highlights some of the positive aspects of capitalist development in the erosion of patriarchy. These contrasting views demonstrate that there are multiple effects arising from economic change, both good and bad.

8 This is not to suggest that there is no workplace resistance taking place; Peña (1987) demonstrates the varied ways in which women protest over work conditions but generally this is individual or in very small groups which has only a local impact and leaves universal standards untouched. If a factory becomes renowned for industrial action it is generally closed or key activists are sacked.

9 The anti-bureaucratisation policies refer to the economy in the Latin American case; I argue below that there has been a bureaucratisation of poverty alleviation policies to remove the issues from protest organisations.

10 See Graham (1994) for a comparative discussion of PAPs around the world; cf. Gideon (1995) for a discussion of NGOs and development in Latin America.

11 Indeed Graham emphasises that '(s)afety nets should not be confused with what the market or the state is expected to deliver; namely, the economic growth and production in the first case and *basic social services in the second*' (Graham 1994: 5; emphasis added).

12 Many donor agencies and governments insist on 'gender-sensitive' projects as part of the aid package.

13 Raczynski and Serrano (1992) stress that states have not abandoned their responsibilities but are trying to focus limited resources on target communities. This reflects discourses in the north, particularly Britain.

14 The term NGO has increasingly become a catch-all term for social organisations. Here I will follow Reilly (1995: 2) and refer to NGOs as '(L)egally constituted, nonprofit associations (which) deliver services, mobilize interests, encourage self-reliance, and act as advocates for improving citizens' life conditions and opportunities.' These can be local, national or international organisations. The literature on NGOs is generally very favourable but below we will be discussing some of their limitations in the current socio-economic situation.

15 There are examples of women transgressing gender stereotypees to participate, such as in projects in rural Mexico to build dirt-tracks, but this is the exception rather than the norm.

16 There appears to be little discussion as to what constitutes 'the community'.

17 Both Gideon (1995) and Graham (1994) show that, although government projects, many PAPs are dependent on external funding which often reinforces short-termism and, in part, explains their emphasis on their democratic credentials in an age where aid and loans are linked to good governance and proof of democratic practice.

18 Also, as Manuel Castells (1982) demonstrated, the illegal status was preferred by some organisations since it gave them more leverage in protest.

19 These structures are frequently traditional vertical ones such as women's sector, youth, peasants, etc. This tendency is particularly marked in Mexico (Craske 1994).

20 Bystydzienski (1992: 3) describes empowerment as the process by which people take some control of their lives by taking 'part with others in development of

activities and structures that allow people increased involvement in matters which affect them directly . . . This process involves the use of power, not "power over" others . . . rather, power is seen as "power to".'

21 Similarly Gideon (1995: 39) argues that NGOs, often used by PAPs, are not having the hoped-for democratisation impact on local politics; she suggests that they fail to by-pass local power networks and may even fail in helping the state to by-pass them.

22 Waylen (1994) details how the democratisation literature also reflects this in its narrow focus and concentration on institutional politics without questioning the distribution of power in society. Indeed, there is the suggestion that popular protest organisations should limit their demands under civilian rule, which could be destabilising (Centeno 1994).

23 Raczynski and Serrano (1992: 18) also comment on the wave of decentralisation promoted through the region which was also assumed to be an automatic good; but, as they point out, if resources are not forthcoming, all that is decentralised are the problems.

24 Women generally have a lesser propensity to participate in formal politics although this is changing; in Chile in 1989 women outnumbered men as voters (Waylen 1996: 10). Many parties have continued to demonstrate the negative qualities which led to their rejection by social movements: corruption, in-fighting, lack of coherent policies.

25 Below we will discuss the shifting rhetoric on gender.

26 Similar discourses emerged in post-communist countries: see Waylen (1994) and Gorbachev (1987: 116–18).

27 Although governments have been quick to give rhetorical support to 'women's issues', some of which has been backed with legal change such as the relegalisation of contraceptives, there is little state-funded activity. There is still a great need for adequate childcare, public contraceptive services, legal advice on divorce and domestic violence, and women's refuges.

28 See Jean Franco's (1996) analysis of the Catholic Church's counterattack against feminism.

29 See Craske (1998) for a fuller discussion of government and party actions regarding women's political involvement.

References

Alvarez, S. (1990) *Engendering Democracy in Brazil: Women's Movements in Transition Politics*, Princeton, N.J.: University of Princeton Press.

Arellano-López, S. and Petras, J. (1994) 'NGOs and poverty alleviation in Bolivia', *Development and Change* 25: 555–68.

Barrig, M. (1992) 'Quejas y Contentamientos: historia de una política social, los municipios, organización femenina en la ciudad de Lima', in D. Raczynski and C Serrano (eds), *Políticas Sociales, Mujeres y Gobierno Local*, Santiago: CIE-PLAN.

Brodie, J. (1994) 'Shifting the boundaries: gender and the politics of restructuring', in I. Bakker (ed.), *The Strategic Silence: Gender and Economic Policy*, London: Zed Press/North/South Institute.

Bystydzienski, J. (1992) 'Introduction', in J. Bystydzienski (ed.), *Women Transforming Politics: Worldwide Strategies for Empowerment*, Bloomington, Ind.: Indiana University Press.

Cammack, P. (1994) 'Democratization and citizenship in Latin America', in M. Moran and G. Parry (eds), *Democracy and Democratization*, London: Routledge.

Camp, R. (1995) *Political Recruitment Across Two Centuries: Mexico, 1884–1991*, Austin, Tx.: University of Texas Press.

Castells, M. (1982) 'Squatters and politics in Latin America: a comparative analysis of urban movements in Chile, Peru and Mexico', in H. Safa (ed.), *Towards a Political Economy of Urbanisation in Third World Countries*, Delhi: Oxford University Press.

Centeno, M.A. (1994) *Democracy Within Reason: Technocratic Revolution in Mexico*, University Park, Pa.: Pennsylvania State University Press.

Chuchryk, P. (1994) 'From dictatorship to democracy: the women's movement in Chile', in J. Jaquette (ed.), *The Women's Movements in Latin America: Participation and Democracy*, Boulder, Col.: Westview Press.

Cornelius, W., Craig, A. and Fox, J. (eds) (1994) *Transforming State–Society Relations in Mexico: The National Solidarity Strategy*, San Diego, Cal.: University of California Press.

Craske, N. (1993) 'Women's political participation in *colonias populares* in Guadalajara, Mexico', in S. Radcliffe and S. Westwood (eds), *'Viva' Women and Popular Protest in Latin America*, London: Routledge.

Craske, N. (1994) *Corporatism Revisited: Salinas and the Reform of the Popular Sector*, Institute of Latin American Studies, Research Paper no. 37, London: University of London.

Craske, N. (1998) 'Mexican women's incorporation in politics in a Latin American perspective', in V. Rodríguez (ed.), *Women's Participation in Mexican Political Life*, Boulder, Col.: Westview Press.

Dresser, D. (1991) *Neopopulist Solutions to Neoliberal Problems: Mexico's National Solidarity Program*, Center for US–Mexican Studies, Current Issue Brief 3, San Diego, Cal.: University of California.

Eckstein, S. (ed.) (1989) *Power and Popular Protest: Latin American Social Movements*, Berkeley, Cal.: University of California Press.

Escobar, A. and Alvarez, S. (eds) (1992) *The Making of Social Movements in Latin America: Identity, Strategy and Democracy*, Boulder, Col.: Westview Press.

Fisher, J. (1993) *Out of the Shadows: Women, Resistance and Politics in South America*, London: Latin American Bureau.

Foweraker, J. (1990) 'Popular movements and political change in Mexico', in J. Foweraker and A. Craig, (eds), *Popular Movements and Political Change in Mexico*, Boulder, Col.: Lynne Rienner.

Foweraker, J. and Craig, A. (eds) (1990) *Popular Movements and Political Change in Mexico*, Boulder, Col.: Lynne Rienner.

Franco, J. (1996) 'The gender wars', *NACLA: Report on the Americas* 29(4): 6–9.

Gideon, J. (1995) 'The politics of social service provision through NGOs: a study of Latin America', unpublished MA dissertation, Faculty of Economic and Social Science, University of Manchester.

Goetz, A.M. (1992) 'Gender and administration', *IDS Bulletin* 23(4): 6–17.

González, G. (1992) 'Organismos no gubernamentales, políticas sociales y mujer: el caso de Chile', in D. Raczynski and C. Serrano (eds), *Políticas Sociales Mujeres y Gobierno Local*, Santiago: CIEPLAN.

Gorbachev, M. (1987) *Perestroika: New Thinking for Our Country and the World*, London: HarperCollins.

Graham, C. (1994) *Safety Nets, Politics and the Poor: Transitions to Market Economies*, Washington, D.C.: Brookings Institution.

Jaquette, J. (1994a) 'Conclusions', in J Jaquette (ed.), *The Women's Movements in Latin America: Participation and Democracy*, 2nd edn, Boulder, Col.: Westview Press.

Jaquette, J. (ed.) (1994b) *The Women's Movements in Latin America: Participation and Democracy*, Boulder, Col.: Westview Press.

Kabeer, N. (1995) 'Targeting women or transforming institutions? Policy lessons from NGO anti-poverty efforts', *Development in Practice* 5(2): 108–16.

Logan, K. (1989) 'Empowerment within a female consciousness: collective actions in Mérida, Yucatán, Mexico', paper presented to the Latin American Studies Association XV International Congress, Miami.

Lustig, N. (1994) 'Solidarity as a strategy of poverty alleviation', in W. Cornelius *et al.* (eds), *Transforming State–Society Relations in Mexico: The National Solidarity Strategy*, San Diego, Cal.: Center for US–Mexican Studies, University of California.

Molinar Horcasitas, J. and Weldon, J. (1994) 'Electoral determinants and consequences of national solidarity', in W. Cornelius *et al.* (eds), *Transforming State–Society Relations in Mexico: The National Solidarity Strategy*, San Diego, Cal.: Center for US–Mexican Studies, University of California.

Montaño, S. (1992) 'Mujer, donaciones alimentarias y poder local en Ciudad de El Alto, Bolivia', in D. Raczynski and C. Serrano (eds), *Políticas Sociales, Mujeres y Gobierno Local*, Santiago: CIEPLAN.

Munck, G. (1990) 'Identity and ambiguity in democratic struggles', in J. Foweraker and A. Craig (eds), *Popular Movements and Political Change in Mexico*, Boulder, Col.: Lynne Rienner.

O'Donnell, G. (1979) 'Tensions in the bureaucratic state and the question of democracy', in D. Collier (ed.), *Authoritarianism in Latin America*, Princeton, N.J.: Princeton University Press.

Pankhurst, D. and Pearce, J. (1996) 'Feminist perspectives on democratisation in the South: engendering or adding women in?', in H. Afshar (ed.), *Women and Politics in the Third World*, London: Routledge.

Pearson, R. (1992) 'Gender issues industrialisation', in T. Hewitt *et al.* (eds), *Industrialisation and Development*, Milton Keynes: Open University Press.

Peña, D. (1987) 'Tortuosidad: shop floor struggles of female maquiladora workers', in V. Ruiz and S. Tiano (eds), *Women in the US–Mexican Border: Responses to Change*, Boston, Mass.: Allen & Unwin.

Perelli, C. (1994) 'The uses of conservatism: women's democratic politics in Uruguay', in J. Jaquette (ed.), *The Women's Movements in Latin America: Participation and Democracy*, Boulder, Col.: Westview Press.

Pringle, R. and Watson, S. (1992) '"Women's Interests" and the post-structuralist state', in M. Barrett and A. Phillips (eds), *Destabilizing Theory: Contemporary Feminist Debates*, Cambridge: Polity Press.

Puar, J. (1996) 'Nicaraguan women, resistance and the politics of aid', in H. Afshar (ed.), *Women and Politics in the Third World*, London: Routledge.

Raczynski D. and Serrano, C. (1992) 'Abriendo el debate: descentralización del estado, mujeres y políticas sociales', in D. Raczynski and C. Serrano (eds), *Políticas Sociales, Mujeres y Gobierno Local*, Santiago: CIEPLAN.

Radcliffe, S. and Westwood, S. (eds) (1993) *'Viva' Women and Popular Protest in Latin America*, London: Routledge.

Rai, S. (1996) 'Women and the state in the Third World', in H. Afshar (ed.), *Women and Politics in the Third World*, London: Routledge.

Reilly, C. (1995) 'Public policy and citizenship', in C. Reilly (ed.), *New Paths to Democratic Development in Latin America: The Rise of NGO–Municipal Collaboration*, Boulder, Col.: Lynne Reinner.

Roberts, K. (1995) 'Neoliberalism and the transformation of populism in Latin America', *World Politics* 48(1): 82–116.

Roldán, M. (1993) 'Industrial restructuring, deregulation and new JIT labour processes in Argentina: towards a gender-aware approach', *IDS Bulletin* 24(2): 42–52.

Sparr, P. (1994) 'What is structural adjustment?', in P. Sparr (ed.), *Mortgaging Women's Lives: Feminist Critiques of Structural Adjustment*, London: Zed Press.

Staudt, K. (1987) 'Programming women's empowerment: a case from Northern Mexico', in V. Ruiz and S. Tiano (eds), *Women on the US–Mexican Border: Responses to Change*, Boston, Mass.: Allen & Unwin.

Stephen, L. (1996) 'Tools for studying women's local political participation in social movements', paper presented at the conference *Women in Contemporary Mexican Politics*, Mexican Center, University of Texas at Austin, April 12–13.

Taylor, L. (1996) 'Civilising civil society: distracting popular politics from politics itself', in I. Hampshire-Monk and J. Stanyer (eds), *Contemporary Political Studies 1996*, vol 2: *Proceedings of the Annual Conference of the PSA*, Oxford: Blackwell, for Political Studies Association, 778–85.

Varley, A. (1996) 'Delivering the goods: solidarity, land regularisation and urban services', in R. Aitken *et al.* (eds), *Dismantling the Mexican State?*, Basingstoke: Macmillan.

Waylen, G. (1993) 'Women's movement and democratisation in Latin America', *Third World Quarterly* 14(3): 573–87.

Waylen, G. (1994) 'Women and democratisation: conceptualizing gender relations in transition politics', *World Politics* 46: 327–54.

Waylen, G. (1996) 'Analysing women in the politics of the Third World', in H. Afshar (ed.), *Women and Politics in the Third World*, London: Routledge.

8   The gendered politics of land reform

Three comparative studies

Susie Jacobs

Introduction

This chapter examines land and agrarian reform policies in the context of gendered state politics and popular, including feminist, movements. I employ three case studies, from Zimbabwe, Vietnam and India, which have had land reforms ranging in extent and aim. All deal with situations of social upheaval and with avowedly socialist/communist movements that, in two cases, came to form the state itself.

Policies concerning agrarian reform are almost universally gender-blind, marginalising women by omission rather (usually) than through explicit intent. However, in some cases state policies have attempted to address, at least in a partial sense, women's lack of secure access to land. Thus, state policies attempting to benefit women exist at times alongside gender-blind ones. Most commonly, the former occur in spheres seen as relevant to women, such as legislation concerning women, or policies addressing some aspects of kinship/marriage/biological reproduction, while agrarian policies are compartmentalised as separate to women's interests.

Three themes inform the article. One is differing state policies towards land reforms and the place assigned to/taken by women within these. A second concerns conceptions of the category 'woman'. A third theme concerns resistance to programmes, policies and images which peasant women see as detrimental to their interests. Such resistance does not always occur in forms that researchers find easy to observe and record. Nevertheless, women have organised within some rural movements, as well as reacting individually, to address needs for land. To some extent, the development of explicitly feminist movements in some Third World settings has facilitated this process.

Definitions and types of agrarian reform

A well-known work in 1974 summarised land reform as comprising 'compulsory takeover of land, *usually* by the state, from the largest land-owners . . . and the farming of that land in such a way as to spread the benefits of man-land relationship more widely . . . Its primary motivation is to reduce poverty . . . via distributionist or collectivist means' (Lipton 1974). In 1993, arguing for the continued relevance of land reform, Lipton queries this definition and proposes a reformulation. 'Land reforms' are only those reforms which enrich or empower the rural poor by transferring substantial land rights (Lipton 1993: 644). Hence some reforms excluded under the previous definition, for instance changes in tenancy laws, such as have occurred in South-East Asia and Latin America, which remove restrictions on tenancy and rights of the poor to purchase land, would in this definition be included. Some use the term 'agrarian reform' to denote more thoroughgoing, widespread change.

Land/agrarian reforms have been favoured by a surprising array of governments with differing political tendencies and state structures. Although the most extensive reforms have taken place in situations of revolution or widespread agrarian revolt, other land reforms have taken place in order to pre-empt such upheaval (see Montgomery 1984). This is particularly the case for some US-backed reforms such as those in South Korea and Japan. Aside from broad questions of strategy, aims of land reform are various and span economic, social and political criteria. Without rehearsing all the arguments for land reform here, the main aims include: increasing production and rural incomes; providing a subsistence base for the landless/land-hungry; decreasing class inequality in the countryside; diminishing patronage relationships; and establishing support for new/existent regimes.

Putzel (1992) distinguishes revolutionary, conservative and liberal reforms, demarcated by the intention of the state enacting policy, with regard to several variables. These include: the form of property rights; the transformation/maintenance of existing state structures; and processes through which such reform is to be achieved (that is, purchase or expropriation); Sobhan (1993) makes similar points. The dominant orientation in 'Third' World nations has been conservative, introducing agrarian reform legislation in response to peasant demands while attempting to minimise disturbance to existent property rights. This approach has dominated, particularly in Asia. The 'liberal' strategy places land reform at the centre of agrarian strategies of transformation; however, it does so in order to consolidate existing state structures or else to pre-empt revolutionary movements in the countryside (Putzel 1992: 10). Revolutionary reforms are usually enacted by explicitly Marxist states following massive upheavals. The ultimate aim has been to form state-held collective farms; however, it is often seen as necessary to form co-operatives as an intermediate step, in order to gain peasant support and to avert the disastrous consequences of Soviet-style forced collectivisation.

The general orientation of land reforms also appears to impact upon the amount of land redistributed in particular situations. Where aims are radical, it is usually the case that larger amounts of land are redistributed and that more men are beneficiaries. In China and Vietnam, over 50 per cent of land was redistributed (Sobhan 1993: 8). By 1993, over 20 per cent of agricultural land had been redistributed in Zimbabwe (ibid., Moyo 1995a). In India, however, only 1.5 per cent of viable agricultural land had been redistributed by 1986 (Sobhan 1993: 10).

Gender concerns

The absence of any discussion above of a gender dimension reflects the near-total absence of such discussion in policy-making. Most policies, whether 'socialist', capitalist or some mixture, converge in the assumption that households/families are unified entities which the 'head of household' manages on behalf of the family, taking all interests into account. In discourses of land reform – and more widely, in much work concerning peasants – women are assumed to 'reside' conceptually and practically within households, and little attention is paid even to the most obvious factor: their productive contribution to household agriculture and petty industry. Such assumptions, of course, have been critiqued by a still-growing body of feminist literature. What is notable is that this large body of feminist work on the household still, in general, exists separately from 'mainstream' literature on land reform. In seven recent books on land reform (Thiesenhusen 1989; 1995; Christodoulou 1990; Prosterman *et al.* 1990; El-Ghonemy 1990; Barraclough 1991; Sobhan 1993), gender divisions are either omitted or else mentioned only in passing. Whatever this omission indicates politically, at the theoretical level it relates to a failure to analyse the complex links between kinship, gender and class relations *within* smallholder households. It has been left to feminists[1] – and not a large group of them – to analyse gender with regard to land reform policies.

The literature indicates that when (as in most cases) redistribution is along individual household lines, land is virtually always redistributed in the name of the household head, who is nearly always considered to be a man. Where women can hold land at all, usually only widows and divorcees are eligible. Married women may lose customary rights to the small amounts of land they control, as in parts of Africa and South-East Asia.

Nevertheless, some effects of land reform are beneficial. First, household incomes often rise for those fortunate enough to take part in what are often limited reforms. One of the main aims of land reforms is increased food security; this often occurs, and is crucial for all. For some women, the importance of this aspect outweighs all others. Other 'positive' changes concern transformations of family structure, usually so that extended families are more distant and so have less control. Particularly when, as in the majority of cases, such families are patrilineal and patrilocal, many younger wives welcome this change to a smaller and/or more nuclear family.

Other changes are more negative. Wives may be under pressure to intensify their work to increase production and to bear more children in order to supply labour for a larger plot. The workloads of many rural women, particularly in Africa, may already be injurious to health, with 15–16-hour days not uncommon. The material benefits of individual family reforms may have to be 'exchanged' for some loss of autonomy. Studies worldwide report increased male control for a variety of reasons, the most straightforward of which is the continuous presence of the man. It is common for husbands to be defined as 'farmers' and for wives to be (re)defined as 'housewives'. Hence any freedom from control by in-laws gained may be traded for an increase in control by the husband (see Jacobs 1996).

A few historical situations have occurred in which land is meant to be redistributed to women as well as men, the most notable case being China in the initial land reform of the 1950s (Frenier 1983; Stacey 1982). In general, however, the notion that married women should receive land along with their husbands is not considered to be within the arena of reasonable discussion. For instance, one astonished Ministry of Agriculture official (in India) said to Bina Agarwal, an authority on women's land rights: 'You want *women* to have land?! What do you want to do? To destroy the family?!' (Agarwal 1994: 53). At a national meeting on land held in Bloemfontein, South Africa, in 1993, a chief put the matter: '"Whom is to *lobola* whom [i.e. to pay bride-wealth to whom]," he asked, "if we are all [to become] equal?"' (Walker 1994).

Where the matter is taken more seriously, as it sometimes is, the argument deployed against equal land rights for women is that holdings will thereby become fragmented (Agarwal 1994; Government of Zimbabwe 1983). Another variation of the argument is that individual land rights for women (even in situations where men already have such rights) are unsocialist (see Moyo 1995b), although the same argument is rarely applied to male beneficiaries (Agarwal 1994).

This brief discussion should perhaps be enough to emphasise that women, whether at the grassroots, party or state level, rarely have any say in land reform policies. No doubt women party activists and cadres and women in smallholder/peasant households have views on this matter, but this is still largely an unwritten history.[2]

It is not surprising that it is difficult for poorer classes of rural women to make their voices heard. Rural smallholders often have great difficulty in organising due to factors such as transport difficulties, relative isolation and the need to tend land and livestock: it is not necessary to see peasants as 'potatoes in a sack' to recognise this. In the case of most poorer rural women, other factors operate as well: domestic responsibilities; the need for male permission to attend meetings; threats of sexual harassment; male violence; and, more simply, ridicule and loss of respectability.

As noted, the literature on gender and land reforms is not yet a large one, and gaps exist. Aside from these gaps, conditions within countries differ, and the literature may reflect differing orientations of authors. Hence, the literature on Zimbabwe concentrates mainly on the effects of land reform upon gender relations; that on Vietnam concentrates on gender divisions within collectivised agriculture and on the processes whereby collective forms have been eroded; that on India concentrates on women's organisation and processes of resistance. The examples used here are chosen to highlight some of the differences, as well as some similarities, in gendered land reform processes. In Zimbabwe, which falls between 'conservative' and 'liberal' strategies (see above), most reform has been along individual family lines with married women usually not in receipt of land titles. Vietnam is an example of one of the more radical land reforms, with largescale collectivisation and with many legal rights granted to women. Here, however, the 'peasant nag' of which Bukharin wrote becomes an apposite term; in face of male peasant opposition and of the general dominance of market mechanisms, some of women's gains have been reversed. India provides an example of a conservative reform; however, it also provides an example of one of the most militant feminist peasant movements to date.

Zimbabwe

The example of Zimbabwean land reform illustrates women's marginalisation when land is redistributed to 'household heads'. Struggles over the conceptualisation of 'women' also exist in Zimbabwe; in some ways, in an acute form. The example also underlines some of the difficulties rural women face in mobilising. Despite these factors, some aspects of resettlement have benefited women farmers.

The ZANU(PF) (Zimbabwe National People's Union – Patriotic Front) was elected to power in 1980, following a guerrilla war from the late 1960s against the white settler regime and a negotiated settlement. The call for the return of lands from white settlers was one important, although by no means the only, impetus for the war. Rural women played an important role in the war, some as guerrilla fighters, but more commonly supplying male guerrillas, both ZANU and ZAPU, with food and acting as go-betweens. However, recent accounts indicate that peasant support, both male and female, was at times grudging (Kriger 1992; Staunton 1990). However, the symbolic role of female fighters remains important: several female MPs elected in the 1995 parliamentary elections are ex-combatants.

Within this framework state policies towards women have always been ambiguous. Rai's (1996) comment, that in many developing countries the state is deeply embedded in civil society, would seem particularly apposite. The Ministry of Community Development and Women's Affairs, formed after independence, was dissolved and attached to the Prime Minister's office in the late 1980s (Sylvester 1991: 150). The ZANU Women's League, led in her lifetime by the Prime Minister's first wife (Sally Mugabe), is used to rally support for the government. This was the case even soon after independence, as I observed on a field trip.[3] From 1983, the government launched several campaigns against 'prostitution' which were, in effect, aimed at all urban women, from urban 'marginalised' people to the middle classes; women were arrested, imprisoned, some interned in camps (Jacobs and

Howard 1987; Batezat and Mwalo 1989; Jacobs 1989b). In general, the state has become increasingly authoritarian.

While rural women, who perform the bulk of agricultural tasks in small-scale agriculture, are frequently ignored in policy-making, it is not the case that rural African women are seen only as 'non-productive housewives'. Motherhood is a particularly important status and aspect of identity in southern Africa, and this too is drawn upon in political imagery: women were portrayed as 'mothers of the revolution' (Staunton 1990). And Nkomo (now vice-president) exhorted the ZANU Women's League:

> the role of women in the Party . . . is to fulfil the objectives of the Party through the Women's League, but the Party would like women to take their role as mothers seriously . . . [in order] to strengthen the nation.
> (Jirira 1995: 12)

A 'proper' Zimbabwean woman is often seen as a rural woman. Since colonial times, when the first wage labouring opportunities for women were in prostitution, urban and waged women have been seen as somewhat suspect. This image may be diminishing: far more African women live in cities, and waged opportunities for them, particularly in the service sector, increased after independence, although they are still highly disadvantaged compared with men. However, the fact that many men have liaisons or secondary wives in urban areas must fan rural–urban female antagonisms. In its 'clean-up' campaigns, the state was able to mobilise many rural women in support. Likewise, it has attempted to mobilise some rural women in its current campaign against gay men. It seems that one state definition of 'woman', particularly rural women, is as passive and easily malleable. However, the Women's Action Group, with mainly urban membership, was formed in 1983 in protest against the 'clean-up' campaigns. It remains independent and a main feminist advisory and campaigning organisation.

Some aspects of state policy, however, have been beneficial for women. After independence, and before the advent of structural adjustment, programmes of primary health care and literacy were significant. Several legal measures promoting gender equality have been passed. The most important of these concern the right of women to vote, to represent themselves and to make contracts (the Legal Age of Majority Act 1982). Other legal changes have reformed divorce law, including allocation of property at divorce; child custody; and rights to maternity leave.[4] However, a proposed Inheritance Act has still not been passed (*Speakout/Taurai* 1996). For a variety of reasons, poorer rural women are unable to avail themselves of new legislation and remain constrained by the customary law constructed under colonialism (Kazembe 1986).

The land issue, linked with beliefs concerning the homes of people's ancestral spirits, has long been important in popular mobilisation. In the land resettlement programme, white-owned land was redistributed to the 'land-hungry'. According to the Lancaster House Agreement, it had to be bought on a 'willing-buyer/willing-seller' basis. Land was redistributed from large estates to 'families' in 5.5-hectare (12-acre) plots. Land is owned by the state but held on a series of permits. The bulk of settlement is along individual family lines. Land permits are allocated to household heads, considered to be men unless women are widowed, divorced or deserted and with dependent children.

Although relatively modest by international standards, the programme has been the largest one in Africa south of the Sahara. Figures from the Auditor General's Report show that by 1989, 47,678 people had been resettled on nearly 3 million hectares (Moyo 1995a: 118), mostly on poor-quality land. Most land purchase took place in the three years after independence; since then, the process has slowed markedly (Alexander 1994).

From the late 1980s, land re-emerged as a major issue, perhaps due to the government's electoral vulnerability (Bratton 1990; Alexander 1994). The land policy statement of 1990 set a target of 5 million *additional* hectares to be acquired for resettlement of 110,000 more households (Moyo 1995a: 245). The 1992 Land Acquisition Act facilitated state acquisition of land; however, some of the land seized was not redistributed but was leased out to senior state officials. About 15 per cent of large-scale agricultural capitalists are now black (ibid.: 252); a proportion of these are government ministers, including the ex-Minister of Lands, and 20 per cent of the powerful Commercial Farmers' Union are black (Beresford 1994.) Thus, one aspect of the renewed focus on land concerns the interests of landowners, not those of the rural poor. The 'land-hungry', evoked though they be in populist rhetoric, are not mythical. At least 300,000 households were on waiting lists for resettlement in 1993; real demand for land is even greater than such numbers indicate (Moyo 1995a: 119).

The exclusion of the majority of women in resettlements, which are meant to be 'self-contained islands of modernisation' (Alexander 1994: 334), seems particularly anomalous. The assumption that land should be held by the household head is common internationally but also reflects colonial assumptions. The resonance of Rhodesian policy is manifested in centralisation, in the domination of appointed technical advisers at many levels and in the role of chiefs. The latter is particularly significant for women, as chiefs help to enforce 'custom and tradition'. The role of Resettlement Officers (henceforth, ROs), who administer Resettlement Areas, also derives from past community development policies, and is akin to that of the old District Commissioner. Despite the establishment of village and ward development committees to ensure popular participation, these are meant mainly to implement policy decided upon at higher levels. Settlers have no elected representation beyond village level, so the RO wields great power, including powers of arbitration.

Research which I conducted in 1984 indicates some positive features of the RO's role, as well as other aspects of land reform; these exist alongside more negative tendencies. Of 204 respondents interviewed in Model A (individual family) schemes, 102 were wives and 41 widows or divorcees; I also contacted approximately 700 women in a series of meetings. Many wives reported an increase in the amount of land that husbands allocated to them to cultivate. Family income increased in the sample I studied, many women reporting higher personal incomes. Women perceived that, although everyone's absolute workload increased with resettlement, men did more fieldwork than previously. They were also reported to be 'better husbands', drinking less and spending less money on extra-marital relationships. This phenomenon is partly circumstantial: beerhalls are further away in RAs. However, I have analysed this as being in part due to the influence of the RO, who encourages settlers to 'behave well'. A man who drinks, is often absent and does not cultivate his fields could, theoretically, lose the permits to land. Another aspect of resettlement is that the husband's patrilineal relatives were usually not nearby; many women welcomed living in smaller families, and those in monogamous households (see below) felt that they had somewhat more say in household matters. None the less, the structural factor of allocation of land to men means that women's dependence upon husbands is exacerbated. Ironically, resettlement may help to promote the idea of female farmers as 'housewives'.

Changes in the selection of settlers which are of relevance to women have occurred recently. In the selection process, wives and husbands are now awarded points separately for various criteria such as education, certification (that is, obtaining a Master Farmer qualification, indicating skill) and capital (Stewart, 1996). However, even if a wife is awarded more points than her husband, he still receives the land permits. In some cases, however, ROs have awarded titles to married women; and a high percentage of Master Farmer students are now female (Goebel 1996).

In another respect resettled women are advantaged over other African women in Zimbabwe, who are subject to the property claims of their husband's patrilineal relatives if he dies. It is the norm for widows to be left with virtually no property, as it is not considered to be hers. In RAs, however, rulings have meant that wives and senior wives inherit rather than husband's brothers. Since many wives are considerably younger than their husbands, a substantial number will inherit (Chenaux-Repond 1994, cited in Gaidzanwa 1995); and the figure of 15 per cent female permit holders cited by Gaidzanwa (1995) is high by international standards. In another study of Wedza one-fifth of tenants are currently widows (Goebel 1996); some ROs are enforcing widow's claims.

While these changes mean that there is some cause for optimism with regard to the status of settler women, other factors mean that they, like other rural women, are severely disadvantaged. Polygyny appears to have increased in Resettlement Areas. I found rates in excess of 30 per cent, and Chenaux-Repond (1994) found a rate of up to 36 per cent. This phenomenon tends to indicate that many junior wives in resettlements are being treated as labourers, similar to the phenomenon found by Weinrich (1975) and by Cheater (1981) in Small-Scale (previously, African) Commercial Farms. As elsewhere in Zimbabwe, women greatly fear divorce, since they are likely to end up impoverished and, despite recent legal changes, lose custody of children aged over seven. In Resettlement Areas, they will also lose access to resettlement land, since upon divorce it is always wives who are ejected, never husbands. Fear of divorce inhibits most rural and many urban women from asserting their needs and rights (Mpofu 1983; Pankhurst and Jacobs 1988).

The government set up a Land Tenure Commission in 1993. However, no specific recommendations to remove gender discrimination were included (Mabuwa 1996). Although ZANU sees rural women as a force to be mobilised, it was not seen as necessary to address their needs. However, some protest against this state of affairs has taken place, particularly from the Women's Action Group.[5]

Women themselves in Resettlement Areas certainly have agency; various documents have indicated their demands for independent access to land (ZWB 1981; Muchena and Government of Zimbabwe 1983; Jacobs 1989a; Chenaux-Repond 1995). However, they are not viewed as powerful social actors. Perhaps one of the few fora in which rural women can discuss matters relatively freely is local Women's Groups, mainly dedicated to forms of income generation within women's homemaking roles. In conditions of political repression, economic constraint (often, desperation) induced by structural adjustment, continued legal disadvantage, and under the implicit threat of divorce, rural smallholder women may find it, to say the least, difficult to protest. The fact that they resist at times, both covertly and overtly, is a tribute to their determination.

Vietnam

The example of Vietnam demonstrates both how collective land reforms may benefit women but cause a backlash of gender and class conflicts, and how lack of an autonomous women's movement may inhibit women's resistance.

Agriculture in Vietnam has long been seen as an activity involving both sexes. Men usually ploughed but could not farm without women to perform tasks such as transplanting rice seedlings (White 1982). Other tasks, such as harvesting, were less gender-stereotyped; women's activities also extended to marketing and to keeping household accounts. Despite having their own spheres of activity, Vietnamese women were subordinate both in village and family. Villages were organised as collectives of male household heads and governed by councils of notables (Eisen 1984; White 1982): kinship systems are patrilineal and patrilocal.

Although there exist hints that indigenous (pre-Chinese colonial) forms were less severe (Eisen 1984: 14; Tétreault 1994), under long Chinese rule the Confucian ethic prevailed. Eisen (1984: 14) cites a commonly quoted proverb which perhaps gives some indication of women's status: 'One hundred women are not worth a single testicle.' Although the Confucian ethic was weaker in peasant families, all women were subject to the 'Three Obediences': to father, husband and then eldest son. In most periods of Chinese and indigenous Vietnamese 'feudal' rule, women could not hold land.

Under French rule, most agriculture remained in peasant hands, but the majority of households became ensnared in bonds of debt slavery (White 1982). In the early twentieth century, many women joined in the anti-colonial movement; however, no Vietnamese intellectuals, including Marxists, advocated legal equality for females (Tétreault 1994: 113). Nevertheless, women in the north were later mobilised by the (then) Indochinese Communist Party, through its organisation the Women's Union (WU), formed in 1930. The WU has existed continually since that time, and it is still the main organisation representing women, especially in rural areas. Eisen (1984) writes that, although a party organisation, it has always had a degree of autonomy.

Women in both urban and rural areas took part in anti-colonial agitation; some women who died became portrayed as revolutionary martyrs. Several accounts note the interrelation between women's later mobilisation, in the war against the US, their politicisation, the eventual success of the war and land reform campaigns (Chaliand 1969; White 1982; Tétreault 1994). Thus the Viet Minh gave women a share of land in areas they controlled (Tétreault 1994: 114). The 1946 Constitution of the Democratic Republic of Vietnam (DRV) proclaimed legal sexual equality and provided for female suffrage. Following the expulsion of the Japanese, the DRV land reform campaign of 1953–6 eliminated land ownership by non-tillers and established a pattern of small/middle peasant proprietorship (White 1982: 46). Women often emerged as radical activists in anti-landlord campaigns, protesting against sexual as well as economic abuse (Eisen 1984). During these campaigns, women were sometimes elected to village leadership posts, an entirely new situation.

The second 'stage' of land reform in (newly divided) North Vietnam involved the formation of producer co-operatives. Unlike in the Zimbabwean example, the Vietnamese government followed orthodox Marxist strictures in aiming for a degree of agricultural collectivisation, partly because this was believed to be more efficient. The movement for collectivisation was party-led, with little democratic participation, but was none the less relatively voluntary and entailed no physical coercion (Deere 1986).

Women, especially young women, were among the first to join co-operatives. White (1987: 229) points out that it was not coincidental that new marriage laws outlawing polygyny, child marriage and forced marriage were introduced at the same time that co-operativisation campaigns attempted to widen the agrarian unit. Women who were trapped in such arrangements as marriage to a young boy (for his family's use of her labour) joined enthusiastically in order to gain independence from their in-laws. In co-operatives, work points were awarded individually, so that women's work was more visible. Women remained disadvantaged *vis-à-vis* men, since they were responsible for domestic labour, work in garden plots (see below) and because much of the work they did gained fewer work points (Eisen 1984; Wiergsma 1988). But in some co-operatives, women's tasks gained maximum work points (Chaliand 1969; Houtart and Lemarchand 1984). Wiergsma (1988: 169–70) writes:

> From the beginning of land reform throughout the collectivisation campaigns, women in northern Vietnamese villages saw these socialist movements as an advance for themselves. Socialists freed them from child marriage, concubinage, polygyny and arranged marriages . . . Even some nurseries were established.

Meanwhile, men remained more reluctant to join co-operatives due to the threat to their independent status and to their control over women. In one village the difference between the sexes was so marked that village land was divided into two, with most women joining the co-operative and most men remaining outside (White 1982: 47).

Particularly during the war years, Confucian conceptions of passive womanhood and the (less explicitly drawn) French and American ideas of Vietnamese women as prostituted became supplanted by images of women as revolutionary heroines. The image projected was of woman as fearless in battle while still managing to fulfil wifely and motherly duties (White 1989). Tétreault (1994), too, cites the importance of the enduring image of the nurturing mother (see also Eisen 1984).

While co-operatives predominated, conflicts between the collective and family economies were apparent. The collectives lacked the administrative capacity to supply many basic necessities. Unlike in China, the plan was never that they would wholly supplant individual household production. The importance of the family economy was most visible in the persistence of garden plots. Officially, the land so designated was 5 per cent of the total, but the amount cultivated in practice was up to 13 per cent. Not only was productivity on these plots far higher than on collective land, as elsewhere crops grown on family land tended to be of higher value than the staple crops grown on collective land. Hence households continued to receive over half their incomes from family rather than collective production (Wiergsma 1988: 161). Although some cadres did express concern about the renewal of capitalism in the countryside, connections were never made between the petty capitalist and the patriarchal nature of the family farm unit. Wiergsma gives a powerful analysis of male peasant influence on the reconstitution of patriarchal authority; she uses the term in its classical sense, and also links the preservation of patriarchy to the preservation of a middle peasantry, which also remained influential at local party levels.

After the war ended in 1975, changes occurred within co-operatives. Many female managers were replaced by returned male officers who considered it demeaning to be directed by women (White 1989). The state's intention was to further collectivise agriculture; however, agricultural productivity, which had risen, fell in the late 1970s. The government's response was to institute a new subcontracting system from 1979, which ceded much more control to 'family heads'. In this system, the co-operative contracted with individual households or groups of households for the delivery of final products. The masculinisation of co-operatives was increased: 'higher'-level, more technical work came to be dominated by men. The return to a family labour system has meant that women's work becomes less visible (White 1987). White (1989: 187) also writes, however, that the advent of the subcontracting system meant that women could again assume traditional roles as market women.

At least in the late 1980s, decades of war had meant a general deterioration for rural women. Where customarily an adult male and female, a water buffalo and a plough constituted a farming household, the man might be dead or absent, the buffalo dead as well, and the plough too expensive. A large minority of women were left to farm on their own, lacking even draught animals (White 1989: 175); it is likely that this is still the case.

From 1988, household rights over land were greatly strengthened and a much fuller decollectivisation was initiated; in 1993 land law was further revised so that, in effect, a land market was permitted (Dao 1995: 157). Recent work indicates that rural incomes (and food consumption) have increased in many regions (Kerkvliet and Porter 1995). This latter volume makes little mention of the effects on peasant women of the momentous changes which have occurred, although presumably the diets of women too have improved. It seems likely that, as in Zimbabwe, rural women may face either 'housewifisation' or (in female-headed households) even more arduous, unassisted labour.

Thus the spheres of family and 'women's issues' continue to be treated as separate from that of agriculture in both policy and academic work. In the sphere of family law, unlike in that of concerns seen as 'agrarian', new regulations benefit women. In particular, the 1986 Family Law, drafted by the WU, affirms joint control of household property, joint consent to economic transactions, and equal household domestic responsibility. It also attempts to protect women against divorce during pregnancy and from spouses' violence. A husband (or wife) convicted of violent abuse may now be imprisoned (Tétreault 1994). Although it is highly unlikely that such provisions operate fully in the countryside, they have raised rural as well as urban women's legal status. Other new developments such as the advent of rural female schoolteachers (White 1987) have demonstrated new roles for peasant women within civil society.

A number of Vietnamese women are active and prominent politically, even at high levels (White 1989). However, rural women are less prominent than during the war. In a 1987 visit, Wiergsma (1991) found that villages were still patrilocal and that mother-in-law's control over sons' wives had only slightly diminished. Official policy, building on the idea of the 'three obediences', now stresses women's 'special' family obligation as well as their responsibility for building socialism. A negative side of extolling motherhood is that childcare workers (and women who employ them) are disdained (Tétreault 1994).

Failure to overthrow 'socialist patriarchy' has had serious consequences for rural women and for the overall shape of agricultural organisation. Many Vietnamese women fiercely resisted colonialism and an imperialist war; they also pursued gender interests both within collectives and more widely. In this, they had a more than usually powerful ally in the Women's Union. However, no widespread independent women's organisation has been possible in Vietnamese conditions, where non-state organisations have not existed; thus it is difficult to ascertain rural women's opinions where they differed from the party line. Although it should not be automatically assumed that peasant women supported collectives, these did present many advantages. The lack of autonomous feminist movements is likely to have been an important element in the eventual demise of a land reform which, for a time, operated in the interests of many peasant women.

India: land rights and the Bodghaya struggle

The Indian land reform has been characterised by stasis, broken promises (Herring 1990: 49) and its narrow scope. It has tended to benefit the intermediate rather than the poorest rural classes (Christodoulou 1990: 145). It is perhaps curious that it is within the context of a (nationally) small-scale and conservative land reform that the Bodghaya movement has taken place. This is the first movement worldwide which has secured independent land titles for wives in preference to husbands. The Bodghaya movement's partial success owed much to the general climate of feminist agitation on the Left.

Unusually, in India the land reform process has been left to individual states not only to implement but to formulate, within the understanding that the process should not be overly radical in nature (Christodoulou 1990). Nearly every state has attempted some limited land reform measures since independence. Many of the reforms which have occurred have come about due to the widespread rural unrest characterising many regions. The Telengana movement and the Naxalite rebellions (in West Bengal) are two of the best-known. Despite prolonged and violent agitation, the end-product of a series of land reforms has been that a class of middle/larger peasants rent land and hire a growing rural proletariat (Sobhan 1993: 65). Only in Kerala state, which has had long periods of communist rule (of a fairly social democratic nature) has tenancy been abolished and the balance of power altered:

over 36 per cent of sown area has been redistriubted to 43 per cent of agriculturalists (Sobhan 1993, citing Herring 1985).

From the 1950s, India, along with other South Asian countries, accepted the principle of women's independent property rights and enacted this into law. However, this acceptance was limited to inheritance laws governing private property in land, rather than state-redistributed land (Agarwal 1994: 8). Where South Asian women have gained land title, usually through inheritance, there have been many barriers to their full use and management of the land. In general, women are not deemed fit to control land fully; this is the case to an extent even in matrilineal systems which tend to grant women higher status: often the actual management of a woman's land is undertaken by a man. Granting women land rights is seen by some as a deliberate and sinister attempt to destroy the family and the patrilineage (ibid.: 273). In communities in which women have never held land, such rights are met with particular hostility: witchcraft accusations, attacks, divorce threats, torture and murder are among the responses reported.

Aside from actions which directly discourage women from claiming land rights, there are other, more indirect considerations. Due in part to norms and ideologies of gender behaviour which enjoin female modesty and seclusion, female purity and male sexual honour, most women are dependent upon male kin: brothers in particular are potential protectors from violence and ill-treatment, particularly from in-laws; so few women wish to break this valued relation (ibid.: 265). However, a woman claiming land to which she is entitled may come into conflict precisely with brothers (Kabeer 1985).[6]

Land obtained through the state, that is through land reforms, carries the possibility of side-stepping these complex knots of relationships. However, as elsewhere worldwide, the emphasis of most reform programmes in the region has been on assigning land to 'household heads'. Even where land redistribution has taken place as a result of popular struggle, as in the 1950s Telengana movement (led by the Communist Party), issues of gender and land were not given priority despite women's prominence in the struggle (Sanghatana 1989). Indeed, the ambivalence of Indian Marxist parties regarding women's land rights – seeing them as 'divisive' – has been an important negative influence (Agarwal 1994).

Agarwal documents some of the early demands for women's rights to redistributed land and some state responses. For instance, in a 1979 Calcutta women's conference, women village council (*gram panchayat*) representatives from West Bengal demanded joint titles to land on behalf of destitute Muslim women (Agarwal 1994: 5). In its Sixth Plan, in 1985, the Indian Ministry of Agriculture and Rural Development stated that the government would endeavour to give spouses joint titles to land. However, such reports gather dust (ibid.: 7). The Eighth Five-Year Plan for India (1992–7) left most responsibility for monitoring gender-related issues in land to the National Commission for Women. This follows the usual pattern of assigning gender concerns to a separate women's body rather than incorporating them into agriculture and lands ministry policy.

The Bodghaya movement, a socialist movement of the rural poor in Bihar, constitutes a landmark for women's land rights, but its achievements have not occurred in a vacuum, isolated from other feminist movements. Indian left movements have for some time been marked by feminist agitation; likewise, feminist movements have been more than usually oriented to the rural poor. The Self-Employed Women's Association, for instance, is one of the first women's trade unions in the world. In 1974 the Progressive Organisation of Women, of Maoist origin, began to raise wide issues of gender oppression (Kumar 1995). In the late 1970s, the renewed sharecroppers movement in Telengana, Andhra Pradesh was marked by feminist agitation against wife-beating and landlord rapes (Kumar 1995: 65). More recently, mass feminist protests against dowry, systematic police rape of prisoners and *sati* (widow immolation) have occurred. A recent significant development is that in one village, Vitner (Maharashtra), women have obtained shares in their husband's land (Gala 1990).

Manimala (1983) gives a detailed account of the origins of the Bodghaya movement in Bihar, India's poorest state. I reproduce this in some detail because of its continued relevance, and because of the farsighted linking of different types of gender issues that women in the movement managed to put forward in the context of a land struggle.

The Chatna Yuva Sangharsh Vahini, formed in 1975, was a socialist movement of the young dedicated to peaceful resistance and to living among the rural poor. The Vahini were always marked by the high participation of women. However, at first 'women's issues' were passed over in favour of organisation among the landless. Manimala relates how, at an early meeting in 1979, several significant events occurred. For instance, Manimala herself decided to speak on land issues while the male organiser, Prakesh, spoke on 'women's issues'; wife-beating and the household division of labour were discussed, for the first time openly. Prakesh suggested that, as a gesture, men assist wives by washing their own dishes. Lest one assume, however, that raising issues openly is sufficient, the outcome should be noted. When one woman that evening handed her husband his plates, he threw them in her face and then proceeded to beat and injure her badly (Manimala 1983: 5). The costs of resistance to women, perhaps especially impoverished rural women, should be seen as a matter for feminist discussion.[7]

From late 1979 it was decided that a struggle against the *math*, a religious body which held land illegally, would be launched. Although this did not cause the Vahini to abandon its focus on gender issues, conflicts within the movement began to surface, particularly concerning the movement's priorities. Should these concern land or issues such as drink and wife-beating? Manimala reports how the movement came to be influenced by the orthodox Marxist idea that economic change had to occur before women's grievances could be addressed; however, many women argued against such assumptions, pointing out that men who had gained land would be even more likely to beat and abuse their wives than would landless labourers – who were not immune to such behaviour despite their own oppression and exploitation (Manimala 1983: 8).

It was in this context of general feminist agitation in the Vahini movement that a woman's meeting first decided that when the land was won it should be redistributed in *women's* names. Despite this ground-breaking demand, movement women still found it difficult to make their views heard. In mixed-sex meetings, when women's concerns were raised, their opinions rarely carried the day.

From 1980, the land struggle escalated and women were the target of violent attacks by the police, being jailed in equal numbers with men. By 1981, a partial victory occurred and the government identified for redistribution 1000 acres illegally held. But when the Vahini put forward plans for redistribution, it emerged that 'landless labourers . . . [i.e. men], the disabled and widows' would receive land (Manimala 1983: 14). Vahini women were furious at this turn of events and at the suggestion that for a man to be without land was equivalent to a woman being without a man. Women in many villages noted that authoritarian behaviour increased as a result of the redistribution. In February 1982, the Bihar state conference of Vahini decided that in future redistribution of land would be in women's names. (It was also said that in the next round of redistribution, husbands would receive land.) Most delegates agreed that the decision was fair. Eventually, in 1982, 10 per cent of land was redistributed in the names of married women (Kelkar and Gala 1990: 94). Women who were widows, destitutes and even unmarried daughters also received land.

Problems, however, did not cease with redistribution of land. Unfortunately, even when the pressure of officials (to redistribute land in the names of both spouses) was resisted, many women found it difficult to cultivate their land. Constraints were presented by restrictions on women's use of space, by the patrilocal residence norms and, importantly, by the region-wide taboo on female ploughing. Despite the great struggle waged, some married women interviewed said that they would pass their land on to daughters-in-law, not daughters; others said that sons would inherit their land so that it would stay within the village.

Despite such difficulties, the rights gained by women in Bodghaya did go along with a general lessening of violence and abuse towards them, and with improved status. Alaka and Chetna (1987: 26) cite a village woman: '*Didi*, earlier, we had tongues but could not speak, we had feet but could not walk. Now that we have got the land, we have got the strength to speak and to walk.'

Significantly, in the late 1980s, women in the movement also launched a campaign against patrilocal residence and for matrilocal residence, seeing this feature of the kinship/lineage system as one which operates against their interests (Kelkar and Gala 1990).

Conclusion

The three cases cited all concern land reforms undertaken either after the victory of a revolutionary socialist/nationalist movement or in conjunction with such an organisation. In the case of Vietnam and India, the movements concerned were strongly influenced by Marxist aims such as bringing women into industrial production and instituting the heterosexual nuclear family (Waylen 1996). In Zimbabwe, such influence was less strong. Peasant women have benefited in each of the three cases discussed, despite the fact that neither the land reforms nor more gender-specific policies have created 'equality'. A third similarity is the importance of patrilineal/patrilocal kinship systems to women's experience of agrarian reform.

The cases also present paradoxes. The outcome of the most widespread, radical and collectivist reform, in Vietnam, meant that peasant farm economies were reconstituted. Women made gains through increased incomes and due to legal attacks on 'traditional' practices such as concubinage and forced marriage. Despite their heavy involvement in agriculture, in the war and in the party itself, women were rarely involved in policy-making, even as cadres. Even though patriliny as a form was weakened, the continuation of the family economy encouraged male peasant interests.

The Zimbabwean example, smaller in scope, has had contradictory effects. Although nearly all land has been redistributed to individual male heads of households, wives have benefited to an extent that makes Zimbabwe unusual among cases of land reform with individual tenure (Jacobs 1996). A large minority of families are polygynous and in some of these, wives may be used as an agricultural labour force; but in many cases (and not only in nuclear families), wives have gained from increased household income, which has been passed on to them; they have also reported that the absence or distance of the husband's wider kin and men's increased involvement in farming have been advantageous.

In the above cases, state policies have also helped to improve women's social position. Such policies have been mainly apparent in marriage and family law, as is also the case in India. In Vietnam, a state feminist organisation, the Women's Union, has had some degree of power and success, particularly in establishing relatively radical family laws in which violence is outlawed, at least theoretically. In Zimbabwe, some ROs have been sympathetic to women settler's demands, intervening in cases of male violence and in disputes over land allocation.

However, whatever gender-sensitive policies exist, these have failed to link the spheres of agriculture and marriage/kinship, or at least not to a sufficient degree. Women's concerns continue to be seen as lying *par excellence* within the sphere of motherhood while agriculture is thought to be either a male or a gender-neutral concern. On one hand, the importance of women holding land on the same basis as men (whatever that may be in particular circumstances) is either ignored or not understood. In this sense, gendered state policies have not been sufficiently 'productionist' – at least in the sphere of agriculture – even in regimes commonly accused of productionism. On the other hand, neither is the role of other factors in barring women's access to land, labour and inputs considered. Prime among these are systems of descent, marriage and residence.

Paradoxically, it has been left to a smaller, non-state directed socialist and feminist movement in a society in which the land reform has been very limited to make the links suggested above. The Bodghaya movement managed not only to gain land rights for women but also raised the issue of patri-local residence. It was able to do this because from the early days of the movement, feminist issues were raised by activists in a context of general rural agitation. These continually made links between such matters as land-holding, alcoholism, violence, women's status in general, the welfare of children, patrilineality, patrilocality and general socialist aims. Although some links (such as violence and consumption of alcohol) are obvious, others are far more opaque.

The fact that the Bodghaya movement is grassroots-based is of great importance; unlike in the other two examples, peasant women have helped to form policy. No such grassroots movement exists in Vietnam, and rural women's autonomous organisation in Zimbabwe is confined to Women's Clubs. I would make the point that the ability to make such connections does not spring automatically from everyday experience, as is held by some versions of feminist theory, although direct experience is one crucial factor in understanding. In the Bodghaya case, much analysis of these complex links had already been undertaken by individuals and groups within wider feminist-influenced movements.

Together, the examples discussed illustrate that were a gender perspective to be integrated into analyses of land reform, their aims, achievements and failures might appear rather differently. To use one example: had Lipton (1993) included 'gender equity' in his revised definition – or had he noted that the the majority of the poor are commonly female – then *most* land reforms would fail to qualify under a broadened definition. Although many reforms raise living standards, including women's, the fact that husbands hold land means that women are often disempowered.

The division between 'land' and 'gender' issues so evident in policy is also a reflection of the sidelining of the former within feminist analyses. Even in a utopia in which wives hold land rights (either individual or collective) equivalent to men's, they would not automatically achieve 'equality'. But reforms of marriage and legal status alone, although important, may mean little for many rural women who lack effective access to land.

Notes

1 The work of Bina Agarwal, Jean Davison, Carmen Diana Deere, Magdalena Leon, Judith Stacey and Nancy Wiergsma with regard to gender and land reform should be particularly noted.
2 It should not be assumed that such unwritten histories are *always* in favour of land for women. For instance, Marcus *et al.*'s (1996) summary of a national South African project on these issues indicates that many women agree that men should hold land; in their view, this is most likely to preserve families, their main hope of security.
3 In 1981 I accompanied the PM's wife and sister on ZANU Women's League rallies in Mashonaland Central Province.
4 The 1985 Matrimonial Causes Act partially removes 'guilt' clauses in divorce suits; section 7 also empowers courts to make equitable reallocation of spouses' property at divorce; however, these clauses apply only to civil and not to African Customary Marriages. The 1985 Labour Relations Act allows employed women paid maternity leave and rights to breastfeed at work (Stewart and Armstrong 1990). More recently, the 1992 Taxation Act stipulates that wives be taxed separately from husbands.
5 The WAG held a series of workshops and the Ebert Foundation held a large meeting to consult female farmers (Chenaux-Repond 1995). The first issue of the new feminist journal *Southern African Feminist Review* (*SAFERE*) addresses land issues.
6 Kabeer (1985) makes this point for Bangladesh; however, it holds true as well for India.
7 I thank Ruth Jacobson, Department of Peace Studies, University of Bradford, for emphasising this point.

References

Agarwal, B. (1994) *A Field of One's Own: Women and Land Rights in South Asia,* Cambridge: Cambridge University Press.

Alaka and Chetna (1987) 'When women get land' *Manushi*, no. 40.

Alexander, J. (1994) 'State, peasantry and resettlement in Zimbabwe' *Review of African Political Economy*, no. 61.

Barraclough, Solon (1991) *An End to Hunger?*, London: Zed Press.

Basu, A. (ed.) (1995) *The Challenge of Local Feminisms*, Boulder, Col.: Westview Press.

Batezat, E. and Mwalo, M. (1989) *Women in Zimbabwe*, Harare: SAPES Trust.

Beresford, D. (1994) 'Mugabe backs down over "land grab" plan', *Guardian*, 24 October.

Bratton, M. (1990) 'Ten years after: land redistribution in Zimbabwe, 1980–90', in R. Prosterman, M. Temple and T. Hanstad (eds), *Agrarian Reform and Grassroots Development*, Boulder, Col.: Lynne Rienner.

Chaliand, G. (1969) *The Peasants of North Vietnam*, Harmondsworth, Middlesex: Penguin.

Cheater, A. (1981) 'Women and their participation in commercial agricultural production', *Development and Change*, 12 (July).

Chenaux-Repond, M. (1994) 'Gender-based land use-rights in Model A resettlement schemes of Mashonaland, Zimbabwe', ZWCN Monographs, Harare; cited in

R. Gaidzanwa, 'Land and economic empowerment of women: a gendered-analysis', *SAFERE* 1(1) (1995); and S. Moyo, 'A gendered perspective of the land question', ibid.

Chenaux-Repond, M. (1995) 'Women farmer's position paper', third draft, Harare, unpublished.

Christodoulou, D. (1990) *The Unpromised Land: Agrarian Reform and Conflict Worldwide*, London: Zed Books.

Dao The Tuan (1995) 'The peasant household economy and social change', in B.J.T. Kerkvliet and D. Porter, *Vietnam's Rural Transformation*, Boulder, Col.: Westview Press.

Deere, C.D. (1986) 'Agrarian reform, peasant participation and the organisation of production in the transition to socialism', in R. Fagen, C. Deere and J. Coraggio (eds), *Transition and Development: Problems of Third World Socialism*, New York: Monthly Review Press.

Eisen, A. (1984) *Women and Revolution in Vietnam*, London: Zed Books.

El-Ghonemy, M.R. (1990) *The Political Economy of Rural Poverty: The Case for Land Reform*, London: Routledge.

Frenier, M. (1983) 'The effects of the Chinese communist land reform on women and their families', *Women's Studies International Forum*, 6: 1.

Gaidzanwa, R. (1995) 'Land and the economic empowerment of women: a gendered analysis', *SAFERE* 1(1).

Gala, Chetna (1990) 'Trying to give women their due: the story of Vitner village', *Manush*, no. 59.

Goebel, A. (1996) Private correspondence, Dept. of Sociology, University of Alberta, October.

Government of Zimbabwe, Ministry of Lands, Resettlement and Rural Development (1983) Interview with official, Harare, September.

Herbst, J. (1990) *State Politics in Zimbabwe*, Harare: University of Zimbabwe Publications.

Herring, R.J. (1990) 'Explaining anomalies in agrarian reform: lessons from South India', in R. Prosterman, M. Temple and T. Hanstad (eds), *Agrarian Reform and Grassroots Development*, Boulder, Col.: Lynne Rienner.

Houtart, F. and Lemercinier, G. (1984) *Hai Van: Life in a Vietnamese Commune*, London: Zed Books.

Jacobs, S. (1989a) *Gender Divisions and Land Resettlement in Zimbabwe*, DPhil. Thesis, Institute of Development Studies at the University of Sussex, Falmer, Brighton.

Jacobs, S. (1989b) 'Zimbabwe: state, class and gendered models of resettlement', in J. Parpart and K. Staudt (eds), *Women and the State in Africa*, Boulder, Col.: Lynne Rienner.

Jacobs, S. (1992) 'Gender and land reform: Zimbabwe and some comparisons', *International Sociology* 7(1).

Jacobs, S. (1996) *Land Tenure and the Politics of Land Reform*, Strathclyde Papers on Sociology and Social Policy no. 10, Glasgow: University of Strathclyde.

Jacobs, S. and Howard, T. (1987) 'Women in Zimbabwe: stated policy and state action', in H. Afshar (ed.), *Women, State and Ideology in Africa and Asia*, London: Macmillan

Jirira, K.O (1995) 'Gender, politics and democracy', *SAFERE* 1(2).

Kabeer, N. (1985) 'Do women gain from high fertility?', in H.W. Afshar (ed.), *Women, Work and the Family in the Third World*, London: Tavistock Publications.

Kazembe, J. (1986) 'The woman question', in I. Mandaza (ed.), *Zimbabwe: The Political Economy of Transition*, Dakar: Codeseria.

Kelkar, G. and Gala, C. (1990) 'The Bodghaya land struggle', in A. Sen (ed.), *A Space in the Struggle*, Delhi: Kali for Women.

Kerkvliet, Benedict J. Tria and Porter, Doug (eds) (1995) *Vietnam's Rural Transformation*, Boulder, Col.: Westview Press.

Kriger, N. (1992) *Zimbabwe's Guerrilla War: Peasant Voices*, Cambridge: Cambridge University Press.

Kumar, R. (1995) 'From Chipko to Sati: the contemporary women's movement', in A. Basu (ed.), *The Challenge of Local Feminisms*, Boulder, Col.: Westview Press.

Lipton, M. (1974) 'Towards a theory of land reform', in D. Lehmann, *Agrarian Reform and Agrarian Reformism*, London: Faber & Faber.

Lipton, M. (1993) 'Land reform as commenced business: the evidence against stopping', *World Development* 21(4):

Mabuwa, C.C. (1996) Interview, Women's Action Group, Harare, July.

Manimala (1983) '"Zameen Kenkar? Jote Onkar!": the story of women's participation in the Bodghaya struggle', *Manushi*, Jan.–Feb., 14.

Marcus, T., Eales, K. and Wildschut, A. (1996) *Down to Earth: Land Demand in the New South Africa*, Durban: Indicator Press, University of Natal.

Meldrum, A. (1996) 'Zimbabwe mob defies gay ruling', *Guardian*, 3 August.

Montgomery, J. (ed.) (1984) *International Dimensions of Land Reform*, Boulder, Col.: Westview Press.

Moyo, S. (1995a) *The Land Question in Zimbabwe*, Harare: SAPES Trust.

Moyo, S. (1995b) 'A gendered perspective of the land question', *SAFERE* 1(1).

Mpofu, J. (1983) 'Some observable sources of women's subordination in Zimbabwe', Harare: Centre for Applied Social Studies, University of Zimbabwe.

Muchena, O. and Government of Zimbabwe, Ministry of Community Development and Women's Affairs (1982) 'Report on the situation of women in Zimbabwe', unpublished, Harare.

Pankhurst, D. and Jacobs, S. (1988) 'Land tenure, gender relations and agricultural production: the case of Zimbabwe's peasantry', in J. Davison (ed.), *Agriculture, Women and Land: The African Experience*, Boulder, Col.: Westview Press.

Prosterman, R., Temple, M. and Hanstad, T. (eds) (1990) *Agrarian Reform and Grassroots Development*, Boulder, Col.: Lynne Rienner.

Putzel, J. (1992) *A Captive Land: The Politics of Agrarian Reform in the Phillipines*, London: Catholic Institute for International Relations Press; New York: Monthly Review Press.

Rai, S. (1996) 'Women and the state in the Third World', in H. Afshar (ed.), *Women and Politics in the Third World*, London: Routledge.

Sanghatana, Stree S. (1989) *We Were Making History: Women and the Telengana Struggle*, London: Zed Books; New Delhi: Kali for Women.

Sobhan, R. (1993) *Agrarian Reform and Social Transformation*, London: Zed Books.

Speakout/Taurai/Khulumani (1996) 'Women cry foul over inheritance law reform', no. 35 (June/July): 2, 13.

Stacey, J. (1982) 'People's war and the new democratic patriarchy in China', *Journal of Comparative Family Studies* 13(3).

Staunton, I. (1990) *Mothers of the Revolution*, Harare: Baobab; London: James Currey.

Stewart, J. (1996) Interview, University of Zimbabwe, Harare, July.

Stewart, J. and Armstrong, A. (1990) (eds) *The Legal Situation of Women in Southern Africa*, Harare: University of Zimbabwe Publications.

Sylvester, C. (1991) *Zimbabwe: The Terrain of Contradictory Development*, Boulder, Col.: Westview Press.

Tétreault, M. (1994) 'Women and revolution in Vietnam', in M. Tétreault (ed.), *Women and Revolution in Africa, Asia and the New World*, Columbia, S.C.: University of South Carolina Press.

Thiesenhusen, W. (1989) *Searching for Agrarian Reform in Latin America*, Boston, Mass.: Unwin Hyman.

Thiesenhusen, W. (1995) *Broken Promises: Agrarian Reform and the Latin American Campesino*, Boulder, Col.: Westview Press.

Walker, C. (1994) 'Women, "tradition" and reconstruction', *Review of African Political Economy*, no. 64.

Waylen, G. (1996) *Gender in Third World Politics*, Milton Keynes: Open University.

Weinrich, A.K.H. (1975) *African Farmers in Rhodesia*, Oxford: Oxford University Press.

White, C.P. (1982) 'Socialist transformation of agriculture and gender relations: the Vietnamese case', *Bulletin of the Institute of Development Studies* 13(4).

White, C.P. (1987) 'State, culture and gender: continuity and change in women's position in rural Vietnam', in H. Afshar (ed.), *Women, State and Ideology in Africa and Asia*, London: Macmillan.

White, C.P. (1989) 'Vietnam: war, socialism and the politics of gender', in S. Kruks, R. Rapp and M. Young (eds), *Promissory Notes: Women in the Transition to Socialism*, New York: Monthly Review Press.

Wiergsma, N. (1988) *Vietnam: Peasant Land, Peasant Revolution*, New York: St. Martin's Press.

Wiergsma, N. (1991) 'Peasant patriarchy and the subversion of the collective in Vietnam', *Review of Radical Political Economics* 23: 3–4.

Zimbabwe Women's Bureau (1981) *Black Women in Zimbabwe*, Salisbury, Zimbabwe: ZWB.

9 Gender politics and the state during Russia's transition period[1]

Valerie Sperling

The political situation is the most important thing, even more important than the lack of money. Here, instead of politics, we have anti-politics. It's not clear what will happen. We live on a volcano. Today it's like this. But tomorrow, the Bolsheviks or the radicals could come to power, and everything will fall apart; nothing will happen.
Moscow activist, commenting on obstacles to women's movement organizing
(Interview, November 27, 1994)

Introduction

In 1979, a small group of women involved in the Soviet dissident movement decided to create their own underground journal, called *Almanac: Woman and Russia*. Inside were descriptions of grisly abortion procedures in the USSR; the conditions in maternity hospitals, and other subjects previously publicly ignored. The KGB got wind of the group's activity and acted swiftly to disband it. Several of the editorial collective's members were imprisoned, others exiled from the country. Only when Gorbachev came to power in the mid-1980s did other women's groups, independent of the state, dare to form and speak out against discrimination. Gorbachev's new policies of glasnost (openness) and perestroika (restructuring), allowed for the legalization of civic associations, through which social groups could formulate new identities and articulate their interests in the public sphere.

As the state monopoly over the public sphere crumbled, power was re-routed to a slowly marketizing economy and an increasingly pluralistic political system. Yet, both the labor market and new political institutions in Russia proved to be highly discriminatory against women. Women's political representation at all levels declined (by comparison with Soviet times), while the market brought massive economic discrimination against women, who in 1994 made up over 70 percent of Russia's unemployed.

Changes in Russia's political opportunity structure have made possible the emergence of a women's movement, consisting of over 300 organizations. Many of these groups are consciously responding to the decline in women's status, and are trying to pressure the Russian state to ensure a non-discriminatory labor sphere, and somehow reincorporate women's voice into political decision-making.

This chapter analyzes the political opportunity structure for women's movement organizations in Moscow since the beginning of perestroika.[2] Although the political opportunity structure has changed, creating new opportunities for the Russian women's movement, there are also significant economic, attitudinal, and historical obstacles to women's organizing success. In this chapter, I focus on the political-institutional opportunities and obstacles encountered by groups hoping to influence the Russian state on women's behalf.[3] For example, whereas the movement can now enjoy public speech without censorship, it has few opportunities to influence members of parliament and government officials. Furthermore, many state institutions remain hostile to women's advancement, and their representatives maintain that women's role should be limited to that of homemaker until the economic crisis has passed. On the other hand, some women's organizations are slowly gaining access to political decision-makers. Highly placed politicians, including Yeltsin, have sworn their support for improving Russian women's status. Yet the Russian state remains notoriously unable to carry out its own decrees and laws supporting equal rights and opportunities for men and women. The political opportunity structure for women's organizations in Russia is thus quite complex.

Political opportunity structure is a multi-dimensional concept enabling us to analyze some of the reasons for a social movement's success or failure. According to a definition compiled by Doug McAdam (1996: 27), political opportunity structure includes four elements:

1   the relative openness or closure of the institutionalized political system;
2   the stability or instability of that broad set of elite alignments that typically undergird a polity;
3   the presence or absence of elite allies
4   the state's capacity and propensity for repression.

Analysis of the shifts in the political opportunity structure for any given social movement reveals a multi-faceted and changing relationship between that movement and the state. Openings in the state may facilitate social movement activity and expansion; likewise, pressure on the state from social movements can give rise to further openness, or to crackdowns and state retrenchment. Instability in elite alignments can present social movement activists with opportunities to find new allies in positions of power, although those alignments can also become too unstable, making the state almost inaccessible to social movement demands. Social movement allies in the state may appear, lending support to the movement; this support may be rewarded with popular political support for the allies in question. Close analysis of the political opportunity structure for a social movement reveals that allies may be located at different access points in the formal or institutionalized political system, and that the state is far from monolithic, its representatives far from uniform in their attitudes toward social movement activists and issues. In studying all four elements of the political opportunity structure, it becomes clear that the relationship between states and social movements is a reciprocal and dynamic one.

In this chapter, I will illustrate four areas of change in the political opportunity structure for the Russian women's movement, with respect to Russia's transition period (beginning in the late 1980s and continuing up to the present day). First, I will examine the decrease in state repression, and the shifts in the degree of openness of the institutionalized political system, with emphasis on changes in the Soviet Women's Committee (a part of the Soviet institutionalized political system directly relevant to the nascent independent women's movement). The chapter then turns to changes in women's political representation, and the appearance of allies in positions of power, as revealed by their discourse and actions. I will focus on one group of allies for the women's movement: the Women of Russia bloc, which won election to parliament in December 1993, with an amazing 8 percent of the popular vote. After considering the role of sex-based discrimination in restricting the women's movement's lobbying success, the chapter will turn to an analysis of shifts in the elite alignments that underlay the Soviet and Russian political systems, focusing on how the elimination of the Communist Party's power monopoly undermined the stability of the polity, affecting the openness and the implementation capacity of Russia's new political institutions, which, in turn affected the political opportunity structure for the women's movement.

Declining repression and increasing openness in the institutionalized political system: glasnost and perestroika

Changes in the political opportunity structure made possible the public emergence and spread of women's groups in the late 1980s and early 1990s. With the advent of glasnost and perestroika, the repressive character of the Soviet state declined substantially. No longer were independent women's organizations persecuted as the *Almanac* group had been.

Until the late 1980s, there was only one women's organization legally operating in the USSR: the Communist Party-run Soviet Women's Committee. But by the early 1990s, there were hundreds of women's organizations functioning in Russia, ranging from politically innocuous women's charity groups to advocacy groups demanding equal treatment of women in politics and in the labor force, and overtly lesbian groups organizing for rights and visibility.

As evidenced by the broad spectrum of women's groups emerging at that time, there was and remained no agreement as to what constituted the set of "women's" most pressing issues. These ranged from consciousness raising, to women's participation in political decision-making, to improving women's economic status, and ensuring state financial support for families and children. Women's interests and priorities vary considerably in Russia, as in any other country, depending on women's financial well-being, age, and a host of other factors. All of these 'women's' issues, however, from raising women's status in the defense industry to the importance of reviewing Russian legislation for its potential impact on women, broke into the public realm during the early 1990s.[4]

Perestroika, in addition to expanding the limits of the permissible, also initiated explicit legal changes in the political system that further made possible the blossoming of women's groups. It became feasible to register social organizations and thus to acquire organizational bank accounts. Glasnost also provided an opportunity to alter the 'universe of political discourse' (Jenson 1987), to put women's issues on the agenda in a more public and contested way. Soviet women took advantage of this in March 1991, at the First Independent Women's Forum, the first nationwide conference of women's groups autonomous of the state. There, for the first time, the issue of violence against women was raised on a national scale, and the fact that women were being left out of the so-called democratization process was emphasized ("Itogovyi otchet . . ." 1991). In order to understand how these changes developed, we must take a short side trip into the history of the Soviet women's movement's origins.

Expanding opportunities and the formation of the first women's movement groups: society organizing itself

The rapidly changing political opportunities for feminist organizing in the USSR's final years can be illustrated by tracing some of the original connections between the women who later formed the first women's organizations independent of the Soviet state.

In the mid-1980s, the discussion of women's issues began in earnest, amidst changes in the institutionalized political system. Seminars on women's issues were initiated by state and Communist Party-related organizations. These events provided an accidental forum in which feminist academics, previously isolated from each other, became acquainted. Said Olga Voronina (interview, April 27, 1995):

> We met at a seminar that was conducted in the Academy of Social Sciences under the Central Committee of the CPSU, about the status of women. The seminar was very boring – those ladies who'd talked all their lives about the Soviet experience in solving the woman question. But each of us took part in the discussion, and we noticed each other. We worked in different places. Natalia [Zakharova] was working for Natalia Rimashevskaia, Valya [Konstantinova] was at that Academy

of Social Sciences, and I worked at the Institute of Philosophy. It was fall 1987.

From such chance meetings among the like-minded sprung Russia's first feminist organizations. Voronina, Konstantinova and Zakharova encountered each other repeatedly at seminars, and then began to meet as a group in their free time, to discuss feminism and ways to counter the reassertion of patriarchal stereotypes, in particular the "return women to the home" campaign that was spreading in late-1980s Russia. In April 1988, Zakharova brought along a new co-worker, Anastasia Posadskaia, who shared the group's passion for feminism. In early 1989, Posadskaia formulated a declaration which became the foundation for their tiny new organization: LOTOS – the League for Emancipation from Societal Stereotypes (*Moskovskii tsentr* . . . 1995: 28–35). Among other things, the "memorandum" called for enriching perestroika with an egalitarian ideology, undoing the sex-based stereotypes that pervaded the political and economic spheres and creating a new ethos whereby women would play a worthy role in the workforce and men would enjoy a worthy role within the family (Memorandum LOTOSA 1989). LOTOS members continued to speak out at academic events, where their critical remarks on women's status in the Soviet Union met with disapprobation:

> We were taken for radicals. And in several seminars, they already knew us and wouldn't let us speak, for instance, in the Academy of Social Sciences. They would invite us because of our status as academics, because we were published, and well-known, but when we started saying things they didn't want to hear, they'd just interrupt us and not allow us to have the floor.
>
> (Olga Voronina, interview, April 27, 1995)

In 1989, the Soviet Congress of People's Deputies approved the idea of preparing a state program on improving women's status and protecting the family, maternity, and childhood. Natalia Rimashevskaia, director of the Institute of Socio-economic Population Problems within the Russian Academy of Sciences, was given the task of collecting a group of researchers and formulating a position paper (*konseptsiia*) on the subject (Elena Kochkina, interview, July 22, 1995). Under Rimashevskaia's direction, several of LOTOS's members took part in the project. The document focused on creating a new, more egalitarian policy, which considered emancipation a "bilateral" issue: freeing women to take a more extensive role outside the home, and men to play a greater role within the family sphere (*Moskovskii tsentr* . . . 1995: 6). In 1990, the position paper was presented to the Soviet government, and Rimashevskaia's institute was allotted five staff positions with which to form the Soviet Union's first women's studies research laboratory: the Moscow Center for Gender Studies (MCGS), with

Posadskaia at its head and the other LOTOS members on staff (ibid.: 38).[5] A few years later, MCGS had become the hub of the emerging women's movement.

Russia's tiny feminist organizations grew and networked, coming together in March 1991 for the aforementioned First Independent Women's Forum. Among the organizers of the Forum were LOTOS, MCGS and several other feminist groups, including SAFO (the Free Association of Feminist Organizations, later the Feminist Alternative), which played a central financial and organizational role (interview, November 21, 1994). The Forum was attended by some 200 women, representing 48 women's organizations. In the words of one of its organizers, the Forum was evidence that a plethora of women's organizations and initiatives had arisen from below, rather than having been organized from above. The Forum operated under the slogan, "Democracy Minus Women Is Not Democracy," and its final document attested to the multiple forms of discrimination against Soviet women, both under state socialism and during perestroika.

Although the First Independent Women's Forum took place several years into perestroika and glasnost, it proceeded not without incident and hints of the repressive state apparatus. On the eve of the Forum, a popular newspaper published an announcement of the conference, portraying it as a meeting of "over-excited lesbians" (Azhgikhina 1993: 92).[6] When the Forum opened, uniformed police were present in the auditorium ("Itogovyi otchet . . ." 1991: 1). Participants in the Forum expressed fear, years later, recalling the event: "There were representatives of the KGB there among us, and . . . I was scared. And why not! I didn't think I'd be sent to prison, but I could have been fired" (interview, name withheld).

The First Independent Women's Forum was followed by a Second Forum, held in late 1992. The Second Forum opened under a different slogan – "From Problems To Strategy" – and had a new agenda: devising strategies for integrating women and women's issues into the economic and political systems developing in Russia and the former Soviet republics. Up to that point, women had been more or less excluded from the "democratization" process. In the words of Anastasia Posadskaia, the director of MCGS, perestroika's attempt to liberate the individual without liberating the sexes had been as unsuccessful as the earlier socialist efforts to emancipate women without emancipating the individual.[7]

As public discourse and networking opportunities at conferences and seminars expanded, a growing circle of women became increasingly aware of the nascent women's movement and active within it.

The Soviet Women's Committee

Glasnost and perestroika not only enabled new women's organizations to appear, but also helped to transform the old ones, such as the Soviet Women's Committee (SWC). The SWC, in the late 1980s, underwent an alteration that can best be understood by analyzing it as a change in the institutionalized political system of the Soviet Union.

The SWC, like all other social organizations of the Soviet era, was subordinated to the Communist Party. Its purpose was in part to convince foreign women's delegations of Soviet women's high economic and political status, and to represent the Soviet Union at international women's conferences (Waters and Posadskaya 1995: 358). SWC representatives stressed the fact that the majority of doctors, lawyers, and teachers were women, with no mention of the miserly salaries and low prestige of those professions within the Soviet economic hierarchy. This hypocrisy turned many women against the Soviet Women's Committee.

Despite its origins, the SWC became an important source of change in the political opportunity structure for Soviet feminists during the late 1980s, opening temporarily to the budding feminist movement. As Gorbachev's "new thinking" toward the West evolved, the SWC became a place for independent feminists to meet foreigners: one of the important factors in the formation of the Russian women's movement.

Opportunities for contact with foreign women through the SWC multiplied quickly at the end of the 1980s. One of LOTOS's original members described the situation:

> The SWC started holding various seminars, started inviting academic women from Russia to these seminars, and they started doing joint seminars with their foreign contacts. And they started very actively inviting us, including me, and Valya Konstantinova, and all of LOTOS. At first I didn't really understand what was going on, but almost every week, I was there, speaking at some seminar or another. And then I understood that we were "exotic beasts" for them. It was perestroika, there was pluralism: Look, we have communists, look, we have democrats, look, we have feminists! Real, live feminists! And we even let them talk!
>
> (Olga Voronina, interview, April 27, 1995)

The SWC also began to send independent Soviet feminists abroad, sometimes with unpredictable results. Valentina Konstantinova, for example, was sent to Finland in 1988 on a delegation to meet with the women's branches of thirteen Finnish political parties. Before the meeting, Konstantinova was asked what she was planning to speak about, by a woman whom she assumed to be accompanying the group as a representative of the KGB:

> Well, when I said what I was planning to talk about . . . you can imagine. . . . it was 1988! I was going to talk about discrimination in all spheres of life, about abortion, about the high maternal mortality rates, the lack of women in decision-making, and say that our women's movement was paralyzed. The woman, having listened, said to me,

"I wouldn't advise you to give that speech, because I know this country very well, and it's not accepted, in their culture, to wash your dirty laundry in public." It was a direct threat. And I, of course, spoke, I said what I'd wanted to say, but I was worried.

(Interview, July 9, 1995)

Konstantinova also ran into trouble after being sent to Czechoslovakia on a similar delegation:

Before the trip [the SWC deputy on international work] called me in and said, "Tell them we're returning to Lenin." It was the fashion then, under Gorbachev, that we were returning to Lenin. I gave her such a look . . . She understood that I physically just couldn't pronounce such a strange phrase . . . Instead of returning to Lenin, I gave a totally feminist speech, which then sounded very revolutionary . . . And my speech created such a tumult, inasmuch as I came in the name of the Committee, but with a totally different position . . . And after that, there was rather a parting of the ways between me and the SWC.

(Interview, July 9, 1995)

The Soviet political opportunity structure for the women's movement had changed, at least for a while, as the institutionalized political system designated to deal with women's issues opened up to independent voices.

Although there was later a closure again on the part of the SWC, as Konstantinova noted, that organization indirectly helped to alter another aspect of the political opportunity structure, namely, the availability of political allies. When the Soviet state collapsed in 1991, the SWC collapsed along with it, leaving its successor organization, the Union of Russia's Women (URW), to inherit its legacy and property. In 1993, the URW served as a founder of the parliamentary bloc Women of Russia (WOR), a potential ally of the women's movement within the Russian state.

Allies and access points for the Russian women's movement

The emergence of elite allies is often a critical component of the political opportunity structure for a social movement. Allies can provide institutional support, an influential channel into the corridors of power, and a public voicing of movement issues. This section examines the various allies and access points available to the women's movement in Russia, and the shifting political opportunities created by the absence and presence of such allies in power, tracing the fluctuations in women's political representation, focusing on the Women of Russia political bloc. I then turn to a brief consideration of other potential allies in the executive branch, as well as exploring the position and power of political opponents, and their influence on the Russian women's movement's political opportunities.

Women's political representation

> Where there's power, there are no women, and where there are women,
> there's no power.
>
> (Russian adage)

The past several years have brought considerable fluctuations in the levels of
women's representation in national politics, particularly in the legislative
branch (the paucity of women in Russia's executive branch remains relatively
constant).

Women regularly attained one-third of the seats in the Supreme Soviets of
pre-Gorbachev days, though the women chosen tended to represent the
"masses" of workers and peasants, rather than being powerful political individuals in their own right (while the male representatives were party leaders,
cabinet ministers, renowned academic leaders and so forth) (Novikova 1994:
17). Moreover, real decision-making power had never been vested in the
Supreme Soviet but, rather, in the Central Committee of the Communist
Party of the Soviet Union, where less than 5 percent of the deputies were
women.

The elimination of the Communist Party's power monopoly, and the introduction of increasingly free elections, altered the political opportunity structure for women's movement and other social activists. In 1989, semi-free
elections to the Soviet Congress of People's Deputies (CPD) were held,
with a significant number of seats reserved for the Communist Party, trade
unions, and other official organizations. These included the Soviet Women's
Committee (SWC), at the time still under the aegis of the Party. Women won
15.7 percent of the seats, largely due to the seventy-five seats reserved for the
SWC. In 1990, when quotas for seats were lifted, the proportion of female
deputies elected to the Russian Federation CPD dropped to only 5.4 percent.
The declining representation of women in parliaments elected in the final
years of the Soviet state further decreased women's access to positions of
political power.

After the collapse of the USSR in December 1991, and the later destruction
of Russia's own parliament at Yeltsin's order (in October 1993), free elections to the new Federal Assembly were held in Russia in December 1993.
Women won nine of the seats in the legislature's upper house – the Federation
Council – and sixty in the lower house, called the Duma. Women's presence
in the Federal Assembly thus reached a total of 11.4 percent, more than dou-
bling the percentage of women that were in the Russian CPD (Novikova
1994: 17). Approximately one-third of women's seats in the Duma were
won by the bloc Women of Russia (WOR), which organized very quickly
in the two months preceding the elections. The rest of the women's seats
were won from a few other parties and from single-mandate districts. To
the extent that the 1993 elections increased women's political representation
in parliament, and thereby potentially improved the political opportunity
structure for women, it was due to the success of WOR.

That success was ephemeral. In the elections of December 1995, WOR failed to clear the 5 percent barrier required for representation in parliament. The number of women in the Duma had dropped to forty-six – only 10 percent. Meanwhile, the Federation Council claimed only one female representative. The opening in the political opportunity structure (as reflected by legislative representation) was closing anew.

Between 1989 and 1995, the emergence of WOR constituted perhaps the best chance for the women's movement to gain a political ally in the legislative branch of government. It is to the experience of this unusually successful women's party that we now turn.

Women of Russia

> Better a woman wielding a rolling pin, than a man with a machine gun.
> (Statement made by a male supporter of WOR, as reported by
> Elvira Novikova, interview, February 17, 1995)

Evidence at the outset of the 1993 campaign suggested that WOR was merely a reincarnation of the Soviet-era SWC, which, upon the Soviet state's collapse, had become the Union of Russia's Women (URW), chaired by the same woman who co-led WOR, Alevtina Fedulova. Indeed, representatives of the independent women's movement were highly suspicious of WOR, both during their election campaign and afterwards. Activists portrayed WOR's deputies as old-style Soviet bureaucrats. Many pointed to Fedulova's previous twenty-year long chairpersonship of the Young Pioneers organization and her leadership work with the Soviet Peace Committee (like the SWC, an organization created and controlled by the CPSU), before joining the top ranks of the URW in 1992. Indeed, when invited to join forces with the WOR, one major network of women's organizations, the Independent Women's Forum (IWF) let the offer slide:

> Lakhova asked the IWF to join WOR for the election campaign. We just didn't answer their request. The IWF isn't a political organization, and we didn't really want to unite with them.
> (Elena Kochkina, interview, July 22, 1995)

Allies may be revealed through their actions and through their discourse. A detailed look at the evolution of the WOR bloc during its two years in office may enable us to develop a more objective assessment of WOR's value to the women's movement in Russia as an ally. Let us examine discourse first.

Much of the feminist organizations' suspicion of WOR was based on its campaign rhetoric. Indeed, some of WOR's election campaign materials failed to stress women's rights specifically, focusing more overtly on the restoration of social welfare benefits (education, healthcare, childcare), and stressing human rights, a stable society, and peaceful solutions to conflict. Moreover, the word 'women' did not appear on a 1993 leaflet listing the ten reasons to vote for WOR (Women of Russia 1993). On the other hand, WOR candidates did talk with the press about women's disproportionate unemployment and about women's low levels of political representation.

While in office, WOR adopted more overtly feminist overtones. For example, the WOR bloc unanimously adopted a political declaration of equal rights and opportunities, calling for the legislative implementation of the Russian Constitution's clause on the subject, and for anti-discrimination legislation guaranteeing equal rights in the labor sphere, in line with the International Labor Organization's Convention 156 (plus the ratification of that document by Russia).[8] By 1995, WOR deputies' discourse had taken an even more radical turn. At a conference in June, Ekaterina Lakhova (head of the WOR faction) condemned the absence of women from high political positions, and argued that the women's movement and the mass media should act to alter societal consciousness about women's proper social roles, and to undo the "patriarchal-conservative stereotypical attitudes towards women" ("Second All-Russian Women's Conference report" 1995: 7). A campaign booklet about WOR declared: "It is evident that women, who the voters increasingly trust, are consciously kept out of power by male administrators" (Zhenshchiny Rossii, 1995: 15). And WOR's 1995 campaign literature mentioned overtly the bloc's support for "equal rights and freedoms, and equal opportunities to carry them out, for women and men," a change from the 1993 flyer that had provided ten reasons to vote for WOR ("Zhenshchiny Rossii za Vera v cheloveka . . ." 1995).[9]

WOR's overt identification with feminism was more hesitant. In an informational campaign brochure on WOR, the answer to the question, "How does WOR relate to radical western feminists?" was: "Radical feminists are . . . warriors against the male principle (*nachalo*), but Women of Russia is intent on collaborating with men, in the name of society's well-being. We stand for a policy of equal rights and opportunities for women and men" (Zhenshchiny Rossii 1995: 2). This question and answer was given a prominent position on page 2 of the brochure, suggesting that WOR believed it important to distance itself from feminism – specifically, the "radical western" variety. Yet in an interview in mid-1995, WOR deputy Galina Klimantova, chair of the Duma's Committee on Women, Family and Youth Affairs, reluctantly admitted to being a feminist:

A: Well, to put it briefly, I think that feminism is a movement of women . . . for upholding their rights, for equal rights with men. Not a "fight," as it is often phrased . . . it's an absolutely insane idea, to fight against men. But to be alongside them, to attain equal partnership, that is how I see the feminist movement.

Q: Do you consider yourself a feminist?

A: [*Sighs*] It's hard to say if I am a feminist. But that I love to work with women, and occupy myself with it professionally, yes, from that point of view, I'm probably a feminist. (Interview, May 15, 1995)

Aside from WOR's unenthusiastic adoption of an overtly "feminist" identity, if we compare their above-noted rhetoric in office with the positions taken by the independent feminists of LOTOS and MCGS, it seems clear that the rhetoric of independent women activists and WOR deputies drew closer over time.

Rhetoric, however, is insufficient as a measure of political alliance. What concrete steps or actions did the WOR take in office that could be regarded as support for the Russian women's movement?

Among WOR's most significant accomplishments was the formation of the Duma's Committee on Women, Family, and Youth Affairs. It is likely that the committee would not have been formed if not for WOR's insistence (Lakhova 1994: 6–7). This committee made a point of meeting with representatives of the independent women's movement, and inviting activists to parliamentary hearings on issues that concerned women. In fact, by June 1995, Klimantova had made an agreement with a network of women's movement organizations to meet with her and other WOR deputies on a monthly basis, to exchange ideas and hear proposals from these groups, thereby establishing a channel between the faction most likely to hear women's issues raised and the organizations that were articulate and driven enough to raise them in the public sphere. It seemed that the groundwork had been laid for a real alliance. If the WOR had remained in office, it is likely that the independent women's movement might have enjoyed greater influence in the Duma over time, through acting directly on the WOR and continuing to influence its deputies in a more feminist direction.

In addition to establishing the Duma's Committee on Women, Family, and Youth Affairs, while in office WOR was able to lobby women's movement causes with the executive branch, maintaining a close relationship with the Ministry of Social Protection's Department on the family, women, and children (Lakhova 1994: 6–7). And Lakhova, even after election to the Duma, remained chair of a Presidential Commission on Women, Family, and Demography. WOR also acted as a conduit between the women's movement and state representatives, by sponsoring several large women's congresses while in office, providing women's movement activists with opportunities to meet and pressure deputies as well as government officials.

WOR also influenced several pieces of legislation that had an impact on women. The bloc's deputies initiated and drafted bills revising the Family and Marriage Code (to alter alimony regulations to reflect the new economic conditions); and on benefits to families (such that welfare benefits would accrue to the family, and its members would all have equal opportunities to fulfill family obligations), among others. WOR deputies amended the budget to protect children's programs, an issue very important to the prag-matic wing of the women's movement.[10] WOR also lent significant support to the creation of a draft bill "On ending violence in the family," an issue taken very seriously by a number of women's movement organizations and activists. The Committee formed a working group, headed by Galina Sillaste, a researcher and activist, to draft the bill. Meanwhile, WOR deputies gave interviews to popular newspapers about violence against women, even pro-viding shocking statistics to support the need for a special law on family vio-lence. According to an interview with Klimantova, in Russia over the course of 1994, 14,500 women had been murdered by their husbands (Drugoveiko 1995).

The WOR faction unquestionably included a number of individual women's movement allies – women who were active members of Russia's independent women's organizations, as well as being WOR deputies. These included several original members of the Moscow-based Women's League and of Dzhenklub, a Moscow professional women's organization (Nina Yakovchuk, interview, May 5, 1995). Furthermore, one of the co-founders of the Moscow Club F-1 (standing for "First Feminist") bragged with good reason that a number of Duma deputies got their consciousness raised originally at the club's monthly meetings, which began in September 1992 (interview, November 15, 1994).

Although alliances can be measured objectively by analyzing the concrete actions of the parties involved in any given alliance, at base alliance is a sub-jective concept, founded on the interpretations of those actions as well as on mutual trust. The alliance between WOR and women's movement activists should thus be measured by activists' feelings toward WOR, in addition to WOR's discourse and actions in office. Sentiments toward WOR in the acti-vist community were mixed. Some groups, such as the Feminist Alternative, lauded WOR's work in establishing a precedent in court against job advertisements that discriminated on the basis of sex.[11] Others supported the WOR's efforts to pass the law on violence against women. Activists from pragmatically oriented groups supported WOR's legislative efforts on behalf of children, especially their program 'Children of Russia' (Nina Tiuliu-lina, interview, May 25, 1995).

Still, many activist women retained a negative attitude toward the WOR. Said one feminist researcher at MCGS:

> The list of bills that they made in 1994, and the list of bills that they adopted, or worked on, is not critical, from the viewpoint of women's interests. Furthermore, they haven't done anything in relation to the Labor Code. And they totally missed the law about social insurance and the amendments made by the Ministry of Health, and now we have to pay for abortions!
>
> (Elena Kochkina, interview, July 22, 1995)

The alliance between WOR and the independent women's movement, shaky at best, was short lived. In the 1995 elections, only three of WOR's deputies (including Lakhova) re-entered the Duma – from single-mandate districts.

Without the WOR, the independent women's movement may have lost ground in the Duma, especially regarding support from the Committee on Women, Family, and Youth Affairs, now led by a Communist Party deputy who seems less amenable to the issues raised by women activists, such as violence against women (Martina Vandenberg, personal communication, June 5, 1996). On the other hand, the Duma's Committee on Labor and Social Policy may be the new site of alliance for the movement; the Committee's deputy chair, Tatiana Iarygina, helped to organize feminist groups' participation in parliamentary hearings on the Labor Code in March 1996, providing an important opportunity for activists to voice their demands for a non-discriminatory labor law.

Allies and access points in the executive branch

If WOR was the women's movement's best potential ally in the legislative branch, then the Ministry of Social Protection was the movement's main supporter in the executive branch. Until her removal in 1996, Liudmila Beslepkina, the Minister of Social Protection, served as an ally for the women's movement, at least indirectly. In her introduction to a 1994 book about integrating women into the process of societal development, Beslepkina referred to growing discrimination against women, and overtly opposed the increasingly popular idea, propagated especially in the mass media, of "returning to the patriarchal past" and relegating women to the kitchen (Beslepkina 1994: 4, 6).

Beslepkina's feminist positions were in marked contrast to the attitudes exhibited by representatives of the Ministry of Labor. A brief analysis of speeches made by Beslepkina and Deputy Labor Minister Valerii Ianvarev at a women's conference in September 1994 illustrates the contrast.

Upon taking the floor, Ianvarev noted that it was the first time he'd been "surrounded by so many beautiful women at once." He also invoked a bureaucratic style reminiscent of the Soviet era, pointing out that the "correlation of labor function and maternity function is determined by the stage of development through which society is passing." Ianvarev's speech was almost schizophrenic: he affirmed that discrimination was extant and that two salaries were necessary for families to maintain the minimum standard of living, but argued simultaneously that women did not mind losing their jobs. In support of his argument, Ianvarev suggested that according to a survey of unemployed women, two-thirds did not think that they would find new jobs, but that it was not a catastrophe, rather, a positive phenomenon. This statement gave rise to a noisy stir in the auditorium, provoking the Deputy Minister to apologize, saying: "I didn't mean to offend the women" (author's notes).

Beslepkina spoke next, on the welfare of women and families during the transition period, making sure to counter Ianvarev's remarks. Unemployment, said Beslepkina, was hard for women, both psychologically and financially. She stressed the Russian economy's need for women's labor, and expressed her opposition to the idea that women should be exclusively the keepers of the domestic hearth. "Women don't want to exit the national economy: it's illiterate and tactless to say so," she lectured.

The Labor Ministry had, at that time, proposed a new labor code to replace the Soviet-era document. The new code was reviled by women's movement organizations for its discriminatory articles.[12] Article 117, for example, stated that fathers could receive certain benefits granted to mothers automatically (limitations on night work, work on holidays, and business trips, for example), only if they were raising a child without a mother. Article 105.3 referred to a list of occupations forbidden to women (but not to men). Also, a series of articles granted maternity benefits and leaves rather than parental benefits and leaves (thus making women's labor less desirable to employers, who would only have to grant the benefits to female workers). These articles were seen as reinforcing extant sex-roles and detrimental to women's labor market competitiveness.

The dynamic between Beslepkina and Ianvarev at the September 1994 conference reveals an interdepartmental struggle over women's treatment in Russian society, with the Ministry of Social Protection speaking out for equal treatment and the Labor Ministry favoring women's exit from the economy. The difference in these Ministries' attitudes on the subject may derive from their respective leaders. Gennadii Melikian, at that time the Minister of Labor, had set the tone for the Ministry's position on women when, in 1993, he made a public statement questioning the value of creating jobs for women as long as men remained unemployed (Posadskaia 1993: 9). In the mid-1990s, the Ministry of Social Protection was thus clearly far more of a mind with the women's movement than was the Ministry of Labor, and therefore provided a better entrance point to policy-making structures than the latter. As demonstrated by this analysis of allies within the executive branch, the Russian state is neither monolithic nor thoroughly closed to appeals by women's movement activists.

The Ministry of Social Protection, in fact, had well-established contacts with women's movement organizations, particularly through the Department on Family, Women, and Children's Issues, formed in January 1992, which was charged with co-ordinating a unified state policy on women, and involving NGOs in the policy implementation process (Samarina 1995: 2; Olga Samarina, interview, March 24, 1995). The main source of contact between the Ministry of Social Protection and the independent women's movement, however, was the National Council on Preparation for the 1995 UN Worldwide Conference on Women. The National Council, established in 1993, provided the first regular opportunity for contact between women's organizations and the state structures (Liborakina 1995: 5). According to Olga Samarina, head of the Department on Family, Women, and Children's Issues, dozens of women's NGOs were invited to National Council meetings, where they could "they take a real part in developing policy" (Olga Samarina, interview, March 24, 1995).

Another access point for the women's movement was the Presidential Commission on Women, Families, and Demography, established in 1992 and headed by Ekaterina Lakhova (adviser to Yeltsin on these issues for two years prior to the Commission's establishment and, later, head of the WOR faction). The Commission was charged with developing position papers and programs about women's and family issues, distributing information to branches of the Russian federal and local governments, and executing presidential decrees on the subjects falling under its purview. It addressed issues such as family planning, abortion (supporting legal, safe, and free abortion), women's unemployment, and domestic violence (Azhgikhina 1995: 10–12). Anastasia Posadskaia, feminist researcher and activist at MCGS, was a member of the Commission.

Yeltsin himself may be viewed as somewhat of an ally of the women's movement, based on his support for the Commission and on a decree he issued in March 1993. The decree called for the creation of a unified state policy on improving women's status, in order to provide for "identical conditions for actual equality for women and men, in the political, social, economic and cultural life of the country, and freely chosen self-realization for women in all spheres of activity" (Ukaz Prezidenta Rossiiskoi Federatsii 1993), in line with the UN Convention on Eliminating All Forms of Discrimination Against Women (CEDAW). According to activist Elena Kochkina, the decree itself "was more or less written" by two researchers at the Moscow Center for Gender Studies, at Lakhova's behest (interview, July 22, 1995). Despite the fact that it was never implemented, Kochkina felt that the decree had a substantial impact:

> Ideologically, it was very important, because that was the first time that a special policy, at the level of state policy, had been formulated, during the transition period in Russia, from the perspective of equal opportunity policy.
>
> (Interview, July 22, 1995)

The presence of new allies in power positions (whether in government ministries, parliament, or consultative bodies) amounts to a change in the political opportunity structure for the Russian women's movement.

Sex-based discrimination in the legislative and executive branches of the Russian government

The mere representation of women in legislative or executive political bodies provides no guarantee that they will attempt to create policies favored by the women's movement. But even if the intention is there, as one could certainly argue was the case at the national level with Women of Russia, women in politics encounter a major obstacle that men in the political arena do not confront: namely, discrimination, which must be considered when examining the political opportunity structure for women's movements.

Discriminatory and patronizing attitudes toward female deputies have been reported from both the Russian Federation's defunct Supreme Soviet, as well as the Duma. In an interview, Alevtina Fedulova, chair of the Union of Russia's Women and leading member of WOR, claimed that the WOR deputies to the Duma "feel comfortable, so far," although she added: "[A]s before, people can still be heard saying, 'Give the girl the floor!'" ("Mnenia zhenshchin-politikov . . ." 1994).

According to eyewitnesses, attitudes toward women in the parliament have remained somewhat consistent since the times of Russia's Supreme Soviet. Asked in 1991 whether it was hard for women deputies to operate there, Lakhova acknowledged that women deputies felt a lack of respect:

> Men see us as women, but not as deputies. You're explaining something to him about infant mortality, and he says that it doesn't become you to talk about such serious things; that you have to be a woman.
>
> ("Nashe interv'iu . . ." 1991)

Women activists have also met with disrespect when addressing state officials. In one particularly memorable instance, movement activist Tatiana Konysheva attempted to find out how familiar the legal institutions in Moscow were with the UN Convention on Eliminating All Forms of Discrimination Against Women (CEDAW). At the People's Court, Konysheva spoke to a judge who dismissed the Convention as being far removed from anyone's interests. When Konysheva asked him about the available statistics on violence against women (one of the points in the Convention), his response was much more unexpected: "How many men have you had over the course of your life?" ("Opyt vzaimodeistviia . . ." 1995: 4–5).

For political opportunities to expand and for allies or women's movement activists to make headway with the state, a certain degree of respect is required. It is far from clear that such respect has been achieved. Sex-based discrimination creates barriers to the expansion of the political opportunity structure for a women's movement, in much the same way that racism restricts the political opportunities of civil rights activists, even if political allies and access points are available.

Instability of elite alignments undergirding the polity

Political instability, in particular, the collapse of the Soviet state and the weakness of the new Russian state, further complicates the political opportunity structure for the women's movement. The rapid succession of political-institutional changes and the state's resulting limited capacity for policy implementation restrict the movement's developmental opportunities.

The rapidly changing political opportunity structure had a retarding effect on women's movement groups' successes. The Moscow-based group Women and Conversion (supporting unemployed women in the defense industry), for example, was forced to start afresh making contacts in the Duma after the destruction of the Supreme Soviet in October 1993:

> We had contacts established in the Supreme Soviet. I talked at the Higher Economics Council, twice, in 1993, in March, and in May, at the Supreme Soviet: they'd agreed to finance our project on re-educating highly qualified women to become world class level managers. Because only men were being trained in that sort of thing. The program was to begin in November. But then the October events occurred, and everything came to naught. Now, in the Duma, we have to start over from the beginning. We're only just now starting to get somewhere in the Duma. It's a hard process, trying to find an entry into the corridors of power.
>
> (Eleanora Ivanova, interview, February 6, 1995)

The extraordinary number of shifts in the political system confronting the women's movement (and other social movements) in post-Soviet Russia, including the disbanding of the USSR and the destruction of the Russian parliament in October 1993, made for a perpetual search not only for new allies, but also a constant struggle to master each new system. While gradual and even relatively sudden changes in elite alignments (such as those that occur with elections) have surely created openings for western social movements, in Russia the continuous systemic political instability during the transition period entailed far more fundamental changes than those usually categorized under the rubric of political opportunity structure in the West.[13] This instability has been deleterious, at least in the short term, to the women's movement.

Moreover, even when women's groups manage to create temporary channels of access to the state and achieve policies consistent with their goals, their efforts can be fruitless because of the Russian state's inability to implement its policies and laws – an element of political opportunity structure more relevant in emerging democracies and other newly established political regimes than in stable democracies. Although it may be perceived as willing to engage in a certain amount of political repression or violence (as in Chechnya), when it comes to running the country the Russian government is perceived as weak, in that its laws and decrees are disobeyed on a regular basis. Wages, for example, are held in arrears for months at a time, despite state declarations making such detention of salary illegal.

The weakness of the Russian state has discouraged women's movement organizations from building large constituencies in order to attract the attention of parliamentary representatives. M. Steven Fish (1995: 217) reached a similar conclusion:

> the decay of state power during the second half of the Gorbachev period, while creating some space for the emergence of independent societal power, may paradoxically have slowed the development of autonomous political organizations. A state that lacks effective administrative capacities and the authority to enforce universalization of the law – and the Russian state currently lacks both – may actually inhibit the growth and maturation of civil society.

This point may be summarized by reversing Tocqueville's inference about state–society relations in America: in the Russian case, a weak state is found together with a *weak* society, not a strong one. A state with limited capacity for policy implementation restricts the political opportunity structure for a social movement. Even if access and allies are available, legislated or decreed changes in the social distribution of justice may not come to fruition, because of the problem of state capacity.

Conclusion

From the evidence presented in this chapter, it appears that the political opportunity structure confronting the Russian women's movement during the transition period is mixed. Although the opportunity structure for the women's movement is immeasurably more favorable than it would have been in the pre-Gorbachev era, the movement is still confronted with significant obstacles in the political arena, not to mention economic obstacles, socio-cultural attitudes obstructing the transformation of consciousness, and a political history that runs counter to the creation of coalitions and various other social-movement-building techniques.

Focusing on the political opportunity structure, however, we may conclude the following. While state repression against independent social movement organizing has unquestionably declined, state capacity, too, has been eroded, leaving movements in the unenviable position of having a largely unfettered voice but little impact. In part, this is the result of Russia's executive-centered political system. Thus far, the women's movement has taken advantage of that system, using activists' ties to Lakhova, in her capacity as chair of the Presidential Commission on Women, Families and

Demography. Such a political system, however, leaves activists subject to the whims of the president, and discourages the building of a mass movement. Moreover, in today's Russia activists confront the fact that, despite Yeltsin's "strong presidency," his power of implementation is insecure and his decrees are not observed.

Analysis of the political opportunity structure for the women's movement during the transition period shows that the Russian state, whatever its implementation capacity, is far from monolithic, and that the presence of elite allies can alter a movement's opportunities considerably. The emergence of the Women of Russia (WOR) political bloc, and even the limited support from the Ministry of Social Protection and the National Council, under Beslepkina, created opportunities for activists to increase their influence on political decision-makers. The failure of WOR in the December 1995 elections and Beslepkina's removal from the Ministry in 1996, however, illustrate the fragility of political alliances. Moreover, while the instability of the Soviet political system ultimately enabled the creation of the women's movement in the late 1980s, the several upheavals in Russia's political system since 1991 have made it difficult for that movement to build consistently on its own successes in making allies within the women-friendly sectors of the state.

The increasing openness of the formal political system and the reduction in the state's monopolistic control over the public sphere, as revealed by analysis of the political opportunity structure for the Russian women's movement, illustrate the dynamic relationship between state-institutional change and social movement development and expansion. Such change was evident in the transformation of the Soviet Women's Committee, which enabled independent women's movement activists to have contact with foreign feminists, an important element in the later growth of the movement. On the other hand, the very influx of foreign financing of some movement activities and of English-language terminology in the Russian women's movement may reinforce the movement's tendency thus far to focus on well-educated women and on influencing the state, rather than on engaging in outreach to the general population.

In sum, the current political opportunity structure for Russia's women's movement has been thoroughly transformed from that in the pre-Gorbachev era Soviet Union. Perhaps the most fundamental change has been the legalization of NGOs, many of which have adopted some responsibility for defending citizens' material interests, and also defining social groups' identities – perhaps a first step in building a civil society. The actual power held by these organizations, however, is quite limited. Russia's women's movement activists today are struggling with economic and political powerlessness, as they strive to improve women's position in society and define their identities – not as the state sees fit, but as citizens, with equal rights and equal opportunities in social, economic, and political life.

Notes

1 The analysis I present is largely based on a set of interviews with Russian women activists, conducted between September 1994 and January 1996, in Moscow as well as several smaller cities. Some of the interviews were conducted anonymously. The research was conducted with the support of a grant from the Internal Research and Exchanges Board (IREX).

2 Social movement organizations' interaction with the state exhibits different dynamics at the local level, in part by virtue of the closer ties between activists and local government officials. For a discussion of political opportunity structure in two provincial Russian cities (Ivanovo and Cheboksary), see Valerie Sperling, "Engendering transition: the women's movement in contemporary Russia," unpublished dissertation, Political Science Department, University of California, Berkeley, 1997, ch. 4.

3 Representatives from nearly all of the fifty women's organizations I interviewed in Russia expressed a desire to influence state policies on their issues, though they succeeded in doing so to varying degrees. The division between social movement groups intent on retaining "autonomy" and those hoping to influence the state does not seem terribly salient in mid-1990s Russia. The issue of autonomy instead arises in relation to particular movement groups that are viewed as being constituent parts of the state bureaucracy.

4 Almost regardless of their issue focus, women's movement leaders and activists in the mid-1990s belonged overwhelmingly to the class of well-educated professionals. Approximately 40 percent of my activist sample ($N = 63$) had advanced degrees. Despite their high educational level, however, the activists did not belong, overall, to Russia's moneyed class. Indeed, the collapse of the Soviet centrally planned and state-funded economy left many of the women in this socio-economic stratum financially insecure. While women's movement activists are not among the most immiserated in Russia, they are far from membership in Russia's emergent *nouveau riche*.

5 Zakharova did not join her former colleagues, having accepted a position in Vienna.

6 The impression that lesbianism was the motif of the Dubna conference remained. Interviewed in 1995, one activist in Ivanovo (who did not attend the conference) said: "I heard opinions about it, in the newspapers. That it was a feminist gathering and sexually preoccupied" (Natalia Kovaleva, interview, April 3, 1995).

7 From the opening speech at the Second Independent Women's Forum, Dubna, Russia, November 1992 (author's notes).

8 The Declaration was distributed at the November 1994 All-Russian Women's Congress. According to a speech there by movement activist Elena Ershova, the declaration was written by feminist activist and consultant to the WOR, Svetlana Aivazova.

9 The focus, however, remained on the resurrection of a social welfare system.

10 For a list of bills initiated and drafted by WOR members and the Committee on Women, Family, and Youth Affairs, see "Otchet o zakonotvorcheskoi deiatel'nosti deputatov fraktsii politicheskogo dvizheniia 'Zhenshchiny Rossii', chlenov Komiteta po delam zhenshchin, sem'i i molodezhi."

11 The suit was successful; the advertisements in question violated the equal rights clause of the Constitution, the Russian Labor Code, and CEDAW ("My ne mozhem izmenit' proshloe . . ." (1994).

12 For a critique of the new labor code, see Marina Liborakina, "Predlozheniia k proektu trudovogo kodeksa rossiiskoi federatsii," distributed and discussed at a meeting of the Women''s Consortium in Moscow, December 5, 1994. The critique was written in the name of the Independent Women''s Forum.

13 Dieter Rucht (1996: 55) argues that, while some instability can create opportunities for social movements, the degree of instability experienced in East
Germany after the collapse of communism was such that it had the opposite
effect.

References

Azhgikhina, Nadia (1993) "Healing the Soviet legacy towards women," *Demokra-
tizatsiya* 1(3).

Azhgikhina, Nadia (1995) Interview with E. Lakhova, "Zhenshchiny dolzhny
pomoch' sebe sami," *Vy i My*, no. 11: 10–12.

Beslepkina, Liudmila (1994) "Gosudarstvennaia politika v otnoshenii zhenshchin,"
in V.B. Korniak (ed.), *Integratsiia zhenshchin v protsess obshchestvennogo razvi-
tiia*, Moscow: Luch.

Drugoveiko, Grigorii (1995) "Schast'e i neschast'e – vse v sem'e," *Moskvichka*, no.
22–3.

Fish, M. Steven (1995) *Democracy from Scratch*, Princeton, N.J.: Princeton University Press.

"Itogovyi otchet o rabote 1 Nezavisimogo Zhenskogo Foruma" (1991) Dubna –
Moskva.

Jenson, Jane (1987) "Changing discourse, changing agendas: political rights and
reproductive policies in France," in Mary Fainsod Katzenstein and Carol McClurg
Mueller (eds), *The Women''s Movements of the United States and western
Europe: Consciousness, Political Opportunity, and Public Policy*, Philadelphia:
Temple University Press.

Lakhova, Ekaterina (1994) "Ia ne prizyvaiu moskvichek vyiti s kastriuliami na
stolichnye ploshchadi," *Moskvichka*, no. 25: 6–7.

Liborakina, Marina (1995) "Obretenie sily," *Vestnik*, no. 4: 5.

McAdam, Doug (1996) "Conceptual origins, current problems, future directions,"
in Doug McAdam, John D. McCarthy and Mayer M. Zald (eds), *Comparative
Perspectives on Social Movements*, Cambridge: Cambridge University Press.

Memorandum LOTOSA/ LOTOS (1989) "Liga za osvobozhdenie ot stereotpiov."

"Mnenia zhenshchin-politikov o politicheskoi situatsii v rossii," (1994) in *Zhenskii
diskussionyi klub*, Interlegal, January.

Moskovskii tsentr gendernykh issledovanii: 1990–1995 (1995) Moscow.

"My ne mozhem iznmenit' proshloe, no my mozhem vliiat'' na svoe budushchee"
(1994) *Feminf*, no. 1.

"Nashe interv'iu" (1991) *Zhenskoe dvizhenie v SSSR*, no. 2.

Novikova, Elvira (1994) "Zhenshchiny v politicheskoi zhizni rossii," *Preobrazhenie*,
no. 2.

"Opyt vzaimodeistviia (skoree so znakom minus)" (1995) *Strategii vzaimodeistviia*,
Informatsionnyi vypusk, October.

Posadskaia, Anastasia (1993) "Demokratiia minus zhenshchina – ne demokratiia,"
Ogonek, no. 38: 9.

Rucht, Dieter (1996) "German unification, democratization, and the role of social
movements: a missed opportunity?", *Mobilization*, 1: 35–62.

Samarina, Ol''ga (1995) "O natsional''nom mekhanizme po uluchsheniu polozhe-
niia zhenshchin Rossii," *Informatsionnyi vypusk*, April.

"Second All-Russian Women's Conference report" (1995) *Moskvichka*, no. 22–3.

Ukaz Prezidenta Rossiiskoi Federatsii (1993) "O pervoocherednykh zadachakh gosudarstvennoi politiki v otnoshenii zhenshchin." (no. 337), 4 March.

Waters, Elizabeth and Posadskaya, Anastasia (1995) "Democracy without women is no democracy: women's struggles in postcommunist Russia," in Amrita Basu (ed.), *The Challenge of Local Feminisms*, Boulder, Col.: Westview Press.

Women of Russia (1993) "Pochemu ia golosuiu za politicheskoe dvizhenie 'zhenshchiny rossii'?!" Moscow: Women of Russia.

Zhenshchiny Rossii (1995) *Informatsionnyi biulleten'*, no. 5.

"Zhenshchiny Rossii za Vera v cheloveka, za Nadezhda na sem'iu, za Liubov' k rossii" (1995).

10 Gender, civil society and the state in China

Jude Howell

Introduction

The rise of the neoliberal paradigm in the 1980s and 1990s has cast doubt over the desirability and capacity of the state to resolve economic and social problems. As former military and authoritarian regimes in Latin America and Africa democratised from the mid-1970s onwards and the socialist states of the Soviet Union crumbled under the weight of popular dissent, politicians and policy-makers have increasingly placed their hopes in the potential of the market and civil society to address issues of economic growth and democratic accountability.

Despite this general context of disillusionment with the state, feminists throughout the world continue to press for a more active state role in the promotion of women's interests and in the reduction of gender inequities. At the Fourth World Conference of Women in the autumn of 1996 over 30,000 women gathered in Beijing to lobby national governments and international organisations on issues such as abortion, the environment and political participation. Whilst there are clearly expectations that national states should and can promote women's interests and rights and address issues of gender-based discrimination, there is less certainty about the most effective and appropriate institutional forms for achieving this.

It is the purpose of this chapter to explore the role of state women's organisations such as Ministry of Women's Affairs, gender units and women's commissions in addressing gender inequalities and promoting women's interests[1] and political rights. Given that the Fourth World Conference on Women was held in Beijing, it seems timely to pursue this question through the case of China. Socialist states have a relatively long history of state feminism and so provide an important pool of material for analysis. As official women's organisations in the former Soviet Union and eastern Europe have tended to meet a similar fate as their respective communist parties, the case of China, where the Communist Party continues to hold power, is of particular interest.

We thus begin by discussing the notion of state-sponsored feminism, its achievements in liberal democratic states and its particularities under state socialism. We then consider the role of the All-China Women's Federation (ACWF) in promoting women's interests after Liberation in 1949, in questioning the social and economic bases of female subordination and in bringing about change in the power relations between men and women. In the final section we consider the constraints under which the ACWF has to operate and the prospects of it becoming more effective as an agent of change in gender relations.

State feminism

The second wave of feminism, which swept across Europe and America in the late 1960s, was crucial in bringing issues such as a woman's right to choose, childcare facilities and domestic violence into the political limelight. The rise of women's centres, the spread of consciousness-raising groups and the formation of women's peace camps such as at Greenham Common pointed to the growing strength, confidence and dynamism of the movements. In the 1980s and 1990s women's groups have proliferated across Latin America, Asia and Africa, providing important points of resistance to gendered structural adjustment programmes (Daines and Seddon 1994). As women organised themselves within the space of civil society to bring about legislative and political change, the role of the state both in perpetuating women's subordination as well as in potentially challenging gender inequities has come under scrutiny by feminist scholars.

As the second wave of feminism put the spotlight on gender issues, the notion that the state should and could bring about positive change in women's social, economic and political status and undermine existing gender inequities began to gain in prominence amongst some feminists, policy-makers and politicians. State feminism became part of feminist discourse, though its meaning has been contested and variously interpreted. It is sometimes equated with femocrats, that is those women employed in government positions to promote women's policy.[2] At other times it may be used to refer to all elected female politicians, or indeed only those who profess a feminist agenda. It is also used to point to those state institutions set up specifically with the goal of furthering women's interests.[3] In this chapter state feminism refers to the activities and policies of structures within the state which are set up officially for the purpose of promoting women's interests and rights.

The United Nations Commission on the Status of Women had been calling upon governments since the 1960s to set up specialised institutions to advance the economic, social and political position of women. With the UN declaring 1975–85 a Decade of Women, pressure was put on governments to give institutional sustenance to their rhetorical pronouncements of concern for gender inequities. Since then specialised state women's agencies have proliferated throughout the world, taking a variety of institutional forms such as women's commissions, women's units, ministries of women's affairs, gender and development units and women's advisory groups.

Whilst the growth of state women's agencies marks an important step in the development of more gender-conscious policies, feminist scholars and activists have queried the extent to which the state itself is 'disinterested' and the implications thereof for pursuing feminist goals. Marxist feminists such as Barrett (1980) and McIntosh (1978) have maintained that the state organises women's economic dependency through social welfare policies, ideology and segregated labour markets so as to ensure the reproduction of the working class and ultimately the perpetuation of capital's interests. Starting from this Marxist premise, feminist theorists such as Eisenstein (1984) have argued that the state is both capitalist and patriarchal, hence the need for a simultaneous strategy on both gender and class. Far more sceptical of the potential of the state to address gender issues are feminists such as MacKinnon (1987) who view the state itself as implicated in more general processes of patriarchal domination, constructing, reflecting and perpetuating gender hierarchies and inequities.

Drawing on the works of Foucault, post-modern feminists seek to escape the pitfalls of an undifferentiated, monolithic view of the state as a structure or actor, preferring instead a conceptualisation which recognises its diversity of arenas and practices. Viewing the state as 'an important site for the construction of gendered power relations' writers such as Watson (1992: 187) foresee the possibility of effecting change upon this site.

While these various theories have come to different conclusions about the potential of the state as an agent or locus of change in the sphere of gender relations, there have been surprisingly few systematic empirical studies of the effectiveness of state women's organisations in pursuing feminist goals.[4] The most comprehensive study to date is Stetson and Mazur's (1995) comparative survey of state women's organisations in fourteen countries in Europe and America.[5] They set out to describe the diversity of state women's organisations formally charged with promoting women's rights and reducing gender inequities in advanced industrial societies, to assess the extent to which they achieve these goals and to tease out the political and social factors which are conducive to creating effective state women's agencies. With the exception of Poland they find that the gender-specialised state structures have all positively influenced the development and implementation of policies that promote women's interests and challenge gender inequalities. Amongst the thirteen successful cases there was, however, variation in terms of the degree of influence of the state women's agencies on policy formation and the access they provided to women's organisations. Whilst Australia, the Netherlands and Norway, for example, scored highly in both terms of policy influence and policy access, Ireland and Italy both fell into the category of low influence and access. They concluded that crucial conditions for the effectiveness of state women's agencies are not only the recognition of the state as a key actor in addressing issues of social inequality and justice but also the existence of a vibrant sphere of autonomous, radical and reformist women's organisations. This latter condition is particularly relevant when we consider the case of official women's organisations under state socialism.

Compared with liberal democratic states the history of sustained state women's organisations has proved to be much longer in socialist regimes such as the former Soviet Union, Cuba and China. For ideological and political reasons socialist states have placed issues of women's oppression and exploitation firmly on the official agenda. Child marriage, polygamy, domestic violence, divorce, participation in the waged economy have all been common themes during the liberation struggles in Nicaragua, Mozambique, China and Vietnam. Once in power, Marxist–Leninist parties[6] have acted swiftly to eradicate some of the worst forms of exploitation and to create the conditions for female employment through the provision of state-subsidised childcare facilities and educational opportunities (Molyneux 1981: 8–10). By providing political and financial support to the official women's organisations they laid the institutional foundations for the promotion of gender-specific policies.

Compared with the pre-revolutionary situation and many capitalist states at a similar level of economic development, socialist states have made considerable headway in increasing women's employment, in passing legislation defining women's rights and prohibiting oppressive practices, in improving female access to education and enhancing women's participation in the political arena (ibid.: 17–35). However, the tendency to focus on socialising some domestic responsibilities without simultaneously challenging the gendered division of labour within the household has meant that waged employment for women has resulted in a double burden. Although women in post-revolutionary states have been drawn into waged employment, their predominance in sectors such as light industry, textiles, health and education, which are considered less central to the economy and where wages are lower, points to a continuing gendered pattern of employment.

There are two key interrelated factors which have inhibited the emergence of more effective official women's organisations under state socialism and so hastened their demise with the collapse of these regimes. These are, first, the continuing pressure to subordinate gender interests to the policy priorities of Marxist–Leninist parties; and second, the absence of a sphere of radical and reformist women's organisations which are autonomous of the ruling parties.

The tendency to give priority to the party's goals was already evident during the liberation struggles in Mozambique, China, Nicaragua and Vietnam, when issues such as polygamy, divorce and childcare responsibilities were only partially taken up. As official theory on the woman's question attributed gender oppression to exploitative class relations, it followed that women's emancipation hinged ultimately on the overthrow of capitalism.

The primacy of party priorities continued in the post-revolutionary situation. Like other mass organisations, the official women's organisations of state socialism served to communicate and carry out party directives. Although they clearly had a mandate to represent women's interests, they did not have the ideological or political room for manoeuvre to challenge the orthodox exposition of women's oppression.

While radical women's organisations and reformist women's groups working within political parties and unions have been a vital ingredient in the success of state women's organisations in liberal democratic states, their virtual absence in socialist states has inhibited any theoretical or ideological challenge to official theory or practice with regard to gender issues and indeed has precipitated the downfall of the official women's organisations following the collapse of state socialism. Once Marxist–Leninist revolutionary parties came to power, they sought to consolidate their hold over society by prohibiting organisations deemed to be counterrevolutionary and by channelling social demands through a limited number of organisations. Like other mass organisations, the official women's federations served primarily as transmission belts between their members and the party, reflecting the interests of women upwards and relaying party policy downwards. There was little political space within which women could imagine organising themselves autonomously. Nevertheless, it should be noted that a tiny minority of women in a few states attempted to organise independently around gender concerns. Molyneux (1990) refers to the emergence of feminist opposition in eastern Europe from the mid-1970s onwards. In 1979 a group of writers in Leningrad managed to publish *The Alamanac: Women and Russia*, whilst in the 1980s a loyal women's opposition emerged in Nicaragua.

Given their close alliance to the ruling Marxist–Leninist parties it is not surprising that the official women's organisations suffered a similar downfall during the tumultuous years of the late 1980s. Had there been a layer of more autonomous women's groups with which they co-operated, strategised and reflected, it is possible that they might have survived into post-socialism. More tragically for women in the former socialist states, many of the gains under the old political regime have been rapidly removed. The apparently democratic trade union leader, Lech Walesa, played a key role in passing legislation severely restricting abortion.[7] Across eastern Europe women became the first to lose their jobs as state enterprises collapsed dominoe-like and kindergartens closed (Bridger *et al.* 1996; Shapiro 1992; Koval 1995; Molyneux 1994). Although prostitution continued to exist on a very small scale under the old regimes, since 1989 it has taken on previously unimaginable proportions, with networks extending way beyond east European borders (Waters 1992). The extremity of the backlash in former socialist states not only underlined the weak social basis and fragility of the official women's organisations but also brought home with a vengeance the regrettable costs of constricting the sphere of civil society and limiting the emergence of more autonomous feminist and women's groups. Whilst the need to challenge the gendered practices in post-socialism is more urgent than ever, for official women's organisations in surviving regimes such as China and Vietnam the question is rather how to avoid such a tragic fate. The attempts of the All-China Women's Federation (ACWF) to adapt to a rapidly changing socio-economic context are thus of particular interest.

The case of the All-China Women's Federation

The establishment of the All-China Women's Federation (ACWF) after Liberation in 1949 marked an ongoing commitment on the part of the Chinese Communist Party (CCP) to the emancipation of women. In the communist-held areas of China during the 1930s and 1940s the CCP had begun to acquire experience of governing and were already implementing policies designed to address gender inequities, such as the prohibition of child marriage, bigamy and wife-beating, and legislation granting women equal rights to citizenship and to land (Davin 1976; Andors 1983; Johnson 1983). By setting up a nation-wide organisation the CCP sought not only to promote gender-specific policies but also to create an institutional channel for mobilising women economically, politically and ideologically.

From its inception the ACWF had the dual and often contradictory task of promoting the interests of both women and the CCP. Like other mass organisations such as the All-China Federation of Trade Unions and the Communist Youth League, the ACWF was to serve as a transmission belt, passing party policy downwards to its constituency of women and relaying their opinions and demands upwards according to the principle of democratic centralism. Faced with this dualism the ACWF was placed at times in an awkward dilemma as to whether to prioritise the interests of its members or those of the party. In practice the goals of national economic development tended to win the day.

With its staff appointed and paid for by the state and its top-down, Leninist style of operating, the ACWF resembles other official organs in China. A woman cadre assigned after high school or university graduation to work in the ACWF would have a job for life and could not be assumed necessarily to have any strong personal commitment to gender issues, at least initially. Like other mass organisations the ACWF disposed of a network of local organisations down to village level such that its institutional reach would be the envy of many a state women's organisation in capitalist economies. Whilst ACWF cadres at city level and above are paid, below that positions are only part-time and either unpaid or poorly renumerated.

The close allegiance of the ACWF to the party has meant that its fate has likewise been governed at times by the vicissitudes of internal party politics. During the stormy days of the Cultural Revolution between 1966 and 1976, when class politics raged and raising gender issues was treated as equivalent to counterrevolution and national betrayal, the ACWF went out of action, reflecting its relative weakness as an organisation and its dependence upon the party (Johnson 1983: 181). It was only in the late 1970s when the reformers consolidated their power that it was able to resume its activities.[8] By 1994 the ACWF laid claim to 68,355 branches, 30 at provincial level, 370 at city level, 2,810 at county level and 65,145 at township level, and employed 80,000–90,000 cadres throughout China (Li 1992). Since Liberation it has enjoyed a monopoly of representation which only began to be challenged in the late 1980s with the rise of semi-autonomous women's organisations and women's studies centres.

Sponsoring feminism?

To what extent then has the ACWF promoted women's rights and interests and challenged gender inequities? We will explore the record of the ACWF with regard to five areas: namely, employment, legislation, family, ideology and education, and political participation.[9] Given that the Cultural Revolution caused a distinct rupture in the activities of the ACWF and that the economic rationale of the reform period differs markedly from that of the pre-1978 era, the achievements will be discussed in terms of pre- and post-reform.

Employment

In line with other socialist states, the CCP considered the participation of women in the waged economy a crucial condition for the enhancement of women's economic, political and social status. After Liberation women in rural and urban areas were strongly encouraged to enter the sphere of production. The processes of collectivisation and communisation not only brought rural women out of the household and into the private sphere, thus increasing their visibility, but also gave them a new form of economic independence, which could improve their economic and social standing within the household. Within a decade after Liberation nearly all women were in waged employment, either full-time or part-time, and had begun to enter predominantly male occupations (Croll 1983).

Whilst the high female participation rates seemed to suggest a new-found equality between men and women, the gendered pattern of employment revealed that bringing women into the workforce was not a sufficient condition for their emancipation. In urban areas women tended to be employed in the least-skilled and lowest-paid jobs, forming the bulk of the workforce in the co-operative rather than the more prestigious state sector (Croll 1983: 6). Although women could be found on the production front of heavy industries such as steel and iron, they were mainly located in light industrial sectors such as textiles and food processing, domains of production which marked an extension of similar activities within the household. In the rural areas they tended to be employed in the least-skilled and mechanised jobs and, despite the rhetoric of equality of pay, were often paid less than their male counterparts, even for the same work (Croll 1983: 6; Andors 1981).

This gendered pattern of employment has not only continued into the post-reform period but also taken on new forms. As state-owned enterprises have struggled to remain competitive and managers have become increasingly conscious of the need to trim down the size of their workforces, women have been the first to lose their jobs. For those in their fifties, ageist attitudes have weakened their chances of re-employment and forced many into premature retirement. Conscious of the costs of providing maternity leave and breast-feeding breaks, state enterprise managers as well as government departments have become increasingly reluctant to employ new female entrants.[10] Whilst the Special Economic Zones on the south-eastern coast of China have provided new employment opportunities, particularly for young rural women, reports of sexual harassment, failure to meet maternity leave obligations and excessive overtime point to new discriminatory practices (Woo 1994). With women concentrated in light industrial sectors such as electronics and textiles and engaged in low-skilled, repetitive assembly work, the arrival of foreign investment has served to consolidate existing sexual divisions of labour.

In response to the new forms of discrimination in the reform period the ACWF has pushed for legislation to protect the interests of women, conducted investigations and research into discriminatory employment practices, and promoted the idea of an employers' fund for childbearing women. With party policy no longer guaranteeing full employment and enterprise managers assuming greater powers, the ACWF has struggled to keep issues of gender discrimination on the agenda, particularly as the trade unions regard urban factories as their terrain (Howell 1996: 134).

Legislation

As in other post-revolutionary states, the CCP has acted swiftly to introduce legislation to guarantee women's rights and interests and to end extreme forms of exploitation and abuse. The Marriage Law of 1950 prohibited child marriage, legalised divorce and gave women and men the right to choose their own spouses (Johnson 1983). By appealing to the law women were able to draw on an alternative source of authority to challenge pressures within the family to remain in abusive or unhappy marriages or to submit to arranged marriages. The Labour Insurance Regulations of 1951 and the Agrarian Reform Law of 1950 gave women the right to engage in waged labour and equal access to land, thus guaranteeing in law the material conditions for women's economic independence. Through regular campaigns the ACWF and other political institutions have been able to popularise knowledge of the law and give more substance to legislative innovations than in many other countries where the introduction and proliferation of laws has done little to change actual conditions.

Due to the chaos of the Cultural Revolution it was not until the reform period that further gender-specific legislation could be introduced. In 1980 minor revisions to the Marriage Law, such as removing the clause supporting exogamy, were made. With the rise of child-trafficking, prostitution, female infanticide and discriminatory employment practices, the ACWF pushed successfully for new legislation in 1992 to protect the interests of women and children. Similarly it contributed to the drafting of the 1995 Labour Law, ensuring that women's legal rights to maternity leave, childcare provision and safe working conditions were given attention.

Family

The prohibition of child marriage and polygamy as well as the legalisation of divorce were important steps towards improving women's position within the household. Nevertheless, the practice of virilocal marriage and the high importance attached to sons who are expected to care for their parents in their later years have continued unabated. The rapid extension of childcare facilities, private canteens and laundries during the Great Leap Forward marked an attempt to socialise domestic responsibilities with the aim of facilitating women's participation in production. However, these new services collapsed almost as quickly as they were set up, prompting the ACWF to focus its attentions on educating men to participate more in household labour (Croll 1983: 7). By attributing gender inequities within the household to the persistence of traditional norms and seeking their redress through ideological means, the ACWF underestimated the importance of developing the household appliances industry and a service sector.

In the reform period the ACWF has continued to emphasise the need for men to take on their share of domestic responsibilities, though the development of the tertiary sector and consumer industry has probably made a far greater impact on the burden of women in the household. As state-owned enterprises have sought to shed staff, some of China's new generation of market economists have begun to argue the apparent logic of women remaining in the home to ease the problem of surplus labour (Xiao 1988). With the introduction of the 'one-child, one-family' policy the prevalence of a preference for sons has surfaced unashamedly, manifested in its most extreme forms in a rapid rise in female infanticide. Whilst initially the ACWF tried to downplay the increase in girl deaths, the startling spread of this abhorrent practice led it to take a more open stance, organising educational campaigns and pushing through punitive legislation.

Ideology and education

By the early 1960s the ACWF was already noting that the participation of women in production was not in itself sufficient to undermine female subordination. With the Maoist emphasis on effecting change through altering people's ideas and attitudes, the ACWF likewise began to draw upon ideology to counter the oppressive attitudes towards women held by both men and women. By constructing images of women as producers, as equals of men, as important players in the future of China, the ACWF sought to challenge notions about the inferiority of women, their dependence and submissiveness, and so to strengthen women's self-confidence and self-respect. However, by juxtaposing the roles of women as mothers and pro-ducers these definitions could not effectively challenge the sexual division of labour within the household nor the expected roles of women in society.

In the reform period women have become subject to a range of competing discourses, making the attempts of the ACWF to construct appealing images much more difficult. Gone are the pictures of steely-eyed women, clad in plain blue Mao suits, looking confidently to the socialist future. In their place have come advertising hoardings showing coquettish, made-up women selling washing-machines, toothpaste and TVs. With the opening up of China, foreign films, videos and songs have introduced images of lux-urious life-styles, promoted new notions of beauty and femininity and endorsed the respectability of consumerism. A perusal of the ACWF's jour-nals, which contain pictures ranging from plainly dressed cadres to skimpily clad fashion models, reveals the lack of clarity within the organisation about which images of women to promote as well as its half-baked efforts to appeal to a new generation. As Barlow (1991a) argues, the ACWF's construction of woman as *funu*, that is as a national woman subject associated with Maoist thought and practice and understood in opposition to bourgeois feminism, imperialism and landlord exploitation, is no longer sustainable. The rise of women's studies in China has introduced other contending subject represen-tations which challenge the hegemony of the *funu* signifier.[11]

With regard to education, the ACWF has played an important role in orga-nising literacy campaigns in rural areas and improving female literacy rates (Andors 1983; Croll 1983). The provision of universal education after libera-tion opened up opportunities for girls unknown in pre-revolutionary China. In the reform period, however, the decollectivisation of agriculture has led to an increased demand for labour within the household and to a rise in female drop-out rates from school (Croll 1994: 110–11).

Political participation

As in other socialist states the ideological emphasis on equality has facilitated relatively high female participation rates in the political sphere. Women have been encouraged to take up positions in trade unions, the CCP, the Commu-nist Youth League and the People's Congresses at national and local levels. Despite this official support and promotion of a greater political role for women, their dual commitments in production and reproduction and the lack of sufficient childcare facilities have made it hard in reality for women to engage to the same degree as men. Not surprisingly then, women are underrepresented within the party and government. There never has been a woman on the Standing Committee of the Politburo and few high-level ministerial or party positions are occupied by women.[12] Moreover, the situation has worsened in the reform period. Following the introduction of the household responsibility system the position of rural cadres was weakened and, indeed, many preferred to focus their energies on cultivating their own plots and developing private businesses. The number of women elected in county, city and provincial elections began to fall. Aware of this new trend and particularly after the decline in the number of women elected during the 1987 elections, the ACWF began to conduct research on this and raised the issue through its journals and the party press. In some cities such as Shenyang the local federations encouraged more women than the quota to stand, in this way increasing the representation of women in the local People's Congress.

Thus, to sum up, the ACWF has partially succeeded in promoting women's rights and interests in the spheres of employment, politics, education and law in China and has sought through ideological means to address submissive and oppressive representations of women. Compared to many countries at a similar level of economic development, and indeed some industrialised countries, China has achieved great steps in enhancing women's economic and political position. The achievements of the first three decades of liberation have been unsettled by the rapid changes in policy in the late 1970s. The introduction of economic reforms has, on the one hand, given women new employment opportunities but, on the other hand, has created new forms of discrimination and inequality, whilst consolidating others. The persistence of a gendered pattern of employment, inequality of wages, son preference and patrilocal marriage, as well as the disturbing falling rates of female political participation in the reform era suggest that the tasks ahead for the ACWF are enormous. Given the rapid pace of socio-economic change, the rise of new women's organisations and the development of more independent women's studies departments and circles, the ACWF will come under increasing pressure to rethink its direction and institutional strategy.

Looking ahead

Having assessed the record of the ACWF in achieving women's rights and interests and reducing gender inequities we should also consider the prospects for the ACWF to become a more effective agency for promoting feminist goals. In doing so we consider not only some of the constraints it faces but also some of the positive factors conducive to improving its work.

In the history of the ACWF since Liberation we can identify three key constraints which have limited the effectiveness of the ACWF: first, its close alliance and dependence on the CCP; second, the restricted nature of civil society; and third, the overall intellectual and political climate.

As a mass organisation the ACWF has faced the classic dualist dilemma of having to promote both the interests of its constituency and those of the party. Whilst the ACWF has sought to further and safeguard women's interests, it has tended to subordinate these at times to the broader goals of national economic development. Its financial and political dependence on the party-state has inhibited it from questioning the theoretical underpinnings of the strategy to emancipate women by drawing them into waged employment and from reflecting more broadly on the multicausal dimensions of gender inequalities. With its cadres assigned to their posts like government bureaucrats the Federation has not benefited from the enthusiasm, dynamism and commitment that can be found in many voluntary, grassroots-type agencies.

As occurred in other socialist states, the CCP has kept tight control over society by prohibiting the formation of autonomous organisations which might threaten its power and by limiting the number of representative organisations. Civil society in post-revolutionary China has been weak. Following the disastrous years of the Cultural Revolution the CCP has constantly struggled to retain its legitimacy, particularly in the eyes of young people. With its close association to the CCP and the rapidly changing needs of women in the reform period, the ACWF has had to make considerable efforts to appeal to an increasingly diverse constituency of women, for whom it is more an arm of the party-state than an organisation which represents or belongs to them. The lack of a vibrant women's movement within the space of civil society has deprived the ACWF of the opportunity to engage with a wide range of women, to comprehend their needs, particularly in the context of rapid economic change, and to challenge its own assumptions about what constitutes 'women's interests'.

Finally, the overall intellectual and political climate has proved a constraint in the development of the ACWF. As mentioned previously, the emphasis on class struggle, class oppression and class relations during the Cultural Revolution brought the work of the ACWF to a halt. The impact of the embargo in the early post-revolutionary years, the break with the Soviet Union in the early 1960s and the economic and political isolation of the Cultural Revolution meant that ACWF cadres had little contact with feminist groups in the capitalist world. As a result ACWF cadres missed out on the heated debates and theoretical developments of the second wave of feminism and had little opportunity to sharpen their theoretical tools or challenge the orthodoxy on the women's question in socialist states.

With the introduction of foreign investment and the expansion of foreign trade since 1978, the reformers have been keenly aware of the need to create an intellectual and political environment conducive to absorbing new technologies. The opportunities for overseas travel and study, translations of foreign literature and academic exchanges have contributed to a much more open atmosphere where ideas of existentialism, democracy and humanism have found expression. Despite the early efforts of radical reformers such as Zhao Ziyang and Hu Yaobang and as a result of the catastrophe of Tiananmen Square, political reform is still far from the political agenda. Given these limitations on political change the ACWF will be hard pressed to seriously challenge the orthodox analysis of gender oppression and to pursue anything less than the party line on a range of issues.

Having noted some of the constraining variables on the effectiveness of the ACWF we might end here on a positive note, by considering the factors which favour a more effective agency. Of relevance here are the potential interaction between the ACWF and the new women's groups, the struggle within the organisation for greater autonomy and indeed a rethinking of the relationship between the ACWF and the party, the more relaxed intellectual climate, moves to seek its own sources of funding and the impact of the Fourth World Conference on Women.

As noted above, the marketisation of China's economy and the development of a private sector have spawned new socio-economic interests and complicated the category of woman. No longer is it sufficient to analyse women in terms of a limited number of classes. Women in China are now entrepreneurs, traders and housewives as well as workers and peasants. The relaxation of controls over residence have enabled rural women to seek employment in the foreign factories in south-east China and so broaden their horizons, develop new perspectives and harbour new aspirations.

With the rapid pace of socio-economic change since 1978, the expansion of the private sector and the emergence of new class divisions, there has been a growing need for new channels of interest articulation. The rise of trade associations, cultural groups, professional bodies, political organisations and learned societies, particularly from the mid-1980s, has provided the ingredients of an emerging civil society.[13] This new layer of intermediary organisations has also included women's organisations such as the Women Mayors' Association, the Women Journalists' Association and women's salons. Although the Ministry of Civil Affairs, the ministry responsible for the registration of social organisations, issued detailed regulations banning the formation of organisations along gender lines, in some cities such as Shanghai those which had organised beforehand were permitted to continue their activities. Otherwise gender-specific organisations have to be secondary associations to major organisations. Thus the Women's Journalists' Association is a secondary body belonging to the Journalists' Association. As these are relatively new organisations the ACWF has yet to define its relationship to them, hovering currently between reluctant toleration of their activities and a desire to co-opt them. Given the limits on its resources the ACWF views some of these organisations as a potential link to different categories of women which it cannot itself easily reach.

The Fourth World Conference on Women held in Beijing in the autumn of 1996 played an important role in strengthening and creating a layer of women's organisations with some independence from the party-state.[14] Foreign donors such as the Ford Foundation provided funding and space for new women's groups to take off whilst the CCP and ACWF took a cautious but tolerant view of these newly emerging associations. With the ACWF hosting this grand event and claiming NGO status it was important that China appear to have some NGOs and more autonomous women's organisations. The tragic events of 1989 had led to a clampdown on associations, and particularly those which were deemed to threaten the power of the CCP. Hence those women's salons which began seriously to discuss issues of gender subordination in China were tolerated but carefully watched by the authorities.

One of the key conclusions of Stetson and Mazur's (1995) comparative study was the importance of autonomous radical and reformist women's organisations which could put pressure on state women's agencies to address gender-specific issues and which could also keep such state bodies in touch with the needs of a diversity of women at the grassroots. The emergence of a layer of more independent women's organisations in China could be a bonus to the ACWF, which is having to deal with an increasingly diverse range of interests in the context of rapid socio-economic change. It could draw on the networks and resources of these groups to carry out some of its own work, as indeed it already has begun to do in some towns.

However, these new women's organisations vary with regard to their degree of independence from the state. Whilst some, such as the professional and trade associations, may receive financial and staff support from the party-state, the more grassroots-type organisations like the salons and women's hot-line enjoy a hands-off relationship, relying on their own funding and voluntary work. Tolerated during the run-up to the Fourth World Women's Conference, it has yet to be seen whether they can continue to enjoy the same room for manoeuvre. For these organisations to influence gender-specific policies and the thinking within the ACWF, the latter has to be ready for a co-operative rather than antagonistic or co-optive relationship with these more autonomous creatures. There is already evidence that the ACWF at national and local levels has reacted in three ways towards the new women's groups and women's studies centres, sometimes financially and politically supporting their activities, sometimes seeking to shape their structures and plans, and sometimes reluctantly acknowledging their existence.

As well as fostering the development of more independent women's organisations, the Fourth World Conference on Women provided the opportunity for ACWF cadres to become more aware of the key issues in international feminist debate, to get a better understanding of the workings of international organisations and especially to have closer contact with a wide range of international and national non-governmental women's organisations. Given the weakness of civil society in China and the lack until recently of any non-governmental organisations, it was difficult initially for both the CCP and the ACWF to fathom the differences between governments and NGOs and the relationships between them. Through the conference ACWF cadres from all over China could note the diversity of non-governmental groups, their enthusiasm and dynamism in taking up gender issues and their imaginative ways of communicating ideas, organising members and lobbying governments. This exposure has contributed towards a more general trend within the ACWF to rethink its nature, purpose and, especially, its relationship with the party.

Like other mass organisations the ACWF has been faced with the classic dualist dilemma of having to promote both the interests of its members and those of the party. Its financial and political dependence on the party has constrained it in taking up issues that might clash directly with party policy. Within the organisation there have been cadres who have sought a more autonomous position. Whilst in the early reform years the ACWF was concerned to re-establish its activities, from the Fifth Annual Congress in 1983 onwards we can detect voices within the organisation calling for greater leeway. This reached a peak at the Sixth Annual Congress in 1988 when there was heated debate about the relationship of the ACWF to the party and the possible options open to it, such as becoming a Ministry of Women's Affairs or a government department or independent of the party altogether. Following the tragic events in Tiananmen Square, the mass organisations were called to heel, muting any further discussion of greater autonomy. Given the exposure of the ACWF to NGOs and state women's agencies during the Fourth World Conference on Women, it is likely that there will be further reflection upon the nature of the organisation, upon ways of making it more effective and upon potential redefinitions of its relationship to the party.

Aware of the need to rein in state expenditures, the party permitted mass organisations in the mid-1980s to raise their own funding through commercial activities. Hesitant to follow up this shift in policy, it was not until after Deng Xiaoping's tour of South China in February 1992 that the ACWF began to think more entrepreneurially about raising funds itself. Encouraged by the Fourth World Conference on Women it has sought overseas funding for projects such as women's reproductive health, education of female children and training of rural women as well as setting up a China Children and Teenagers Fund which has sought, *inter alia*, to reduce the drop-out rate of girls from primary schools. By increasing its own sources of financing the ACWF lessens its financial dependence on the party, thus giving it potentially the material conditions for a more autonomous relationship with the party. This in turn would allow it to focus more squarely on and prioritise women's interests.

Finally, the general intellectual and political climate has an important bearing on the possibility for change in the ACWF. In the reform period there has been a significant relaxation over the content and extent of debate within academic and policy circles. Although the party has tightened its control over the media in the past two years, still the issues that are discussed openly amongst academics and policy-makers and the degree of controversy tolerated compares favourably with the preceding decade. Thus the intellectual and political conditions for a more general rethinking of theoretical assumptions about gender subordination and of the appropriate role and nature of the ACWF are ripe.

Conclusion

There is no doubt that the ACWF has played an important historical role in promoting women's rights and interests in China and in reducing gender inequities. However, its close links with the party have meant that it has often subordinated gender interests to national economic development goals. Moreover, with the party striving to regain its legitimacy after the Cultural Revolution and later Tiananmen, the credibility of the ACWF as a representative agency has also been affected. The rapid pace of socio-economic transformation brought about by the reforms has led to changes in the structure, mode of operating and range of issues taken up by the ACWF. However, as Stetson and Mazur (1995) concluded, a vibrant autonomous women's movement which is given access to the policy process is crucial for ensuring that state women's organisations are effective in their goals. Although more autonomous women's organisations have begun to emerge in post-Mao China, they are still few and far between and their relationship with the ACWF has still to be defined.

The fate of state women's organisations in former socialist states presents a pessimistic scenario to the ACWF, if any fundamental political change occurs. Whilst in the near future the succession appears to be peaceably secured, it would be premature to predict what changes might occur in the international order and within China over the next few decades. The pace of events in the late 1980s caught many a pundit unawares. For the ACWF the key lifeline will be the nature of the relationship it builds up with the emerging women's groups and women's studies centres. If it seeks to co-operate with these rather than co-opt them or act antagonistically towards them, then its chances of survival and becoming a more effective state women's agency will be greater.

Notes

1 It should be noted that the notion of women's interests is contested amongst feminist scholars and activists. It cannot be assumed that there is a consensus amongst women about their interests, as 'women' cannot be treated as a unified category. Gender, class, age, ethnicity and culture are but some of the dimensions of difference which undermine the notion of an essential interest (see, for example, Pringle and Watson (1992: 53–73)). Nor can it be assumed that women's interests and feminist goals are necessarily treated as equivalent. Women's articulated interests may not always include an explicit challenge to gender subordination.

2 As Sawer (1995: 22) points out, the term femocrat itself has acquired different nuances, starting off as a term of abuse, later associated with feminist involvement in the state, and referring also to feminists in mainstream positions in the bureaucracy.

3 It has also been applied in widely differing contexts such as Europe, Australia, state socialist countries and Latin America, where the process of state formation, the character of the regime and the nature and history of women's oppression and struggles vary considerably.

4 Given that the notion of 'feminist' goals is highly contested, the task of embarking upon such an empirical study appears even more daunting. Stetson and Mazur (1995) address this by not only providing their own definition but also by inviting contributors to their edited volume to clarify their meaning of this term in their chapters.

5 Prior to this major study there have only been a few empirical case-studies of state feminism such as Stetson (1987) and Watson (1992, 1990).

6 'Marxist-Leninist parties' is used here as a generic term to refer to the ruling parties in actually existing socialist states. Although their actual names differed, they were all premised on an ideology which derived from Marxist–Leninist philosophy and practice.

7 On 30 August the Polish parliament overturned this legislation. Ironically the former communists along with various women's groups were crucial in pushing this through. Right-of-centre parties and Solidarnoszc have indicated their intention of reversing this if they win the 1997 elections. See A. Bridge, 'Church outcry as Poles reform abortion law', *Independent*, 31 August 1996: 9.

8 According to Davin (1976: 57, fn8), an attempt was made to revive the ACWF in the early 1970s and municipal women's congresses were organised in Tianjin, Beijing and Shanghai. Johnson (1983: 195) records that the ACWF was resurrected up to the provincial level in 1972 and 1973.

9 These five areas were addressed by Molyneux (1981: 17) in her comparative assessment of changes brought about by socialist states and so provide a useful starting-point for analysing the Chinese case.

10 In early 1996 the ACWF called for more policies and laws to protect women's right to work, as 27 ministries and departments attending a talent exchange fair organised by the Ministry of Personnel had refused to employ female graduates. See *Summary of World Broadcasts*, Far East, 2514 G/7, 20 January 1996.

11 In particular these are the concepts of *nuxing* and *nuren*. The former is understood as woman as 'sexed subject' (Barlow 1991: 339) and is also opposed to *funu* in the works of writers on culture, thus signifying an alternative to the ACWF's concept of *funu*. *Nuren* is used by women's movement historians to refer to woman as an extra-statist subject, as a social science category.

12 For example, in 1992 women formed only 16 per cent of government staff and workers and accounted for only three ministers and 13 vice-ministers (7 per cent of the total) (Li 1992).

13 For further details about the rise of civil society in China, see White *et al.* (1996); Howell (1993, 1994).

14 For a more in-depth analysis of the impact of this conference on women's organisations in China, see Howell (1997).

References

Andors, P. (1981) 'The four modernisations and Chinese policy on women', *Bulletin of Concerned Asian Scholars*, 13(2): 44–57.

Andors, P. (1983) *The Unfinished Liberation of Chinese Women, 1949–1980*, Bloomington, Ind.: Indiana University Press; Brighton, Sussex: Wheatsheaf Books.

Barlow, T. (1991a) 'Theorising women: funu, guojia and jiating [Chinese Women, Chinese State, Chinese Family]', *Genders*, no. 10: 132–60.

Barlow, T. (1991b) 'Politics and protocols of *funu*: (un)making national woman', in C. Gilmartin, T. Barlow, G. Hershatter, L. Rofel and T. White (eds), *Engendering China: Women, Culture and the State*, Cambridge, Mass.: Harvard University Press, 339–59.

Barrett, M. (1980) *Women's Oppression Today*, London: Verso.

Bridger, S., Kay, R. and Pinnick, K. (1996) *No More Heroines? Russia, Women and the Market*, London and New York: Routledge.

Croll, E. (1983) *Chinese Women since Mao*, London: Zed Press.

Croll, E. (1994) *From Heaven to Earth: Images and Experiences of Development in China*, London and New York: Routledge.

Daines, V. and Seddon, S. (1994) 'Fighting for survival: women's responses to austerity programs', in J. Walton and D. Seddon (eds), *Free Markets and Food Riots: The Politics of Global Adjustment*, Oxford: Blackwell.

Davin, D. (1976) *Woman-work: Women and the Party in Revolutionary China*, Oxford: Clarendon Press.

Eisenstein, Z.R. (1984) *Feminism and Sexual Equality*, New York: Monthly Review Press.

Howell, J. (1993) 'The poverty of civil society: insights from China', Discussion Paper no. 240, School of Development Studies, University of East Anglia, Norwich.

Howell, J. (1994) 'Refashioning state–society relations in China', *European Journal of Development Research* 6(1): 197–215.

Howell, J. (1996) 'The struggle for survival: prospects for the Women's Federation in post-Mao China', *World Development* 24(1): 129–44.

Howell, J. (1997) 'Post-Beijing reflections: creating ripples, but not waves in China', *Women's Studies International Forum* 20(2): 235–52.

Johnson, K.A. (1983) *Women, the Family and Peasant Revolution in China*, Chicago: University of Chicago Press.

Koval, V.V. (1995) 'Women and work in Russia', in V. Koval (ed.), *Women in Contemporary Russia*, Oxford: Berghahn Books, 17–33.

Li, Jingzhi (1992) 'The history and current situation concerning the participation of Chinese women in private administration', *Zhongguo Xingzheng Guanli*, March, Beijing, 42–3.

McIntosh, M. (1978) 'The state and the oppression of women', in A.M. Wolpe and A. Kuhn (eds), *Feminism and Materialism*, London: Routledge.

MacKinnon, C. (1987) *Towards a Feminist Theory of the State*, Cambridge, Mass.: Harvard University Press.

Molyneux, M. (1981) 'Women's emancipation under socialism: a model for the Third World?', *Institute of Development Studies Discussion Paper*, 157, January.

Molyneux, M. (1990) 'The "woman question" in the age of perestroika', *New Left Review*, 183 (September/October): 23–49.

Molyneux, M. (1994) 'Women's rights and the international context: some reflections on the post-communist states', *Millennium: Journal of International Studies*, 23(2): 287–313.

Pringle, R. and Watson, S. (1992) '"Women's interests" and the post-structuralist state', in M. Barrett and A. Phillips, *Destabilising Theory: Contemporary Feminist Debates*, Cambridge: Polity Press.

Sawer, M. (1995) '"Femocrats in glass towers?": the Office of the Status of Women in Australia', in D.B. Stetson and A.G. Mazur, *Comparative State Feminism*, London: Sage, 22–39.

Shapiro, J. (1992) 'The industrial labour force', in M. Buckley (ed.), *Perestroika and Soviet Women*, Cambridge: Cambridge University Press, 14–38.

Stetson, D. (1987) *Women's Rights in France*, Westport, Conn.: Greenwood Press.

Stetson, D. and Mazur, A. (eds) (1995) *Comparative State Feminism*, London: Sage.

Waters, E. (1992) 'Victim or villain? Prostitution in post-revolutionary Russia', in L. Edmondson (ed.), *Women and Society in Russia and the Soviet Union*, Cambridge: Cambridge University Press.

Watson, S. (ed.) (1990) *Playing the State: Australian Feminist Interventions*, London: Verso.

Watson, S. (1992) 'Femocratic feminisms', in M. Savage and A. Witz (eds), *Gender and Bureaucracy*, Oxford: Blackwell, 186–206.

White, G., Howell, J. and Shang, X.Y. (1996) *In Search of Civil Society: Market Reform and Social Change in Contemporary China*, Oxford: Clarendon Press.

Woo, M.Y.K. (1994) 'Chinese women workers: the delicate balance between production and equality', in C.K. Gilmartin, G. Hershatter, L. Rofel and T. White (eds), *Engendering China: Women, Culture and the State*, Cambridge, Mass.: Harvard University Press, 279–98.

Xiao, Ming (1988) 'Four serious obstacles facing women's political participation', *Zhongguo Funu* August: 12–13.

11 Gender and power

Women engage the state

Vicky Randall

Introduction

This concluding chapter reflects on issues raised by the separate contributions, focusing specifically on women's active engagement in politics and with the state. To that extent its perspective could be seen as 'bottom up', as distinct from the 'top down' perspective of the opening chapter. However heuristically and organisationally helpful such a distinction may be, it must be qualified.

For, as suggested in Chapter 1, it is in many ways misleading to present the relationship between women and the state as either top down or bottom up. It is clearly neither. Nor do we face a simple contrast between women appearing in politics largely as the passive objects, and to an extent even the constructs, of policy or state effects, on the one hand, and women, as a pre-existing, unproblematic gender category and collective actor, (increasingly) participating in and determining the outcome of an in principle gender-neutral political process, on the other. Rather we must recognise that relationship more as a mutual engagement or interrogation, in which to an extent power or influence circulates.

To describe the relationship between women, politics and the state as circular is still a simplification. It implies that the main points of interaction are at two poles of intersection, where policies affect women or where women impact on the policy process, whereas they are in reality much more numerous and diffuse. It also implies a degree of equality in the influence exercised by women or the state, whereas that is both unlikely in most cases and a question to be ascertained more empirically. Related to this last point, it understates the variability, temporal and spatial, of the relationship. None the less, this circular model is one that does more justice to the interdependence and interaction of its central elements.

Having said that, the present discussion will complement Chapter 1 through its focus upon women engaging with and having effects upon the political process, the state and its outcomes. Such a focus, incidentally, can be linked with a concern amongst a number of feminist authors to endow women as subjects with agency, not simply depict them as victims or vehicles for the realisation of transcending systems or projects. The discussion will begin by briefly rehearsing arguments within (western) feminism about the forms, meaning and efficacy of women's political participation. *Should* women participate in mainstream politics in the first place? We then need to consider who these women are: how are gender differences of male and female to be conceptualised and how is such a conceptualisation to be reconciled with the need to recognise the differences among women? How do these competing bases of identity and interest shape the manner and content of women's intervention in the political process?

Having raised, if not resolved, these underlying questions about the value and basis for women's political participation, the discussion will move on to examine the nature and impact of such participation in practice. It will consider both the constraints and openings presented by the 'political opportunity structure', understanding that term to comprise a number of different dimensions. Finally, it will reflect on the different strategies women have employed in their encounter with the state, including the extent to which they have themselves succeeded in modifying the political opportunity structure.

Given the generality of these questions, in the way they are posed, and the variety and specificity of the case studies the discussion is primarily drawing upon, there can be no claims here to produce an exhaustive analysis. The more modest object is to identify some of the key issues and variables such an analysis would need to embrace, thereby helping to clarify and advance debate.

Feminism and political participation

It is widely recognised that early radical feminism brought two, interconnected, perceptions to the women's movement's understanding of politics. These are the calling into question of the public–private distinction and the condemnation of male-dominated mainstream politics and the state. The former has stood the test of time rather better than the latter but both are logical consequences of a more fundamental perception of male power as systematic and omnipresent, as encapsulated in the concept of 'patriarchy'.

Since in early radical feminist thinking the battle of the sexes was taken to be the primary division within society and since it was manifest everywhere and perhaps most of all at the level of personal relationships, the argument was that 'the personal is political'. Further, the notion of a distinct public political sphere was seen as an ideological construct to legitimise the exclusion of women, typically confined to the domestic sphere, and of their interests and concerns. This refusal to accept the public–private distinction went, of course, with a certain kind of practical politics, centring on women's psycho-sexual autonomy, as signalled by such issues as abortion and rape, so that awareness spread as much through practice as through theory. Influenced by such arguments, feminist political theorists exposed the confusion and inconsistency in liberal conceptualisations of public and private spheres (Moller Okin 1991).

It is true that some feminist political theorists were always alarmed by so blithe a rejection of the notion of a distinctive public political realm, since they argued this ignored such a realm's creative potential (Randall 1987: 12). Subsequently, as described by Kate Nash, who is herself critical of this move, feminist theorists like Anne Phillips and Iris Marion Young, influenced by the idea of 'deliberative' or 'communicative' democracy developed by Jürgen Habermas and others, have renewed the call for a distinct public political sphere in which participants, though selected in a more truly representative manner, should then precisely leave behind personal identifications and interests in order, through deliberation, to arrive at some consensus on the public good. Feminist arguments have also emerged for the retention of some conception of 'privacy' (see Phillips 1991).

It can none the less be affirmed that the public–private critique has had an enormous and continuing impact on feminist thinking and politics. Thus in the present volume we hear of how women mobilised in the Bodghaya land reform movement, in India, found the courage to demand that their husbands help with the washing up – and of the sometimes violent response this occasioned (Jacobs, Chapter 8 in this volume). That is, they understood that this challenge to male authority within the home was political. At the same time, women have campaigned to bring concerns bound up with their 'private' and domestic lives on to the public political agenda, as in the case of women's participation in popular social movements under authoritarian rule in Latin America, described by Craske (Chapter 7).

Second, radical feminism rejected mainstream politics and the state because they were seen as instrumental to and an expression of patriarchy and because as such they were infused with male assumptions, a male style of politics or political culture. In Britain, such attitudes became for a time characteristic of the wider Women's Liberation Movement. However, in Britain and elsewhere, there was always in practice more political engagement with conventional political structures and processes than this might suggest. Women could be 'against the state' but they made demands upon it, for instance for 'the right to choose' whether or not to have an abortion. Even where the emphasis of feminist activism was to create 'self-help' networks and organisations, in practice and over time these often developed a more symbiotic relationship with the 'local state'.

At the theoretical level, a less categorical rejection of conventional politics was complemented and assisted by the changing feminist conceptualisation of the state, or at least the liberal state, as described in Chapter 1. There was increasing recognition within Marxist or socialist feminism of the state's plural character, of the multiplicity of its sites and agencies with their distinctive perspectives and interests and of the range of political possibilities this opened up. By the 1990s erstwhile socialist feminists evinced much greater interest and faith in the possibility of working through the liberal democratic state. Thus Nash (Chapter 4) examines the attempts of three important contemporary feminist theorists – Young, Phillips and Chantal Mouffe – not to reject but 'to re-think the liberal state'. Within western feminism, then, arguments about the character of the state and whether feminist ideals can be realised through it continue. Sceptical voices are still heard but the weight of opinion leans heavily towards the optimistic pole.

What is interesting is the way that similar debates now seem to be emerging in many other regions, especially in the context of 'democratisation'. For instance, Lievesley (1996) describes the arguments between the *indepen-dientes*, favouring autonomous organisation and the *politicas* working within left-wing political parties, amongst feminists in Peru. The question is posed, more or less explicitly in Craske's discussion (Chapter 7) of the combined effects of democratisation and the adoption of neoliberal economic policies in much of Latin America. Thus she notes that the social movements in which both women and 'women's issues' featured prominently have tended to be replaced rather than assimilated by re-emerging political parties. Within these parties, 'Since women's issues are not seen as central to party platforms, they often disappear from the political terrain altogether'(p. 110). At the same time Craske acknowledges the gains that women have made both in terms of political representation, with the introduction of gender quotas, and in institutional terms, with the creation of women's ministries, women's sections in parties and some beneficial legislation. By way of contrast, however, Sperling (Chapter 9) comments: 'The division between social movement groups intent on retaining "autonomy" and those hoping to influence the state does not seem terribly salient in mid-1990s Russia.' Representatives from nearly all the fifty women's organisations she interviewed 'expressed a desire to influence state policies on their issues' (p. 163). This is an interesting exception, reflecting perhaps the impact of a strongly statist tradition.

Gender and representation

But if, within western feminism at least, there is growing readiness, both in practice and in theory, to participate in the politics of the liberal democratic state at the very same time the subject of such participation, 'women', has been increasingly problematised. Not simply radical but all early feminist theory talked comfortably about 'women' as a self-evident and straight-forward category. This was in large part a function of feminism's central concern at that time to contest the way male-dominated society tended both to exclude women and to subsume them in such ostensibly universal but actually male-derived concepts as humanity or mankind. The object was to make women visible. But in asserting the claims of women, it became increasingly difficult to avoid questions about the ontological basis of that category, and from there further questions seemed inevitably to flow about differences not only between men and women but among women, and about the nature of 'difference' itself.

It is in the context of analysing male–female differences that the original distinction between 'sex' and 'gender' came to be deployed. Going back once more to the early Radical feminist literature, certainly in the writing of Shulamith Firestone or Susan Brownmiller, men and women were understood as opposing sexes; the basis of the distinction was physiological (although not entirely so). As other kinds of feminist began to engage more directly with this question, however, it became more usual – and the title of our book reflects this trend – to counterpose sex and gender. Linda Nicholson (1995), who provides a useful overview of this debate, describes how the notion of 'gender' came to be used to refer to socially constructed personality traits and behaviour in distinction to the biologically given bodily differences. Such a contrast, for instance, underlies Gayle Rubin's concept of a 'sex–gender system'. In fact, conceptualisations of gender, in distinction to sex, have taken varied forms. Terrell Carver (Chapter 2) in this book, notes that in some usages the notion of sex differences almost disappears but 'gender' comes to operate on very similar lines, that is it comes to denote men and women as largely self-evident categories, or worse, to serve as a synonym for women, thereby losing all sense of the actual and potential variability of social constructions of gender and of the part played in these constructions by relations of power. Rather than seeing gender mapped isomorphically onto sex, Carver maintains, depending upon our understandings of sex and sexuality, we could distinguish any number of different genders.

Nicholson (1995) develops a critique of *all* forms of the sex–gender approach by employing the analogy of a clothes rack. She argues that the clothes rack or body is still understood to be a relatively unchanging given, even though what society makes of it, or the clothes thrown upon it, can vary radically. This means – and here we anticipate the questions of the differences among women – that it is assumed that underlying bodily differences have been the same, everywhere and through time. To that extent, and despite the tremendous culturally determined variations of experience, there is some underlying commonality among women, to which feminism can appeal. Even while criticising the essentialism of radical feminist accounts, Nicholson argues, the clothes rack approach remains itself guilty of an underlying essentialism. If this is not 'biological determinism', says Nicholson, it is 'biological foundationalism'.

Nicholson describes approvingly a further stage in the conceptualisation of gender in which the body, or the clothes rack, is itself problematised, and which we could broadly label 'post-structuralist'. That is, it is argued that our perceptions of supposedly given sex differences are themselves shaped by gender ideology. In this formulation, gender comes to refer to 'any social construction having to do with the male/female distinction, including those constructions that separate "female" bodies from "male" bodies' (Nicholson 1995: 39). In this way it escapes, according to Nicholson, the biological foundationalism of the clothes rack approach. This post-structuralist perspective has become increasingly influential and is most evident in Nash

(Chapter 4 in this book). While sympathetic with feminist concerns, she warns against invoking essentialist conceptions of 'woman': 'the imposition of identity on lived possibilities is the problem and it is not dealt with by further and more fully taking on that identity'.

Here is not the place to embark on a detailed evaluation of these arguments. It is difficult to return to the intellectual innocence of the earliest understandings of sex difference. It is difficult even to disagree that our perceptions of bodily differences are themselves influenced by gender assumptions (as amusingly demonstrated by Emily Martin (1991) in her analysis of the language used in 'scientific' accounts of the process of human procreation). But that does not seem to me to imply that there *are* no significant and shared bodily characteristics, differentiating most men from most women. It may be impossible to think about these differences in some entirely objective or neutral way, to determine what their intrinsic significance is or to disentangle them from the way they have been constructed historically. But it also seems perverse entirely to disregard them. They have almost everywhere formed the basis for socially elaborated patterns of differentiation, no matter how varied. Very often, in the past at least, such differentiation has included a power dimension and male traits have been valued more highly than female.

As already implied, however, even if there are held to be non-trivial physiological differences underlying societies' elaboration of masculine and feminine, it is not clear what the implications should be for feminist political strategy. As is well known, liberal feminists, while not denying physiological differences, have tended to emphasise the extent to which men and women resemble one another in possessing a capacity for reason. From this came the demand for women to be treated equally, or the same, as men. The early radical feminists, who in one sense stressed sex differences, advocated political separatism and eschewed the patriarchal state. In the longer term, however they envisaged an androgynous world in which sex differences would no longer matter. Such a perspective is still apparent in the writing of the contemporary radical feminist, Sheila Jeffreys (1990). On the other hand, cultural or pro-woman feminists came to celebrate and explore the differences between men and women, looking forward to an era when gynocentric or maternal values would prevail.

With the passage of time, and as feminists have grappled with the realities, and theoretical complexities, of liberal democratic institutions, understandings of the way women are to be 'represented' politically have inevitably become less categorical and more cognisant of the demands of different contextual settings. Feminists more directly and practically involved, through politics, as lawyers or trade unionists in the development of policy, came increasingly to see their strategy in terms of balancing or negotiating the tensions between women's claim to equality of status and opportunities and the need to recognise that this might require difference in treatment (Evans 1995). At a more theoretical level, these questions about the nature and implications of gender differences have been rehearsed, for instance, through feminist contributions to the recent revival of interest in the concept and connotations of 'citizenship': should feminists subscribe to the classical liberal conception in which the category of citizen transcends particular attributes, including in theory those of gender; should they seek to replace the hopelessly masculinised current conception of citizenship with one that is more woman-friendly; or should they reject the universalising premise underlying the whole project (Phillips 1991; Dietz 1987). In Chapter 4 in the present volume, Nash explores, with particular reference to gender, how difference is to be represented in the democratic political process. As she writes: 'The problem is how to take differences between the sexes into account without freezing them in their current forms and without denying the importance of other differences which may cut across that of sex.' She tends herself towards the most open conceptualisation of identities, as advocated by Chantal Mouffe. Mouffe does not entirely dispense with essentialism – or a kind of contingent and rhetorical deployment of essentialist categories – but ultimately favours a radical form of democracy which 'privileges the continual disruption of gendered identities'.

So far I have deliberately, some might feel artificially, kept to one side the question of differences among women and among men, but of course this will not do. For, as Nash makes clear in her reference cited above to 'other differences which may cut across that of sex', the objection to essentialist conceptions of sex difference has been not only that they tend to reify and freeze those differences in some way but that they thereby obscure the differences amongst those labelled 'women' and likewise amongst those labelled 'men'. We have already referred to differences concerning sexuality. But in addition, there are all the differences of class, ethnicity, culture and so forth that were always there but which the feminist project itself has served to rearticulate. Even if we accept what Nicholson calls the 'biological foundationalist' position, it does not in any way follow that all women everywhere actually have major interests in common, outweighing their differences, still less that they believe they do. Women themselves do not necessarily see their gender as the single most important attribute defining their social identities and political interests, and even if they do they may construct their interests as women very differently.

The case studies in this book provide vivid illustrations of these problems concerning the identification and political representation of women, demonstrating the necessity, complexity and dangers of articulating and mobilising around a shared identity as 'women'. At times we hear how women have been rendered virtually invisible within political discourse and policy. Thus Craske describes how in Latin America neoliberalism has tended to promote a universalising discourse centred on the individual, understood as a rational, self-seeking man: 'the whole project is gender-blind and makes assumptions about citizens and individuals which indicate a conceptualisation which is masculine and ignores women's unpaid labour essential for the reproduction of the productive labour force and which underpins SAPs' (p. 106). Jacobs refers to the virtual absence of an explicit gender dimension in land reform policy-making: 'Most policies, whether "socialist", "capitalist" or some mixture, converge in the assumption that households/families are unified entities which the "head of household" manages on behalf of the family, taking all interests into account' (p. 123). In such contexts, where male interests and perceptions so dominate policy-making, it may seem that the first priority is to make women *qua* women politically visible.

Even then, problems can arise. Craske, for instance, describes the ambiguous victory or concession entailed in getting governments to provide some kind of space for 'women's' projects within PAPs. This does mark a degree of recognition and demonstrates how official discourse has been made to shift, but on the other hand such projects frequently reinforce stereotypes of women's role. They 'tend either to focus on local income-generation projects frequently emphasising "feminine" characteristics such as needlework or cooking, or service provision which can reinforce gender stereotypes around women's domestic role' (p. 107). Again we must be careful here not automatically to condemn women's mobilisation on the basis of their 'traditional' identities and concerns as mothers and home-makers. In the first place, this may represent a transitional stage. Thus Craske suggests that in Latin America 'initially motherhood played an important role' in women's mobilisation in anti-authoritarian struggles, but 'this did not stay static'. Some women came to question gendered power relations within the home as well as in the public sphere, including the paid workforce and trade unions. But second, we should try to understand such activism in its own terms. Haleh Afshar has written critically of the way it has often been 'ignored and undervalued' not only by orthodox academics but by a first generation of (western) feminist analysts. As she points out, we need to recognise that women have to use the resources and discourses available in a given cultural and political context. Understanding this,

> it will be easy to see that women use concepts like 'motherhood', or 'complementarity' rather than 'equality', to pursue particular goals such as seeking resources, welfare and/or freedom from oppression for their children. Their forms of negotiation with the state must not be equated with weakness nor should their strategies be classified as either temporary or unimportant.
>
> (Afshar 1996: 1)

But the case studies in this book also make abundantly clear the extent and political salience of divisions amongst women. Whether or not they enter politics on the basis of a shared identity as 'women', their subjective understanding of their own identity and interests is infinitely varied. Women do not enter politics, at whatever level, as a united force but often in conflict with one another. This is illustrated, for instance, in Barbara Gwinnett's account of the politics of prostitution (Chapter 6 in this volume). Prostitution is not of course correctly described simply as a women's issue: in fact it involves more men than women. But it has tended to be identified as a women's issue and has been much debated by feminists. However, Gwinnett points out, first, that both feminists and prostitutes themselves have been divided over whether to oppose prostitution or to tolerate it. Second, she shows how, in the specific circumstances of the conflict over prostitution in Birmingham's Balsall Heath area, women as prostitutes have been aligned against women as residents, though Gwinnett also refers to the *social* elaboration of this distinction into 'bad women' versus 'good women', thereby seeming to draw attention to the extent to which this opposition is manufactured by dominant male interests. In a similar way, Barry Gilheany (Chapter 5 in this volume) considers the politics of abortion in the Irish Republic, where women have been central actors both in the pro-life movement and amongst their opponents. Jacobs (Chapter 8) cites instances of conflicts between women's perceived interests in Zimbabwe. Since colonial times rural women have been hostile to urban women portrayed as prostitutes and 'secondary wives' enticing their husbands. Jacobs also discusses the differential impact of policies within resettlement areas on senior and junior wives.

Participation and political opportunity structures

If the object of the previous section has been to explore what can be meant by 'women' and the implications this has for an analysis of how women should or do represent themselves in politics, we must now move on to consider the *context* of women's political participation and the opportunities and constraints this presents. Again, as the quotation above from Afshar underlines, the character of women's self-representation and the 'political opportunity structure' do not exist completely independently of each other. As will be discussed further below, women's intervention can itself significantly modify the political opportunity structure. But also the political context, including the state, will, in ways partly suggested in Chapter 1, both help to shape women's sense of themselves and their own interests and offer specific incentives and disincentives for different ways of representing themselves. Afshar, concentrating on the example of Iranian women under the rule of Islam, cites the concept devised by Kandiyoti (1988) of a 'bargain' that is struck with patriarchal authority. Although some Iranian women have openly resisted Islamic dress codes, others have, temporarily at least, accepted the obligation to wear a veil but, according to Afshar, this bargain 'has enabled them to negotiate better terms' in the spheres of education and employment.

The concept of 'political opportunity structure' has a long pedigree, emanating from social movement theory in the 1960s. It has been valuable in getting away from an excessive emphasis on the internal dynamics of social movements. But, partly because of its association with more rational-choice type approaches to social movement theory – as opposed to sociological or cultural approaches (for a fuller account of this distinction see Scott 1990) – the tendency has been to elaborate the notion of political opportunity structure primarily in terms of political institutions and elites and the way that specific changes or realignments in these open up or close off avenues of possibility for the social movement concerned. Such an emphasis is apparent, for instance, in the definition used in Sperling's chapter (Chapter 9) and borrowed from McAdam. Political opportunity structure is understood to include: the relative openness or closure of the institutionalised political system; the stability or otherwise of elite alignments; the presence or otherwise of elite allies; and the state's capacity and propensity for repression.

While such a conception is undoubtedly useful, it is open to criticism on at least three counts. First, it tends to accept and even reify the very demarcation of a distinct public political sphere that social movements like feminism have sought to contest. What this means is that, especially perhaps when considering women's political participation, the McAdam type of conceptualisation of the political opportunity structure needs to be either amplified or, if it is considered this makes the concept too broad, supplemented by a consideration of the wider context of social and economic change. On the one hand, we want to keep in view all arenas of women's political intervention or resistance, whether in mainstream political institutions, in 'civil society' or the home. On the other, women's political participation cannot be understood in isolation from developments beyond the formal political sphere, for instance the impact of economic 'restructuring', as suggested in the contributions by Craske, Howell and Sperling.

Second, such characterisations of the political opportunity structure tend to neglect the level of ideology or discourse. Of course, it may often be difficult or simply misguided to seek to separate out discourse, in the sense of shared ways of describing or understanding, from policies or overall 'projects'. This is suggested, for instance, in Craske's account of neoliberalism in Latin America. None the less, discourses, dominating or competing, are important features of the political opportunity framework for women. For instance, a growing literature discusses the implications of discourses of nationalism for women's political participation, both the openings they can provide, especially where combined with ideologies of modernisation, and the limits they place on the representation of women's claims (Rai 1996). This is touched on in Jacobs's chapter, where she describes how individual women acquired political prominence in Zimbabwe, through their role in the guerrilla war for independence, and in Vietnam, through their participation in the DRV and later in the war with the US. In this book, in particular, we hear much about the two powerful contemporary discourses of neoliberalism and democratisation. Craske's observations on the 'gender-blind' nature of neoliberal discourse, and its negative consequences for women's political participation, have already been noted. Conversely, the discourse of democracy as it has emerged revitalised in the recent 'wave' of democratisation has provided new opportunities to legitimise women's claims for representation. Sperling cites the slogan of the so-called First Independent Women's Forum in Russia, which came together in March 1991: 'Democracy Minus Women Is Not Democracy'.

Third, and to the extent already questioned that this is separable from discourse, an adequate concept of political opportunity surely needs to embrace actual policies and their resource implications, as these affect women. Thus Craske discusses, in addition to its gender-blind character, two ways in which the neoliberal project impacts upon women's political participation in Latin America, contributing to what she sees as a 'remasculinisation' of politics. It has altered the nature of women's employment so as to make work-based political activism more difficult:

> The new regime of accumulation has increased women's participation in waged labour as well as increasing the importance of the informal sphere; however, since women's wages generally remain lower than men's there is a need for women to work longer hours to maintain family incomes, and conditions are often worse as well. Furthermore, the type of work available under export-led development tends to be short-term contract and the informal sector, neither of which offer much potential for workplace political activity.
>
> (Craske, p. 106 in this volume)

Women have also been particularly affected by reductions in social spending and by the character of such social welfare programmes as survive, together reinforcing women's responsibility for the social costs of reproduction and reducing their availability for political participation. An interesting contrast emerges here between Craske's largely negative assessment of the implications of neoliberal policies for women's political participation and Howell's analysis of their impact in China (Chapter 10). Admittedly, women's participation in formal political spheres seems to have declined following decollectivisation of agriculture and concomitant growth in the demand for labour within the household. However, the All-China Women's Federation has been able dramatically to expand its activities and branches, while Howell notes the emergence of an incipient civil society in the form of a layer of intermediary organisations, including women's organisations, ranging from professional bodies to women's salons and the women's hotline. Part of the contrast must presumably be explicable in terms of the kind of economic regime that preceded these reforms.

That being said, the political opportunity structure in the narrower sense remains crucial for women's participation. As one of the Moscow activists interviewed by Sperling affirms: 'The political situation is the most important thing.' Here, first, we must reiterate the important truism, already emphasised in Chapter 1, that in analysing the opportunities presented by the political system or the state for women, adequate account must be taken of the variation in the overall form or type of the state, for instance whether authoritarian or liberal-democratic, whether capitalist or state socialist, whether 'developed' or 'post-colonial'. Thus Rai (1996: 5) is critical of the extent to which 'western feminist state theory has largely ignored the experience of Third World women under the post-colonial state'. She singles out three characteristics of the Third World state with particular potential implications for women's participation: the combination of, first, a developmental rhetoric, and, second, the relative autonomy of state institutions that can in some contexts provide openings for women's political intervention, but on the other hand, a third characteristic, the state's weakness in terms of policy implementation and the extent of corruption constitute serious obstacles and challenges. But the chapters by Sperling and Howell in this book also demonstrate that a distinctive pattern of opportunities and constraints is associated with state socialism.

Second, we must reiterate the need to recognise the multiple arenas of state activity. No state form is completely monolithic although the extent to which a given political system provides plural points of access and of determination is itself a crucial political variable. While most of the case studies in this volume focus on the national level, Gwinnett (Chapter 6) concentrates on the local level, examining the interplay of community, local and national government pressures. Sperling also notes that, in contemporary Russia, '"social movements"' interaction with the state exhibits different dynamics at the local level, in part by virtue of the closer ties between activists and local government officials' (p. 163). And Craske expresses concern at the way that PAPs have served to co-opt and bureaucratise women's participation at local level. Similarly, the studies indicate how at any given time opportunities for women may vary across different kinds of state institution, even, as in Sperling's account, from one ministry to the next.

Yet a further modification to a focus simply on 'the state' is required here. For, as the case studies illustrate, political opportunities for women have been created by the interaction of numerous states. At the international level, the momentum originally generated by the UN Commission for the Status of Women which led to the holding of a succession of international conferences, culminating in the meeting in Beijing in 1995, has significantly helped to legitimate women's demands within the confines of the nation state. In China itself, Howell relates, the Beijing conference 'played an important role in strengthening and creating a layer of women's organisations with some independence from the Party-state'. Sperling describes how, in Russia, the National Council on Preparation for the 1995 UN Worldwide Conference on Women, established in 1993:

> provided the first regular opportunity for contact between women's organisations and the state structures. According to Olga Samarina, head of the Department of Family, Women, and Children's Issues, dozens of women's NGOs were invited to National Council meetings,

where they could 'take a real part in developing policy'.

(p. 158)

Also noteworthy is the positive response of the Russian President, Yeltsin to the UN Convention on Eliminating All Forms of Discrimination Against Women (CEDAW). Craske likewise acknowledges the role of international pressure in keeping the issue of women on the agenda in Latin America, although she emphasises the largely negative reaction of leading politicians in debates preparatory to the Beijing conference.

One dimension of the political opportunity structure already noted is its relative openness or closure. To this we can link McAdam's further criterion of the incidence of repression. It is obvious and yet often seemingly forgotten that women's political gains in the West have to an extent been premised upon the existence of liberal democratic assumptions and institutions. Several of the contributions to this volume consider the implications both of authoritarian rule and of liberalising trends for women. Craske describes how, under authoritarian governments in Latin America, a paradoxical effect of the suppression of political activity within mainstream political institutions was to increase the importance of women as political actors, through their central role within the social movements. Women in a sense came into their own in this community-based mobilisation. In both China and Russia, however, communist rule provided some limited opportunities for individual women to participate politically, within the narrow parameters of officially permitted policy and discourse, while ensuring that their political contribution would only be marginal. The various degrees of political opening in Latin America have clearly offered a range of new political opportunities for women within political parties and representative bodies, but at the same time, and in conjunction with neoliberalism, have tended to undermine the activities of the social movements, leading Craske to speak of a 're-masculinisation' of politics. In the former Soviet Union, the space opened up by glasnost and perestroika seems much less ambiguously to have provided new opportunities for women to mobilise on their own behalf. As Sperling (p. 145) notes:

> Until the 1980s, there was only one women's organisation legally operating in the USSR – the Communist Party-run Soviet Women's Committee. But by the early 1990s, there were hundreds of women's organisations functioning in Russia, ranging from the politically innocuous women's charity groups, to advocacy groups demanding equal treatment of women in politics and labour force, and overtly lesbian groups organising for rights and visibility.

On the other hand, with the emergence in Russia of a more genuinely pluralistic political system, in which representative political institutions enjoyed greater autonomy and influence in the political process, women's representation within such institutions declined.

A further feature of the political opportunity structure highlighted in Sperling's account is the degree of stability or fluidity in political arrangements and alignments. One would expect, especially where women as political subjects and as bearers of distinctive interests have been largely excluded from forums of state power, that destabilisation could provide new opportunities for political intervention. And to some extent this seems borne out by women's experience in the early phase of democratic transition both in Russia and in Latin America. However, Sperling makes the interesting observation that in Russia in the longer run political instability has created many problems for women's politics: 'The rapid succession of political-institutional changes, and the state's resulting limited capacity for policy implementation, restrict the [women's] movement's developmental opportunities.'

The third dimension of the political opportunity structure identified by Sperling, following McAdam, is the nature of elite alliances and the extent to which they provide women or women's groups with opportunities to collaborate with specific elites. In general terms, this is an issue that has often arisen, within the context of western European politics and more recently of Latin American politics, in relation to the possibility and desirability of various forms of alliance with parties of the Left (Randall 1986). In Britain, it was posed sharply under the political regime of 'Thatcherism' when both the Labour Party and the trade unions, partly under the threat of political marginalisation, became much more receptive to feminist arguments and demands (Lovenduski and Randall 1993). Lievesley (1996) discusses similar debates about the wisdom of working within or outside left-wing parties within the women's movement in Peru. Sperling's own discussion concerns the possibilities for co-operation between autonomous women's groups and the Women of Russia bloc, originating out of the Soviet Women's Committee, and the Ministry of Social Protection, under its sympathetic Minister, Liudmila Beslepkina. This latter possibility raises the question of state-sponsored feminism, examined further below.

Strategies for women

In this section, I shall consider some of the ways women have made use of, or indeed expanded, existing political opportunities. Reference has already been made to the way that women have utilised different discursive openings, exploiting their symbolic status as mothers, for instance, or demanding their democratic rights. I have earlier argued that accounts of women's political participation should not be confined to their activities within the sphere of formal political institutions, such as parties and legislatures. The example cited above of women in the Bodghaya movement challenging their husbands to help with the washing up illustrates politics in the private or domestic

sphere, though incidentally Jacobs's warning should be heeded: that feminists should be aware of the possible repercussions when inciting this kind
of resistance to male domination.

But between the sphere of family relations and that of formal, or public
politics, is the area of the 'social' (demonstrating of course the inadequacy
of existing conceptualisation of the public–private divide). Women's political
participation in this sphere, often currently referred to as the realm of 'civil
society', is described in a number of the contributions to this volume, whether
in residents' associations in Birmingham, in the village and ward development committees of the Resettlement Areas and local Women's Groups in
Zimbabwe, women's organisations in Russia or China, or social movements
and PAPs in Latin America. In the literature on women's political participation, it is sometimes suggested that women find involvement in this level of
politics easier to negotiate because of its relative informality and nearness
to home. The idea of 'civil society' also tends to be depicted in very positive
terms, especially in the democratisation literature. Under authoritarian
regimes the scope for civil society is enormously reduced. Civil society can
only regroup as authoritarian rule is weakened, as in the cases of Latin
America and of China described in this book, where economic liberalisation
has served to strengthen civil society and correspondingly to weaken the
state's ability to control it. Civil society then comes to be seen as an area
of freedom in opposition to the overweening state. This positive reading of
civil society chimes with Craske's (p. 108) description of the way that oppositional social movements in Latin America

> tended to have very localised and small meetings and some groups
> deliberately encouraged women to take on roles which challenged stereo-
> types . . . Although they could not completely escape the influence of
> clientelism and caudillismo there was an attempt to develop new ways
> of 'doing politics' which did facilitate women's participation.

However, there is no reason to suppose, as Rai (1996: 14) has reminded us,
that 'civil society' is automatically more benign and accommodating of
women's political claims than are state institutions. Certainly in the context
of the Third World, for women 'the state and civil society are both complex
terrains – fractured, oppressive, threatening, while at the same time providing
spaces for struggle and negotiation'. While autonomous organisation might
seem, in many contexts, to offer women the optimal political strategy, the
opportunity structure outside of formal political institutions will often rule
it out. In fact, rather than there being a simple choice for feminists between
mobilising within civil society and invading state arenas, it is more generally
the case that, in those societies where possibilities for autonomous organisation are greatest, so too are the opportunities and rewards for participation in
mainstream politics. In extreme authoritarian systems neither are possible,

although where such rule is weakening, renascent civil society may offer new opportunities for women's political participation not yet matched in the formal political sphere.

Women's movements, as has been noted in Chapter 1, are located above all within this sphere of civil society. Here we must remind ourselves that the social collectivities indicated by this term 'women's movement' in reality may be widely divergent both in terms of their goals – by no means all such movements are primarily concerned with the pursuit of gender interests, as they understand them – and in terms of organisational autonomy. Autonomy is of course not only a matter of strategy but of history. In this context, Molyneux (forthcoming) makes a valuable distinction, however much in practice boundaries may blur. There are, first, 'independent movements' in which women organise autonomously and set their own goals (though there is no logical reason why these goals should be 'feminist'). In 'associational linkages', second, these autonomous women's organisations choose to form alliances with other political organisations some of whose objectives they share. As she observes, this kind of linkage avoids the dilemma of 'autonomy or integration' that has beset women's movements; but, on the other hand, to the extent that the women's organisation yields control over agenda-setting it can risk the danger of co-optation. The third organisational situation, 'directed mobilisation', is one where authority and initiative clearly come from outside, so that 'there is little, if any room for genuine negotiation over goals'. This third situation itself takes different forms; in some cases women are mobilised, for instance by a nationalist movement, to help achieve a general goal, with no specific commitment towards furthering their interests, or even at the risk of losing some of their already existing rights. Alternatively, 'women's interests' may form part of the overriding objectives but as defined by external leaders, as in some socialist or communist movements. Such a form of mobilisation is clearly of relevance to the history of the ACWF, discussed by Howell.

In addition to questions about whether and how to form alliances with other movements or organisations within civil society, feminists, as we have seen, have persistently debated whether or not to engage with institutionalised politics and the state. Clearly, there are contexts where such participation achieves relatively little. Thus Howell notes that in China the rate of women's formal political participation is quite high but this in no way ensures them political influence. However, for many feminists, that point is no longer at issue; the state *must* be engaged and the question now is what are the most effective strategies for empowering women in this engagement. While the options open clearly vary with the specific context, I shall briefly consider two kinds. One strategy, which has gained increasing currency within the movement, and relates primarily to the issue of women's political representation with liberal democracies, is that of introducing 'gender quotas', whether in political parties, in local or national legislatures.

The evident success of such polices in the Nordic countries has inspired imitation elsewhere. Although only implemented for a short while, its adoption in Britain's Labour Party in 1993 contributed to a dramatic increase in the numbers of Labour women MPs following the 1997 general election. Gender quotas have recently been adopted in South Africa in the ruling African National Congress and implemented in India at the local level. As Craske notes, in Latin America many parties have introduced internal quotas to increase women's representation while Argentina has a national quota law as part of its electoral code.

While the moral justification for imposing quotas has been much debated, with feminists deploying arguments about the need to compensate for past discrimination *against* women or about the need to distinguish formal from substantive justice (Radcliffe Richards 1980), in her discussion of the issue, and reflecting the influence of post-structuralist concerns, Nash focuses upon the question of representation. As we have already seen, for Nash there is a serious problem posed by the need simultaneously to represent women and to avoid essentialising a given identity. Iris Marion Young argues in favour of 'group democracy' in which there are a range of mechanisms to ensure the representation of different groups, including women, within state decision-making arenas, amongst which gender quotas could be expected to feature. Phillips distances herself from the essentialising implications of Young's approach, but still favours gender quotas, which however, Nash notes, she presents as a way of equalising participation within representative democracy, rather than a way of 'representing' women in the traditional sense of the term.

While discussion of gender quotas has been largely confined to the sphere of representative politics, and has concentrated on how women break into this sphere, a rather different but feminist-informed literature has looked at women's participation in government, both as elected representatives and as state employees. This, in a sense, brings our examination of gender, politics and the state full circle: but instead of asking what impact does the state have upon gender, we are now asking how a politics based upon redressing gender power imbalances can make use of the state. What difference can having women in government make? Here an initial concept we have to deal with is 'state feminism'. It is clear that this term has been used to mean at least two rather different things: it can be used to refer to the tendency for feminists to achieve positions of influence within government, whether in elective positions, in the bureaucracy as 'femocrats', or both (with Scandinavian countries seen as presenting perhaps the paradigm case); or it can be intended to indicate state policies and procedures, however these are determined politically, which are in some sense designed to improve women's status and opportunities, that is, a situation where the 'state', whatever that may be, acts in a quasi-feminist way. This seems to be the sense employed, for instance, in the recent collection of essays on

Comparative State Feminism, edited by Stetson and Mazur (1995), where 'state feminism . . . refers to activities of government structures that are formally charged with furthering women's status and rights' (1–2).

In practice the distinction between these two kinds of state feminism may not always be so easy to make. And yet it is important and has particular implications both for the extent and for the meaningfulness of women's political participation. Craske, for instance, observes that the women's ministries, which exist in some form or other in most Latin American countries by now, 'tend to concentrate on women's role in the economic or social spheres, rather than promoting the development of an inclusive citizenship or encouraging women's political involvement'. In their contributions to this book, both Sperling and Howell refer to a kind of state feminism – Howell calls it – 'state-sponsored feminism' – deployed under communist rule in the Soviet Union and China respectively. As Howell notes: 'For ideological and political reasons socialist states have placed issues of women's oppression and exploitation firmly on the official agenda.' Although women have played their part, especially through the Soviet Women's Committee and the All-China Women's Federation, this has been severely circumscribed by the overriding priorities and perspectives of the extremely male-dominated party-state hierarchy. In such a context, there must always be scepticism as to what increasing women's participation in formal governmental structures could achieve. Even so, Sperling describes how the Soviet Women's Committee evolved with the advent of political liberalisation; it came to form the basis of the Women of Russia bloc, which won 8 per cent of the vote in the parliamentary elections of 1993, though its fortunes subsequently waned, and which served as an 'ally' of the women's movement. Howell also speculates on ways in which changes associated with economic liberalisation in China may spur the ACWF into adopting a more proactive stance.

These cases may be seen to fall at one extreme. At the other, liberal or socialist feminists have opted to work within and through the state. Here, usually, the question of numbers is considered of crucial importance, with familiar arguments about what constitutes a 'critical mass', and so forth. This obviously links with the issue of gender quotas discussed above. But even where numbers of women in government are limited, individual women can make a difference, as Sperling shows through the example of Liudmila Beslepkina, Minister of Social Protection, who for instance provided a spirited defence of women's need for paid employment against suggestions that the increase in female unemployment was not a problem.

The essays in this book, then, have raised questions about the extent, means and desirability of women's participation in representative and executive political institutions. But perhaps most striking of all has been the recurrent suggestion that in order for women's political participation to be effective there needs to be a *combination* of an autonomous or grassroots feminist movement with women's significant presence within state institutions. Such a view is at the least implicit in the discussions by Craske and Sperling. Reflecting on the experience of the All-China Women's Federation, Howell concludes that state women's agencies have to be matched by 'a vibrant sphere of autonomous, radical and reformist women's organisations'. It is the absence of such a force which 'has deprived the ACWF of the opportunity to engage with a wide range of women and to comprehend their needs'. Jacobs reaches a similar conclusion. In Zimbabwe, when the government failed to direct the newly established Land Tenure Commission to remove discrimination against women, neither ZANU nor its completely subservient Women's League protested; that was left to the independent Women's Action Group. In Vietnam, 'the lack of an autonomous feminist movement is likely to have been an important element in the eventual demise of a land reform which, for a time, operated in the interests of many peasant women'. Jacobs contrasts this with the achievements of the Bodghaya movement in India, in which both feminists and feminist analysis played a prominent role.

Conclusion

Essays in this book have highlighted different aspects of women's participation and this concluding chapter has sought to bring some of their central findings together. There is growing recognition of the complex issues raised in demanding the political representation of 'women' as a discrete category. To the extent that the need for such representation is based on the existence of 'women's interests', Phillips (1995) points out that this does not have to imply that all women share the same interests: 'the variety of women's interests does not refute the claim that interests are gendered'. For instance, 'That some women do not bear children does not make pregnancy a gender-neutral event' (ibid.: 68). Even so, and as the legion splits and arguments amongst feminists themselves make clear, there can be no simple and singularly constituted political subject, 'woman', nor any simple reading off of their interests, and our analysis of gender and politics must incorporate this understanding.

The studies in this book illustrate the importance of the 'political opportunity structure' for women's political participation, while at the same time suggesting the need to widen or supplement our understanding of this concept in order to take account of contextual factors and of different levels, dimensions and sites of politics. Women can seize opportunities presented but their intervention will simultaneously be constrained and even shaped by the character of these political openings. Through such participation, women may be able in turn to modify the political opportunity structure itself, so redefining their terms of engagement.

We have seen that in any given context feminist strategy may focus more on mobilisation within civil society or upon penetration of the state, though it is unlikely that opportunities in one sphere will exist for long in the absence of opportunities in the other. We have also seen that success is most likely where participation in state institutions is reinforced by the activities of a vibrant autonomous movement. None the less, and returning to the central theme of Chapter 1, the studies included here have underlined the significance of the state for women. Feminists will continue to debate whether women *should* participate in institutional politics. The issue cannot be simply resolved, and is regularly re-articulated in new political and cultural contexts. However, many would now accept with Ann Stewart (1996: 39), that women cannot give up on the state, 'not least because it will not give up on women'.

References

Afshar, Haleh (1996) 'Introduction', in H. Afshar (ed.), *Women and Politics in the Third World*, London: Routledge.

Dietz, Mary (1987) 'Context is all: feminism and theories of citizenship', *Daedalus* 116: 1–24.

Evans, Judith (1995) *Feminist Theory Today*, London: Sage.

Jeffreys, Sheila (1990) *Anticlimax*, London: The Women's Press.

Kandiyoti, Deniz A. (1988) 'Bargaining with patriarchy', *Gender and Society* 2(3): 271–90.

Lievesley, Geraldine (1996) 'Stages of growth? Women dealing with the state and each other in Peru', in S.M. Rai and G. Lievesley (eds), *Women and the State: An International Perspective*, London: Taylor & Francis.

Lovenduski, Joni and Randall, Vicky (1993) *Contemporary Feminist Politics*, Oxford: Oxford University Press.

Martin, Emily (1991) 'The egg and the sperm: how science has constructed a romance based on stereotypical male–female roles', *Signs* 16(31): 485–99.

Moller Okin, Susan (1991) 'Gender, the public and the private', in D. Held (ed.), *Political Theory Today*, London: Polity Press.

Molyneux, Maxine (forthcoming) 'Analysing women's movements', in R. Pearson and C. Jackson (eds), *Divided We Stand: Gender Analysis and Development Issues*, London: Routledge.

Nicholson, Linda (1995) 'Interpreting gender', in L. Nicholson and S. Seidman (eds), *Social Postmodernism: Beyond Identity Politics*, Cambridge: Cambridge University Press.

Phillips, Anne (1991) 'Citizenship and feminist theory', in G. Andrews (ed.), *Citizenship*, London: Lawrence & Wishart.

Phillips, Anne (1995) 'Quotas for women', in A. Phillips, *The Politics of Presence*, Oxford: Clarendon Press.

Rai, Shirin M. (1996) 'Women and the state in the Third World: some issues for debate', in S.M. Rai and G. Lievesley (eds), *Women and the State: International Perspectives*, London: Taylor & Francis.

Randall, Vicky (1986) 'Women and the Left in Europe: a continuing dilemma', *West European Politics*, 9(2): 307–13.

Randall, Vicky (1987) *Women and Politics*, London: Macmillan.

Richards, Janet Radcliffe (1980) *The Sceptical Feminist: A Philosophical Inquiry*, London: Routledge & Kegan Paul.

Scott, Alan (1990) *Ideology and the New Social Movements*, London: Unwin Hyman.

Stetson, Dorothy McBride and Mazur, Amy G. (1995), 'Introduction', in D.M. Stetson and A.G. Mazur (eds), *Comparative State Feminism*, London: Sage.

Stewart, Ann (1996) 'Should African women give up on the state? The African experience', in S.M. Rai and G. Lievesley (eds), *Women and the State: International Perspectives*, London: Taylor & Francis.

Index